Rock 'n' Blues Stew II

Tasty tales and tuneful stories from the music and lives of Levon Helm, Delaney & Bonnie and Friends, The Allman Brothers Band, Eric Clapton, Danny O'Keefe, Rory Block, The Mahavishnu Orchestra, Peter Green's Original Fleetwood Mac, and others in the world of classic rock, blues, jazz, and country.

The Musings of a Music Journalist

MITCHELL D. LOPATE

ISBN 978-1-95081-804-4 (paperback)

Copyright © 2019 by Mitchell D. Lopate

All rights reserved. No part of this publication may be reproduced, distributed, or transmitted in any form or by any means, including photocopying, recording, or other electronic or mechanical methods without the prior written permission of the publisher. For permission requests, solicit the publisher via the address below.

Rushmore Press LLC
1 888 733 9607
www.rushmorepress.com

Printed in the United States of America

Contents

Preface...7
Foreword..9
Introduction..11

CD Reviews

Soup: *A Tour of Two Cities* 17
Albert King and Stevie Ray Vaughn: *In Session* 21
The Mahavishnu Orchestra: *Birds of Fire*.........................24
Duane Allman: *An Anthology Vol. I and II* 28
Delaney and Bonnie & Friends: *On Tour with Eric Clapton*........32
The J. Geils Band: *Full House* 35
Danny O'Keefe: *Don't Ask*..38
Eddie Hinton: *Letters from Mississippi*.............................40
John Lennon: *Imagine* 43
Fleetwood Mac: *Kiln House* 46
Mr. Lucky: *Satisfied*...49
Swag: *Catch-all*..51
E.G. Kight: *Trouble*...53
B.J. Thomas: *You Call That a Mountain?*.........................55
Richard Thompson: *Action Packed – The Best of the Capital Years*....57
George Harrison: *All Things Must Pass (remastered)*.......60
Danny Brooks & the Rockin' Revelators: *Soulsville –Souled
    out 'n Sanctified* 66
Derek and the Dominos: *In Concert; Live at the Fillmore* 68
Leo Kottke: *6-and-12-string Guitar* 72
Leo Kottke: *My Feet are Smiling*......................................74

Barbara Blue: *Sell My Jewelry* 76
The Allman Brothers Band: *The Allman Brothers Band;*
    Idewild South; The Allman Brothers Band at the Fillmore
    East; The Fillmore Concerts; Eat a Peach 79
Paul Marshall: *Weed and Water* 85
Duane Allman: *In Memorium: 1946-1971 (bootleg)* 88
The Decoys: *Shot From the Saddle* 94
Bobby Whitlock: *It's About Time* 97
Luck Brothers: *Pain* 100
Judi Jetsunn: (untitled studio project) 102
Honorable Mention for a few good people 104
    Sly and the Family Stone 104
    Otis Taylor 105
    Edgar Winter's White Trash w/Jerry LaCroix 106
    Rory Block 107
    John Lisi & Delta Funk 107
    Various Artists – Remembering John Lee Hooker 108
    Northernblues Gospel Allstars 108
    Joe Richardson Express 109
    Jody Williams 110
    Harry Manx 110
    Bill Withers 110
    John Ussery 112

Essays and Reflections

Jam for Duane, 2nd Street Music Hall, Gadsden, AL, 2005 115
Buddy Guy at the Count Basie Theatre, Red Bank, NJ 121
Women Who Cook; The Count Basie Theatre, Red Bank,
    NJ, featuring Koko Taylor, Deanna Bogart, Janiva
    Magness, and Jennifer Wright 124
Roy Buchanan: A life-and-death grip on guitar 129
Robert Randolph & the Family Band at the Stone Pony,
    Asbury Park, NJ 133
Jackie Greene (opening for Buddy Guy); The Count Basie
    Theatre, Red Bank, NJ 136

Bobby Whitlock – The Domino Effect..................................139
Fleetwood Mac (featuring Peter Green): "How Blues can
    You Get?"...145
David Crosby and CPR; William Paterson University,
    Paterson, NJ..150
Wildflower Festival (featuring Judy Collins, Roger
    McGuinn, Janis Ian, and Richie Havens); Count Basie
    Theatre, Red Bank, NJ...154
Rory Block; The Tin Angel, Philadelphia, PA............................157
E.G. Kight; The Tropicana Billiards Room, Chattanooga, TN.....160
Mike Nesmith: From the Monkees to a millionaire, you
    can't argue with a man in a wool hat...............................163

Interviews

Bobby Whitlock *(Layla and Other Love Songs; All Things
    Must Pass)*..169
Bonnie Bramlett *(Delaney and Bonnie & Friends; On Tour
    with Eric Clapton)*..199
Levon Helm *(Music From Big Pink; Rock of Ages; After the
    Flood (with Bob Dylan)*..212
Danny O'Keefe ("Good Time Charlie's Got the Blues";
    "The Road"; "Magdelana")..226
Delaney Bramlett *(Delaney and Bonnie & Friends; On Tour
    with Eric Clapton)*..234
Paul Marshall *(Incense and Peppermints – The Strawberry
    Alarm Clock)*..251
Dick Cooper (Road manager, Lynyrd Skynrd; journalist)..........265
Larry Byrom (lead guitar, Steppenwolf).....................................279
Jack Tempchin ("Peaceful Easy Feeling") 287
John Wyker (Sailcat; "Baby Ruth")..297
James Dalton (solo artist): The Stone Pony venue, Asbury
    Park, New Jersey..306

About the Author...313

Preface

The inspiration of this book is dedicated to Duane—Duane "Skydog" Allman, of course. As an astrologer, I wanted to know his time of birth, and so I posted my question on a fan blog site. A response came from a lady, Karen, who said she knew Duane and Gregg in the early days of the HourGlass, back in St. Louis—and why did I want to know Duane's information?

The answers that flew back and forth were validations of our own birthdays being nearly identical in day but not year; her enthusiasm to talk about him encouraged me to write something about Duane: an essay on my regards for him. Since the early '70s, I had been immersed in the writings of the Rolling Stone Rock and Roll review guide books that were a fantastic guide to the best and worst of rock, country, blues, and jazz.

Sometimes, it's the dreams that we keep alive that in turn become some of the most precious gifts and treasures received from others. In the fall of 1999, I began to submit some reader replies and comments to the editorial staff at the Allman Brothers Band's fan magazine, Hittin' the Note. Encouraged by the fact that they liked my material, I sought out other free-lance chances, one of which being an interview: Delaney Bramlett, the man who taught Eric Clapton to sing with a soulful voice. Delaney opened a doorway to other musicians to me that included Bobby Whitlock, ex-wife Bonnie Bramlett, Levon Helm, Danny O'Keefe, and others. The miracles still continued to happen: friendships, collaborations, articles, essays, and a chance to move from Eureka, California, in Humboldt County to Boaz, Alabama, and finally up to the Seattle area.

It goes back to the early '70s days when the greatest FM station in New York history, WNEW, ruled the airwaves. They were unparalleled; kind of a <u>Rolling Stone</u> of the media, with brilliant knowledgeable disc jockeys like the Professor, Scott Muni, a friend of the Beatles; Pete Fornatele, Dave Herman, the brilliant Jonathan Schwartz, Vin Scelsa, Richard Neer (then known as Dick Neer), and a lady late in the evening whom I considered someone close to being other-worldly: a beautiful redhead, the Nightbird, the late Allison Steele.

I used to hungrily listen to her whispery, sexy voice describe the music roster that she had selected, which might include some electronic gems like Tonto's Expanding Headband's "Jet Sex," Greg Lake's rich pipes on King Crimson's "In the Court of the Crimson King," or on some lucky evenings, a band from Macon, Georgia: The Allman Brothers. When I first heard Gregg Allman grievously crying, "I'm hung up on dreams I'll never see!" the world stopped. I almost fell out of bed: who on earth was this group and why was this guy singing like someone had ripped out his heart with a fishhook and then set his body on fire?

I began to read the <u>Rolling Stone Record Review Guide</u>, desperate to understand this new awareness of music. I didn't know the performers nor did I have access to their works, but I could understand the tremendous impact of writers like Tony Glover, Langdon Winner, Ed Ward, John Mendelsohn, Ben Gerson, and the incredible Lester Bangs. The essays and reviews of Captain Beefheart and his Magic Band drove me to a frenzy: I had never seen such vibrant words and descriptive statements crashing and colliding so colorfully. Someday, I swore, I would write about this: the music I was learning to understand and grasp. I later wrote things like "Beefheart juxtaposed avant-garde jazz and Delta blues into a new form: Delta jazz and avant-garde blues." You just listen to that growl of his—it's part Howlin' Wolf and part volcanic lava. As for his time signatures and rhythm, just go for "Click Clack" on the *Spotlight Kid-Clear Spot*CD, and tell me that's not a train's wheels banging away behind the drummer's pounding intentions. That's what Lester Bangs said for <u>Rolling Stone</u>. These essays and interviews are a continuation of that dream.

Foreword

I can't really remember the first time I met Mitch Lopate, but it was not long after I started a web magazine called GRITZ in 1998. My original vision was that of a website dedicated to all the music I grew up with in Southern rock: great acts like The Allman Brothers Band and Lynyrd Skynyrd. Mitch was the first to expand my boundaries.

When Mitch first contacted me about writing, I knew right off the bat he was a kindred spirit. We spoke at length about mutual heroes like Duane Allman and Delaney Bramlettas well as a lot of great record reviews and our dreams and love for the music they made.

As the years passed, Mitch and I became good friends, and my respect for him as a writer continued to flourish. He has always been a generous fellow, sharing music with me that I may have otherwise never heard. And much like Mitch, music is my life.

In this collection, Mitch mixes up yet another musical treat for us all to savor. Get a ladle and scoop it up hot from the stove: here's the chance to dish up some rock and blues stew! Taste the music!

Michael Buffalo Smith,
GRITZ.NET/Writer,Editor:
Kudzo Magazine, Musician

Introduction

Everyone needs a passion in his or her life—something that connects an individual to their own personal source of motivation, inspiration, or creativity. For some, art fills that niche; to others, dance, or other forms of movement. Even sports activities or good cooking offer this capacity. Writing is yet another form. Worldwide, perhaps the oldest form of communicating our passions is the rhythms and melodies that have made music.

Music has become a necessary passion for me: I live my day surrounded by it in various formats and types. It brings a kaleidoscopic display of thoughts to my mind, much like an ever-changing background of healthy emotions that uplift and inspire. However, in some cases, music helps me connect to grief, pain, and patience. Hearing how musicians celebrate their own personal insights with their compositions, songs, instrumentals, and writing has been a guide in my own efforts as a writer and instructor of English.

Along with friends in other countries and across the 50 states, involvement in music has established a priority in my activities. A magnificent range of new opportunities exist within each genre of music: I have learned to appreciate classical, hip-hop, blues, jazz, and Third World artists. Music gives me a chance to travel the world while sitting at my desk or driving in my truck—and be united with anyone else who is sharing that same interest in that style of entertainment. I have connected with people as far away as the beautiful Seyschelles Islands in the Indian Ocean, competing for a rare CD online, and discovered a man in the Netherlands who collects concert recordings of one of my favorite performers, Leo Kottke.

My best friend, Mike Michel of Glen Cove, NY, is singularly responsible for much of what I have learned—and I have reciprocated in kind, sharing with him and others the gifts that I uncover from the industry. I cannot name everyone, but special love and thanks go to the late Delaney Bramlett for being the first artist to open the door; to Bobby Whitlock, for his zest and enthusiasm as well as friendship; to Michael Buffalo Smith and the late Jill McLane for giving me wings to fly; Ann Sandlin, for being a Wise Woman and Guide; the late John Wyker and the Mighty Field of Vision friends; Karen Rocchio for challenging me to write; and special memories, love, and admiration for Danny O' Keefe, Bonnie Bramlett, the late Levon Helm, Rory Block, andBram Bessoff and Erik Rowan: the guys from the jam band known as Soup; Danny Brooks, and the distribution of NorthernBlues.com. You all share in the magic that I have found I can give to the world of music with my words. Also, a year's supply of printer's ink in thanks to Tony Mastrianni, former contributor of *Creem* Magazine, for encouraging me to persevere.

I need also to honor the work and brotherhood of the authors from a now-ceased blog site: the Floppy Boot Stomp. The Floppy Boot Stomp deserves separate mention here because of its unique nature. A blog by its nature is dedicated to the views or slant of the particular author—and the FBS was dedicated to an underground nature of bootlegs, demos, outtakes, concerts, and out-of-print music. Because of those qualities and copyright issues, the site was under constant threat of being shut down—"nuked" is the common language—but for over 3200 posts, it was one of the most unique sources for a variety of music that ranged from Ella Fitzgerald, Tool, The Levellers, Merle Haggard, and Parliament-Funkadelic. Thanks to the opportunity to become part of the FBS and the contributing authors, my range and awareness of music has increased in measures beyond any scale of reckoning.

Cheers and a round of drinks and a few tight-and-twisted ones for the authors and brothers who contributed: our Boss and founder, Silentway, Jobe, Doomcan, Detroit Rock City, El Kabong, Subadoo, Woody, Slik, and our buddies, Voodoo Chile, RoBurque, High Ping Drifter, Snowmonkey, BLTSFAN, Axe, Emjota, Boboquisp,

Zigzagwanderer, Lakersfan, and a host of others on other continents. Thanks, fellas, for the fun and games. This book goes out to you all as well for the effort we gave and the music we found.

From 1999 through 2010, here are some of the essays, reviews, and interviews with the people who have made a difference with their ideals, talents, and vision through the world of music. I hope you will enjoy sharing their craft as much as I do.

CD Reviews

A Tour of Two Cities

Soup (Phoenix Presents)

(Alas, Soup broke up due to the nemesis of all musicians: a recording deal never manifested to truly bring this immensely talented group of men the fame I believe they deserve. But I know every Soup fan cherishes their recordings and memories of their performances. I caught them (and carried gear off-stage) at the Mercury Lounge in NYC one autumn evening. Erik, Andrew, Kevin, Bram, Lee: you guys will always be on top in our memories. Look for Bram at http://soundart.us for creative musical marketing ideas and rhythm), and check out Amazon.com for "Soup Jam Band."

I have said it before and I am more convinced than ever: the musical Garden of Eden is alive and flourishing down South. We have been privileged to witness a new generation of tremendously talented young men and women (The North Mississippi All-Stars immediately come to mind), and to the rest of the world, I proclaim: let there be Soup. Captured at two gigs (The Cotton Club, Atlanta, and The Wetlands Preserve, NY), this set packs more muscle-building music than a creatine shake.

You can make all the creative puns you want, but the hottest band I have heard to date—the one that I will stake my reputation upon for anyone who wants to cover the odds—are the five guys from Atlanta who play on this double disc. Soup is hot—no, try scalding—and I'm too serious to be joking. As an audiophile and CD collector, I'm guarding this one with a passion. Imagine, if you will, a musical burrito: wrap it all around the combination of Little Feat and the Dave Mathews Band's herky-jerky rhythms and vocal gyrations, add in the singing whirlpools of Phish and the Spin Doctors (as well as their instrumental nimbleness and enthusiasm), and add in some Cajun chortling and carousing on accordion.

Can you believe it? An accordion as a major player (yes, he cooks), as well as doubling on a harmonica hornet's nest that would make John Popper's and the Blues Travelers's eyes water with joy. Spike this with guitar—an acoustic-lead player whose fingers pulsate wah-wah/chord and jazz ripples <u>and doesn't tear it up</u>—he's so good that you don't notice it's not done on pure electric. Team him up with another guitarist with chords as thick as chocolate pudding, and drop in the funk—a slapping, bopping, and hopping bass, and a drummer who lashes his set like the Feat's Richie Hayward with a new array of toys and tools, including some cartoon woodblocks.

There's also hip-hop, a capella gospel, pop, classic rock, and cool-whip jamming. When was the last time that this much came from a band that is so fresh with material that they have more layers to explore than a geological site?

Work that volume control knob for the first tune, "Squirrels," because it's the only song that features Kevin Crow's slide as it brays and sneers like a trombone with a wicked treble head cold. Erik Rowen's frantic and panicked vocals set up his pickup truck-sized chords and rhythm playing alongside Kevin, and Andrew Margolious skitters and careens over the squeeze box behind the 4th-of-July celebration of Bram Bessoff's drum detonations and Lee Adkins's dancing bass. Margolious switches off mid-song to harmonica and scatters the four winds with a mad outburst, and Crow slices through the air again with a slide solo like a raging sword. The boys play and sing together throughout this rave-up with bank vault tightness—as they do for the entire show.

Everything else that follows is a five-star banquet of sounds and styles: "Salley's Sister" is a tongue-in-cheek love song (that you'll never see in a Hallmark card) that makes lust a joyful word with a pinch of respect. Kevin's solo sounds as if it was lifted from a jazz directory, and the singing is a magnificent percussive display of delightful vocal comedy. Lace that capo on a 12 string and let the richness of the arrangement of "Scratches on the Coffee Table" melt against Andrew's romantic accordion (absolutely showing how effective it is as a rhythm instrument). Listen again how Kevin modulates his acoustic-lead notes—this guy has enough ideas on technique and sound to make a video on his own.

With Kevin's wah-wah dancing like a hop-scotch game, it's essential to catch his stuttering solo on "Cybil Rivalry," and don't you dare overlook Lee's flashes on bass—or you'll find yourself mesmerized by Erik's carpet-thick strumming. The boys have an agenda, and with a hip-hop statement that lays down the rules (with that outrageous guitar orchestrating the pattern), they take the covers off *Neil Diamond*, of all artists, with a hint of "America." Of course it works! Someone lets out a birthday cheer, and it's back to business: "Get Me Back Groove" has enough lift to take to the air on its own like a glider riding thermals. (Is that a reference to Steppenwolf's "The Pusher" that I heard? These guys must have been plowing through a music encyclopedia to find some of these cameos.)

The next four songs have their own magic, but I have a special preference for the vocal textures and happiness of "Lucky's Not a Beggar" (supported by special guest Walter Absher's violin and cello), and the drum corps march of "Jefferson." As a compact unit, the band shows the precision of a football half-time parade that just hits every cue and marker (Bram is determined to show off every tone and highlight on his drum kit throughout this entire package—he's a Rock of Gibraltar, too, as a power surge), and Andrew doubles back and forth between vintage harmonica and accordion. In fact, he's so excited that he blows a clarion call on harp to announce "Get Me Some Action/Need a Little Bit," and the boys sing of a very potent psychedelic substance. Margolious honks again with glee and mischief, and no, that's not a synthesizer, Kevin has found another trick to show on guitar. The last song probably gives away the foundation of their musical repertoire: they close with the Beatles's "Dear Prudence."

Wait, the show's not over yet!!—drop on disc two and groove on the New Orleans-meets-Frank Zappa cavorting of "Marvin Wright." I swear Bram hits everything in sight that he can reach to check out its sound. With an intro beat that eerily echoes of Fleetwood Mac's "Tusk," check out the reggae pulse on "Eweh," and catch the texture on Kevin's elastic solo from the stop-and-go "King of 18." They're not even warmed up yet—lock up the house on the stew-thick chords and the vocal choruses on "Charlie Don't Know." Oh, and you need to have your future told by "Voodoo Lady" and that scamp on accordion during "Come Up for Air."

Lee Adkins gets the spotlight on "Breakdown," and he pushes the envelope to new unexplored heights with a daring, echoing bass wah-wah solo behind Bram's percolating drives. I sold the farm for the rights to "Leisure Suit," and if you feel aches and pains, it's because your muscles are trying to get in the mix via air guitar and that funky beat. You'll definitely need to take your shoes to be resoled if you catch up to Kevin's hypnotic chant. They go for the fences on "RainKing," and their gorgeous vocals just raise your hands in praise for the brief gospel-like "Bid You Goodnight." Well, it's time to pack up and say farewell, and "Papa Says It's Alright" lets the audience share the lyrics—even if they just pretend. Curtain call: Mr. Dylan's "Tangled Up in Blue," and when would you pass up a chance to salute the author when your band has so much skill?

With so much to offer, why haven't we heard more about these guys? I lay that at the extinct offices of Phoenix (who are no longer in action; Bram Bessoff is still in contact with me, and I thank him for that). Hey, there's some studio CDs, and if you think they're superb in concert, then you need to hear them in a different setting—just to compare. I am rejoicing at the opportunity to start these guys with a tie for the #1 slot (with the previously reviewed Richard Thompson) at the end-of-year Best Group nominations for 2001. So, drop me all the jokes, puns, and quips you can, but I'll say it again: brew me some more Soup—this is the tastiest music you'll find.

In Session (Stax)

Albert King with Stevie Ray Vaughn

(When Delaney Bramlett told me Albert King was a friend and inspiration, I was caught off guard. That only took 10 CDs of Albert King material to correct! Worth every penny and minute of effort, too. It's too bad that Albert never learned to read—I wish he could have seen this. Farewell, Stevie Ray. We lost you too soon.)

The old saying is true: when the student is ready, the teacher will appear. In the case of Stevie Ray, his apprenticeship reached a new peak on December 6, 1983, when he was asked to share a stage with the legendary Albert King for an independent television station gig in the Canadian province of Ontario.

This was not their first meeting: Albert had been observing Stevie's career burn like a bonfire when the veteran guitar player caught an introductory 1973 show at the Coliseum Club in Austin. The skinny Texan with the gravelly voice and blazing hands left a lasting impression on the big man with the arrow-shaped guitar, and Albert acknowledged that he stayed back without revealing his personal interest in order to better watch the fiery youngster perform.

Stevie had earned Albert's curiosity the hard way: he had paid his dues by studying the tone, the string-bending, and the blues-drenched statements that made King famous. This album, just released in 1999, simultaneously captures the two-fisted sledgehammer power of both men's hands and fingers—but also demonstrates the delicate caresses on their instruments with which they lavished their love for the blues. More importantly, the fondness and adoration of the master for his pupil (and vice versa) is clearly heard throughout the running comments and patter throughout this set. Albert confidently encourages, coaxes, praises, and blesses his protégée. In return, Stevie's worshipful delight and authentic "aw, shucks" simple appreciation literally shines like a beacon from a lamp with faithful friendship. The two men were perfectly at ease with each other; both locked in synchronicity.

Joined by Gus Thornton on bass and the Llorens brothers (Tony on piano and organ; Michael on drums), the set ran for 105 minutes, but an hour's worth is preserved here as a musical documentary. "Call it Stormy Monday" lays down a tutorial in driving nails with guitar strings as hammers, with Albert cutting a path on first solo, then gleefully urging his partner throughout the blistering reply. Both men pass verbal snapshots of nostalgia after the song is finished, and it's obvious that they totally enjoyed this opportunity and the craftsmanship that it produced.

Albert then beckons Stevie to do "that fast thing—that *rap* thing—*that* had a heckuva groove to it!"—and Stevie muscles his way into "Pride and Joy," much to King's radiant delight. The rhythm section hauls their heavy load like a big trucker's rig, and Stevie's coarse-grit sandpaper voice and jack-hammer fingers work on the Strat's jumbo strings like a pneumatic drill on concrete.

King then asks Vaughn if he would help out on "Ask Me No Questions" (a song covered by B.B. King), and they pack a front-and-back galloping display of firepower pulls and pushes as Tony Llorens nimbly dances over the piano keys. There's a verbal celebration on the sidelines when the song ends, and the electricity between these two is crackling with excitement and potential.

Albert handed out some meaty praise to Stevie when he asked him to fill the shoes of the late Jimi Hendrix (no surprises there!) on "Blues at Sunrise." King bends his intro notes and solo with blow-torch heat on his Flying Vee (they say Albert bent strings that *stayed* bent!) and instructs his student to come on in just like Jimi did. Vaughn takes the task with concentration and deliberation, laying off the volume control to keep things at a savage hum.

With that, Albert calls for new strings and says it's time to sit back and watch the younger generation call the plays at quarterback. The signal is for "Overall Junction," and Stevie and Tony L. make the most of the double-reverse play. One can only imagine that Albert looked back and contemplated the horizons that beckoned to his young scholar. "Put this on your next album," he mentors, and "Match Box Blues" is laid out for Stevie's infusion. Pumped with vitality, "Don't Lie to Me" lets King crush his strings beneath those immense hands (that's why he couldn't hold a pick, right?), and Vaughn steam-rolls a reply, flagged on by his proud coach. The rhythm section has their cross-traffic patterns locked, and this magnificent encounter closes with both men in a musical arm-wrestling match.

God bless them both for giving us such a treasured fruit of their labor. And dear Lord, we miss them dearly. Play the blues, everyone, for Albert and Stevie Ray! They're playing together again, you can bet on that. So, today's assignment is to get your copy of this disc. Albert King wouldn't have it any other way—and anyone with a sense of self-preservation knew not to upset him. And Stevie would just as quickly bull-whip you with a song—so follow in their footsteps and party hearty!

Birds of Fire

Mahavishnu Orchestra

(I argued for years with Buffalo Smith about getting this into print---and he is as big a fan of the M.O. as I am! "Too vivid" was one way he described this essay. Damn right—this is a monster of a recording! I've virtually memorized every note. John McLaughlin and the band raised the stakes with his compositions. Bassist Rick Laird also gave me a personal thumbs-up after reading this.)

Let's play a mini-version of 'Six Degrees of Separation, Allman Brothers/Southern Style' in regards to this selection.

(1) Who did Jaimoe say that Berry, Duane, and he sounded like in Fame studios when they first met and decided to jam? The Mahavishnu Orchestra. (2) What guitarist (as well as Duane) was heavily inspired by John Coltrane and Miles Davis's collaboration on Kind of Blue: John McLaughlin, leader of the M.O. (3) Who is one of Joseph "Red Dog" Campbell's friends? Billy Cobham, drummer for the Orchestra. (4) What's one of Warren Haynes's personal favorite albums? Look closely: Birds of Fire. (5) Leo Kottke, who recorded Duane's "Little Martha," (three times) toured with which group at one time? Of course—the Mahavishnu Orchestra. (6) Speaking of Billy Cobham, when he first heard the Allman tandem of Butch and Jaimoe in a typical battering-ram drum solo, was convinced that it was one man overwhelming the kit, and even more impressed to hear it was a duo. I wouldn't pass up the opportunity either to ponder whether Derek Trucks has had this in his CD player, would you?

This album, released in 1973, has enough energy and power to have been recorded in the birth of a supernova. Only the inner sanctum of guitarists had known a few years earlier of McLaughlin's arrival from England as a living legend, but the message quickly flew to the general public.

The Orchestra featured McLaughlin's double-neck blinding speed; Jan Hammer's keyboard outcries; Jerry Goodman's electric violin playing both classical themes and twin lead lines; Rick Laird's trembling bass, and Billy Cobham's super-speed percussion and footwork. If you need any more help, think of the legendary live Fillmore track of "Elizabeth Reed" and consider that as close kin. Pure kinetic outbursts of notes and turbulent rhythms whip and rage on these 10 cuts, but there's also a few brief glimpses of relative calm in the eye of the hurricane.

It's perhaps appropriate that Cobham's gong splashes and rolling percussion alongside Goodman's chanting violin herald the title song with an Asian Indian-like mantra, as McLaughlin awakens with a piercing, rising flurry that sounds like a peacock in a courtship frenzy. The ritual reply comes back from Hammer's synthesizer, and then it's back to the guitar and violin as they weave and intertwine like DNA strands. "Miles Beyond" (dedicated to the late trumpeter) emerges slowly from the jazzy fog of electric piano, and then watches as Laird and Cobham raise the curtain for an opening statement by McLaughlin and Goodman.

What follows next requires headphones—as much as you want to believe it's muted electric guitar, it's really a fascinating pizzicato on Goodman's violin, supported by more electric piano musings. The band then throws themselves into a brief summary, only to have McLaughlin and Cobham devastate the landscape, sounding like a ferocious firefight from the worst days of warfare, with machine gun-like guitar bullets flying in front of a bombardment of cymbal-and-drum mortar explosions. The song ends as the opening phrase is once again firmly planted in the ground like a waving banner.

Like a scurrying swarm of ants in action (or New York City in rush hour), "Celestial Terrestrial Commuters" features more electric guitar/violin duets and twin lead lines, swept along by the pace of

Cobham and Hammer like two men with push brooms in a hyperactive frenzy to clean up after the crowd. It's followed by the brief (23-second) bit of electronic chatter of "Sapphire Bullets of Pure Love." The M.O. then offers one of the most delicate electric pieces ever recorded, "ThousandIslandPark," with McLaughlin's flamenco-like acoustic performing a jazz ballet movement with Hammer's piano as his partner, praised by Laird's bass.

With almost poetic resolution, "Hope" builds in what can be best considered grandeur, strengthened by Cobham's percussion and Laird's upright bowed bass, capturing some of the rich arrangement ideas that George Martin used so effectively with the Beatles on albums like Magical Mystery Tour's "I am the Walrus."

Track seven, "One Word," was born in the deep realms of space in a galaxy that contains life-forms unlike any found on Earth. Beginning with Cobham's skintight inside-out snare solo, the band frantically careens through the narrowest of channels like a bobsled race without brakes. They miraculously arrive unharmed with the rescue effort of Laird's solo, only to mutter and fuss behind his melodic tumbling notes.

However, it's too easy to be safe, and in a three-way argument of "my opinion, and yours-be-damned," McLaughlin, Hammer, and Goodman take turns venting their thoughts and gestures like a three-headed alien being with dramatic, flamboyant phrases. The climax is reached as each man/creature tries to shout down his colleague with overlapping statements that sound like a marriage counselor's nightmare day in the office, and Cobham steps up to clear the brawl. A muscular drum solo follows as he rolls effortlessly back and forth on his tom-toms, and the double bass drum pedals thump like a dangerous blood pressure reading. A series of staccato notes signals that the band is ready to snap its chains again and breaks into a final exhausting sort of cosmic orgasm.

Something is sure needed to calm down the fury, and it's time to seek "Sanctuary," a song that must be a eulogy from the casualties of all this turmoil. Hammer's grief-stricken synthesizer solo weeps behind the wails of dual violin-guitar lead, and there appears to be no light at the end of the tunnel. However, this isn't the case, as "Open Country

Joy" (a song that Kottke did on Dreams and All That Stuff and the newly-reissued 1971-1976: Did You Hear Me?) awakens like the first warm day of spring. Gliding violin and 12-string guitar preface the false ending, which bursts into full bloom behind McLaughlin's electric warbling, Hammer's return calls, and Goodman's ecstatic freedom. Cobham unleashes a summer shower while the sun shines, then pulsates away, switching to brushes while the others frolic and dance.

All these adrenalin rushes have to find the time to regenerate, and "Resolution" closes out as the band redoubles its intention and vigor with a "you haven't seen the last of me" conviction that is almost patriotic in its foundation. If anything is needed, it's a towel and a shower as these five musical massage therapists have just finished pummeling the daylights out of your mental muscles.

Do not, under any circumstances, give this CD to anyone who is under a doctor's supervision and requiring bed rest. On the other hand, if you need to paint the entire house in one day (or build one) and don't mind doing the job yourself, the Mahavishnu Orchestra will gladly haul any gear or heavy construction material you need with the pure power of sound at its best—and it could move a mountain. I'll bet they don't require a ladder, either, because they know your speakers will use anti-gravity to get the job done. Crank it up and watch!

An Anthology Vol. I and II

DUANE ALLMAN

(He ranked only 2nd to Jimi Hendrix in a poll by <u>Rolling Stone</u>. Goodbye, SkyDog. The Road Goes On Forever.)

The Hourglass were a blues crew waiting for distribution: a young band work up B.B. King, John Lee Hooker, and Mel London with such passion. That grieving, woeful organ player is Paul Hornsby; Gregg melts the microphone with anguished howls and heart-wrenching pleas. B.B. taught Duane how fingertips cut diamonds. Note the Albert King-like influence (on "Loan Me a Dime") formation of his style, including the repetitive phrases that follow one-two in milli-second quickness, lay down a note, ring it again in a bell-like manner, or pull it off on the second try.

Wilson Pickett's scalding cover of "Hey Jude" would praise the Beatles, the Muscle Shoals players, or Pickett himself, but Duane's great white shark bite solo made the hair stand up on the back of your neck. On "The Road of Love," Clarence Carter proudly said, "I like what I'm listening to!" as he admired the fuzzy distortions of Allman's slide. Contemplate, however, when Duane reunited with Hourglass friends Hornsby and Sandlin, and added newcomer Berry Oakley for a string-bending prophetic eulogy on Champion Jack Dupree's "Goin' Down Slow." Duane's vocals could handle slow crooning without being annoying, and his guitar wept where his voice wouldn't go.

Other good people lent Duane their voice or let him be their spokesman: just imagine him nodding his head in agreement, his slide dancing to Aretha's statements when she belted out "The Weight," or the slinky, sinewy electric sitar that pulsated alongside buddy King Curtis, a man with talent to blow--a Meerschaum pipe if possible?--and make notes this beautiful on "Games People Play." A ventriloquist throwing his voice, Duane added a 'talking slide' dimension to his bottleneck on John Hammond's version of Willie Dixon's "Shake for Me," mimicking human frustrations and gestures that hoot and wag wildly beside the unbridled, frenzied vocals.

Perhaps "Loan Me a Dime" is the tune that describes Duane's closeness in letting his instrument speak the words that the soul cannot say. Boz Scaggs carries the heavy hurtin' blues, but Duane's introductory solo also cried to the heavens like his heart had been pulled from his living, beating chest. Boz faces his last day on Earth with no love or hope, and Duane plays as though he's losing his, too. The follow-up solo, criticized for engineering coordination (Duane's mix get buried midway), is apparent that he did not stop playing this tune--ever. The recording session ended, the sun went down, the band went home, but Duane played this way every time: nothing came between him and the feelings he needed to release.

Sensitive regional touches and dobro/slide playing find themselves nestled in the comfort of the Delta's warmth as he, Johnny Jenkins, and Berry settle back at the old farmhouse, finding shelter from that summer heat in Muddy Waters's "Rollin' Stone." Visualize baking-hot red earth beneath your bare feet back as the three men pick and pluck those strings.

Delaney & Bonnie & Friends were Duane's second family unit; his slide has the wildest time with pals "Out on the Open Road," continuing when Johnny Jenkins comes back again in "Down Along The Cove." Gentle times return when Scott Boyer and Cowboy hitch their wagon and give the reins a tug in "Please Be With Me," and Duane shimmers on dobro. Eric Clapton gives/gets a lesson in acoustic slide with Duane on *Layla*'s "Mean Old World." The final songs embrace the group scene, and his five-alarm siren call at the opening of "Layla" make it the epic monolith of unreturned love affairs. Happily, the other five cuts are as fundamental as the laws of gravity: "Statesboro Blues"; "Don't Keep Me Wondering" (the studio version); "Stand Back," and "Dreams": the very best that modern recording could portray in bottleneck phrasing, tone, composition, and originality. By the divine right of kings, Duane had sole ownership of the inner secrets of electric slide. "Little Martha" wraps up (but not the *Dreams* box set with Berry's bass foundation).

Volume II holds true that teamwork aside, Duane's briefest of fills totally complemented the action. Therefore, solve the puzzle for what Rick Hall overlooked when Duane recorded an original composition that sounds like it has tongue-in-cheek honesty: "Happily Married Man." His rhythm guitar sounds like it's waiting for something to develop, galloping joyfully alongside Berry, Paul Hornsby, and Johnny Sandlin--but when it's time for a starburst solo...there's nothing but the same chords.

More fun abounded when Duane sat in with Aretha Franklin; King Curtis was back beside him. Lady Soul drowns her sorrow when she cries, "It Ain't Fair," and she could make a glassblower's lungs look weak. The real charm is David Hood's bass, which skips along beside Curtis's sax. Duane does play sidekick, but with deliberate slow-as-ketchup lines.

This CD reminds us that "You Reap What You Sow," and Otis Rush knows the Laws of Karma. Duane buzzes like a huge angry hornet, but Otis's Cobra Recordings shows that he could do 6-string surgery. Ronnie Hawkins and friends come to the rescue, as Carl Perkins's "Matchbox" sparks up everyone, Duane chirps and glides again, and the house was rockin'. Wilson Pickett was also nearby, "Born To Be Wild." There's no standout artist solo here (except for Pickett), which makes the song fit so well. Speaking of fast cars, Duane's Aladdin's Lamp wishes for a customized set of wheels in "No Money Down" must have been a salesman's nightmare, and Chuck Berry was the co-signer of this loan. More a novelty song (especially with Duane's vocals), his sincere singing makes you expect he found the object of his wishes.

The Hourglass re-appear with "Been Gone Too Long," a tune that could have been taken elsewhere. Arthur Conley's "Stuff You Gotta Watch" follows, featuring Duane's insect-humming tone. With politeness to LuLu, you tried, dear, but you didn't light the pilot flame in the stove for that "Dirty Old Man." Duane's tingling lead sings on her shoulder, but she doesn't have enough heat to melt butter (Bonnie Bramlett hickory slow-smoked it on D&B's *Accept No Substitute*.) The first side ends with "Push Push," with Duane joining flautist Herbie Mann, future Stuff members Richard Tee and Cornell Dupree, a syncopated percussive motor run by Ralph McDonald and Bernard Purdie, and Chuck Rainey's bass. This jam really has fine moments; it's more of a subtle, sensuous, recreational ritual, letting the players use touch and tone to mold rich textures.

A Johnny Jenkins voodoo-enhanced performance calls for disciples to "Walk on Gilded Splinters." Duane quacks away on slide dobro, and a percolating rhythm section bubbles away with help from Butch Trucks, Jaimoe's timbales, Pete Carr's guitar, gospel-rich backup vocals, and Paul Hornsby's keyboards. Boz Scaggs also shows up, "Waiting for a Train," and Duane's dobro yodels as much as Boz. That twang came in handy when Ronnie Hawkins delivers the news: "Don't Tell Me Your Troubles," and Duane's resonator dances a lively jig.

Sam Samudio kept the groove belonging to John Lee Hooker's "Goin' Upstairs" while Duane cross-stitched slide, and reunited with Delaney & Bonnie for a live recording in New York, using an acoustic shuffle. All's fair in love and music at Ludlow Garage in 1970: "We don't do this song very much, but I feel like singin', so I guess that's what we're gonna do," taking the Brothers through a raucous romp on Hooker's "Dimples." Dickey's solo really rasps and files as well as Duane's, and his (Duane's) rough vocals really work here. Duane, aka the Dog, lent his chugging bottleneck to The Duck (Johnny Sandlin) and the Bear (Eddie Hinton). Eddie's lead guitar is overmatched by Duane, so 'enjoy my company while there's time' may be the answer.

The final three songs bring Duane back with the Brothers, sawing away on "Done Somebody Wrong,' cutting a funky "Leave My Blues at Home," and "Midnight Rider" closes the Fillmore East as he and Dickey really play up each other's strengths. Duane did that for everyone, so eat that peach for peace—and his music!

On Tour with Eric Clapton (Atco)

Delaney & Bonnie & Friends

(Ladies and Gentlemen, in my opinion—and one echoed by fans and friends throughout the country and around the world: perhaps the purest rhythm and blues band to ever be recorded: Delaney & Bonnie & Friends.)

If it is true that we are judged by the company we keep, then Delaney Bramlett has the musical wisdom of Solomon. Can you imagine having an on-stage lineup of this proportion: Dave Mason, Jim Gordon, Bobby Whitlock, Carl Radle, Bobby Keys, Jim Price, Rita Coolidge, Bonnie Bramlett, Tex Johnson, and a fella named Clapton. Lord have mercy!

Maybe the Beatles said it better: "I Get By With a Little Help from My Friends." Delaney knows the merits of that—just look again at those names and you know that his little black book of phone numbers belongs in the Smithsonian. I mention the Fab Four because Delaney played with them, too—and George was another Friend of this widespread family. In fact, both he and Ringo were at one of these shows—and stood on their chairs during the applause to show their enthusiasm.

You could add another Beatles phrase in here, too: "…you're gonna carry that weight": this band's power and energy moved <u>fixed stages</u>. But when there was this kind of power coming from the set, they probably needed steel reinforcements.

From the first notes, Delaney's relentless driving pace and Bonnie's crackling, tearing voice rips up the set for this awesome, blistering performance as "Things Get Better" literally kicks off like a revved Harley. Whitlock's steaming organ fires up beside the horns and a great jangling guitar solo takes your breath away. By the way, the man who truly held the helm throughout this show was Carl Radle—just see how quick his fingers jumped as he guided the pace while letting his bandmates enjoy the spotlight. Radle is, in my book, a forgotten mentor for bass players who need to learn how to handle a band in the manner that a trainer works a Kentucky Derby winner.

D&B's souls come with a deep love for two vital ingredients: Robert Johnson's blues and gospel, and "Poor Elijah—Tribute to Johnson (Medley)" lets this good man and woman tell their stories as they set their voices aloft like kites dancing in a summer wind. Mr. Clapton scampers and jumps like an enthusiastic, happy puppy during his solo, with notes that are just down-to-earth delightful and honest in their directness—just listen to his sincerity.

In case you overlooked it, Dave Mason had a well-known hit that Delaney covered: "Only You Know and I Know," and when the band takes it, everyone gets a chance to show off their strengths—especially the guitar solos that challenge each other in a magnificent duel, but please thank Jim Price and Bobby Keys for their horn work and tremendous efforts as they project a panoramic wall of sound as a backdrop.

If anyone in the audience wasn't torn to a frenzy during the Bacchanalian-like festivities of "I Don't Want to Discuss It," I'd like to know if someone checked their pulse. The band races on a hell-for-leather mad dash behind Delaney's ecstatic zeal—just pick any player, follow them over their own off-road rally, and be sure your seat belt is buckled, <u>'cause this is free-wheelin'</u>! Have you ever seen those speeded-up old-time films—the Keystone Kops come to mind—where everything seems to be in double-time? Imagine a song at that pace. Wait a minute--when the party is over, Ms. Bonnie has the spotlight—and a red one, please—the lady asked for it--as "That's What My Man is For" calls for some sweaty swayin' and bumping and grinding. And tell it, tell it righteously she does, just the way it is, two-fisted, rich and raw, as she puts her pipes through a session that would make Janis Joplin stand up and pump the air with a proud salute.

In another of those "here-we-go-again!" escapades, "Where There's A Will, There's a Way" sets Olympic records for enthusiasm, excitement, and all-around musical marksmanship, and that's why fire extinguishers are made—to put out blazes like this--sho' nuff, honey. Follow this up with "Coming Home," as Dave Mason's snaky slide guitar taunts Eric's lead, and the horns make it clear that this destination can't be denied.

So what do we do for a finale? Whop-bop-a-loo-bop!—dance yer shoes off (and anything else that comes loose, but don't stop!), as a Little Richard medley demolishes "Tutti-Frutti," grooves into "The Girl Can't Help It," flaunts a passionate "Long Tall Sally," and escorts sister "Jenny Jenny" for all the right, naughty reasons. Get up, get down, get it on, and best of all, get to it! And if you can catch yourself from dancing in the street, then you need another listen. Memories are made from shows like these—may I be lucky enough in my lifetime to meet more people who were in England on this magic night and hear their testimony.

Full House

J. Geils Band

(Before there was ADHD, there was Peter Wolf. They didn't make fire-breathing dragons any better than the J. Geils Band in concert.)

Crash-bam-boom! This is the musical equivalent of a 4th of July fireworks display by one of the hottest groups ever to soar onstage, and one of the most ferocious shows of its time. If crackling energy is what you need and explosive rock 'n roll is your medicine, this band was made to order. Recorded live in 1972 at Detroit's Cinderella Ballroom on two steamy nights, the place jumped like a pogo stick with mad springs as Peter Wolf lived up to his name and yowled, yelled, screeched, and bawled alongside his five locomotive bandmates.

This Boston-based band plays like they are trying to sprint a marathon, and it's absolutely magnificent to hear these guys work out their love for R&B smokers. "First I Look at the Purse" leaps for the jugular as the band takes no prisoners at the opening signal onslaught of Stephen Jo. Bladd's rollercoaster drumming, and Seth Justman whips up a thunderstorm on shrieking organ. However, they just toy with your excitement, because Magic Dick jumps in (yes, that's his stage name) to kick down the door and demolishes the place with raging harmonica. Crunching mega-ton choruses pound away as Wolf hammers relentlessly on vocals, and without a moment's hesitation, they zoom straight into Otis Rush's "Homework". I've heard Peter Green's Fleetwood Mac do this, but not this volatile, and this is definitely street-wise schooling from the rough end of town that can't be found on any diploma. Wolf and Dick pair off like two angry cats, J. Geils throws some darts with quick guitar licks, and Justman spray-paints clouds again on organ. Hot, hot, hot!

All Peter Wolf needs is to hear the audience goading him on, and he gives it right back, tantalizing them: "This is called 'Take Out Your False Teeth, Momma—<u>I wanna Suck on Your Gums!</u>'" Justman bangs out piano boogie like Jerry Lee Lewis and races ahead of everyone as "Pack Fair and Square" hoots and squeals. Do these guys ever come up for air? It's not possible, especially when Wolf is feeling his adrenalin rushes, jabbering on the edge of pure gibberish to signal Dick's virtuoso special, Juke Joint Jimmy's "Whammer Jammer."

The audience immediately picks up on the coming storm with handclaps—a hip black gal beckons "Come on!" to get everyone into the mix, and what follows is a kaleidoscopic squall by the man "on the lickin' stick." The rhythm section is towed along like a game fish running the line with the hook and bait, and everyone grinds to a finish when they bring the ending onboard. What a fight! No time to look back: here comes more boogie, as "Hard Drivin' Man" is in town and there's no brake pedal on this machine. Justman dances wildly on piano as Wolf cavorts behind the mic, and J. Geils struts on guitar behind Danny Klein's bass and Bladd's threshing percussion. Wolf lashes the crowd for yet-more momentum, and the only thing that can stop them now is a brick wall.

They have that looming dead ahead, and it's the size of a mountain: John Lee Hooker's "Serves You Right To Suffer." Ghostly, dark organ rises and falls like a spectre in the gloom as Wolf begs for mercy, and Bladd and Klein are framed against Dick and Justman's Chicago-style moaning and wailing, mocked by guitar. There's room for one more, and Geils comes in with a banshee solo that batters anything and anyone left standing. However, this band believes in redemption—they're already "Cruisin' for a Love," and Dick's cheerful harp whoops provide forgiveness, followed by an exuberant Geils. Stand back—the prey is in sight, and like a pack of wild dogs, they give chase in a classic Canned Heat groove.

The winner—and they are all first-place champs—is Stephen Bladd, because he runs away with "Looking for a Love" as his partners carry him off on their shoulders. Imagine a team of football players doing acrobatics on the high wire and trapeze while playing some monsoon-style rock 'n roll, and that's how this show ends. It's all muscle and power, and they come back for a raging finale—twice!

These guys were the late Bill Graham's *real* favorite band at the Fillmore East—it's right there in his autobiography. When a band plays like they've got nitroglycerine in their veins and it's about to blow, then there's no doubting that this must have been one helluva show. By the way, I can vouch for them: I saw—honest—U2 <u>open</u> their show in 1982 in Phoenix, AZ. They owned the town that night—just give them the keys to the city and let the music run away with your ears and backbone. You'll have the nail your furniture to the floor before you finish this CD, but it's worth every minute of the show.

Awwooooooooo!!!!

Don't Ask

Danny O'Keefe & Bill Braun

Let's say there's a special party you want to give for an elite gathering of young sophisticated friends. All the arrangements are made for the best atmosphere, and you want to impress a special someone with the time to dance, romance, and be witty. What you need, my friend, is *songmeister*Danny O'Keefe's terrific new collaboration with Bill Braun, *Don't Ask*. O'Keefe has always had the versatility to handle other styles (boogie-woogie, ballads, blues, and crooning like nightclub performer), and it's all available here.

Assure yourself that this is the right choice: Danny's voice is as smooth-and better-than any pop tunes Boz Scaggs ever did. This compilation actually runs on the same circuit as Don Henley's solo work, but Danny sands away all the rough edges that crept into Don's griping.

In fact, the versatile O'Keefe can maneuver like an ice skater anytime he chooses on the jazz rinks occupied by Al Jarreau, Steely Dan's Donald Fagen, or Ricky Lee Jones. But the gold medal here goes to the terrific A-Z catalogue of killer hooks that Braun has unveiled on a panorama of instruments. Snarling guitars, rippling drums, whizzing keyboards, and a scampering bass make these 11 tunes go round and round in a never-ending spiral of slinky (sometimes teasingly sarcastic), poetic rhythms. A virtual one-man orchestra, Bill takes on everything and anything with potent riffs. Go instantly to "Speaking of Destiny," and feel yourself shudder as though Braun's opening guitar creates a musical catastrophic blast of global warming behind Danny's apocalyptic view of life.

There's hope for Earth: "Suddenly the Celestials" shines a funky spotlight from above on the rat race of the morning commute and road rage. Imbedded in this song are the simple-but true jagged twists of Wall Street's roller-coaster mood swings:

> "Shuck the suckers
> 'Til you think you're tough
> In this town, baby
> That ain't enough
> Money cripples people here
> It's a very expensive source of fear
> In this town it ain't funny
> I mean people get mean
> When they're losin' money
> You ask them who they pray to thank
> They'll say, "The Big Guy
> The one who runs the bank"

Be warned, Humans. O'Keefe has your number. And the rest of the galaxy is watching you groove. That also goes for the boppin' and hoppin' "Turn That Damn Thing Down!" as Braun tattooes the 'boards and electronic drums with a finger-snapping beat behind Danny's chanting. No, the ice isn't going to melt in your drink-it's too cool in your hands. Just be sure your threads are tight, because "Jody" comes out as a cross-dresser, and O'Keefe raises eyebrows when he asks, "Why do you wear your sister's clothes?"

Letters From Mississippi

EDDIE HINTON

(John Wyker of Decatur, Alabama, deserves credit for fanning the embers in behalf of Eddie Hinton. No man tried harder to make his song burst forth from the depths of the heart than Hinton. For Eddie, the throat and palate were only obstacles for the raging volcano of passion and sound that burned in his chest. I personally received a letter from Eddie's mother, thanking me for this review.)

Why do musicians give so much of themselves?—they too often end like exhausted supernova stars, and all that's left is a pinpoint of light in the sky. Maybe that's part of the answer: they leave a token of their existence that shines for years. Letters From Mississippi is hands-on proof that Eddie had a burning love for the magic of rhythm and blues—but at a price of a life-and-death bond of opportunity. We need the sun to bring us life, right? When a supply comes with this much joy and intensity, it brightens up our hearts like a solar presence for the soul.

I know of only one other man today who can sing off-key with as much passion and enthusiasm as Eddie did on certain cuts of "Letters," but this other fella carries it with justice, too, and that's Bruce Springsteen. If only they could have met: the possibilities would have been a glorious Circus Maximus. Perhaps then, Eddie was a forerunner, a torch-bearer to show what dedication and sacrifice can mean for the spirit of music, just as Bruce has done throughout his "give-it-all-you've-got" career. Word comes from good inside sources that this set has been heard playing many times backstage when Springsteen was in town.

Eddie's influence on and by Otis Redding has been chronicled, but I say that he leans close to the style of two men who are as inspired on stage as Eddie sounded in the studio—and they have led lives of social unrest that need no extra publicity: Rod Stewart (especially in his days with the Faces), and another guy from New Jersey (who's been onstage many times with Bruce): Southside Johnny Lyons (of the Asbury Jukes). Don't compare the lifestyles—that's too easy—look at the vocals. Eddie could hack and scrape his throat for a note as zestfully as the former, and his "home-grown" style is remarkably like the above-mentioned two heroes of the Jersey shore boardwalk. He clearly loved what he did for a living, and Eddie's playing and singing on this collection is as close to a brief "Greatest Hits" as we'll ever have—and that transcends all the shaggy awkwardness that could be critiqued for technical adeptness.

Like the Boss, Eddie played and sang as he did—because that's who he was from within—he virtually turned himself inside-out to get the sound from his heart to the microphone.

If I had the chance, I'd shuffle the order of songs. Start me off with "Everybody Meets Mr. Blue"--Eddie lays down a sales pitch like a carnival barker behind the crisp metronome-like drumming of Roger Hawkins, and Ronnie Eades's saxophones chime in like a scolding jaybird. Eddie gallops through "Uncloudy Days" like a man on horseback over rough terrain by Jeffrey Simpson's drums, and we briefly catch his zeal through his slogan, "A mighty field of vision!"

Bring it right back home: Eddie's exuberance can't be hidden any longer, as "My Search is Over" plays with matches near the gasoline can, and Ronnie's horns bleat and galumph between high and low ranges. "Sad and Lonesome" shows the gentle, soulful side of Eddie in a song that I would gift-wrap to Messrs. Stewart and Lyons. Once again, Ronnie's horns provide the perfect shades of tone to compliment an excellent arrangement, and don't miss Roger's nifty tom-tom roll just before the song closes. "Everybody Needs Love" is cushioned by Joe Walk's B-3, and the rhythm guitar holds up like a sturdy fence for Eddie's "let-your-conscience-be-your-guide" voice.

The title song holds to a simple pattern (yes, I know there's a basic two-chord structure), but Eddie's unbridled energy and growling enthusiasm make this a keeper. "I Want a Woman" would have made Otis proud, and Eddie really is pleading with his heart in his hands for security and happiness. Maybe that's the secret theme of this set: "Ting-a-ling-ling" is as natural and innocent a bouquet of flowers as any farm boy with straw in his hair and hat ever picked for his beau, and "Wet Weather Man" lets that grown-up plowboy plead his case behind the snickering saxes and Clayton Ivey's nimble, scurrying piano.

There's nothing deeper and stronger than Eddie's testimony that can't be denied when "I Will Always Love You" bends to one knee. There's a determined man on a mission, and "It's All Right" carries the message "like a straight shot from Cupid!"—just listen to him bite out that remark with a smoldering passion, followed by primal yells of lust. However, I think Eddie was in love with a Muse: Erato, the goddess of love poetry, and music was his gift. She's waiting for him at the end of his rainbow, as "I'll Come Running Back to You" is ferried along with Ivey's piano and Eddie's downcast, plaintive singing.

I'll keep Eddie's life story and excessive habits with the memories of those who knew him—what I want to say for all time is that this man had a special feeling for his music, and its unquenchable fire was too quick to consume him. However, like all phoenixes, Eddie's songs have risen from the ashes and are in the process of being reborn. If he truly had forecast his fate, then he knew he was destined to blaze in the sky like the aforementioned stars—it's what he called himself in "I Will Always Love You." It's a cold, clear night tonight, and I'm going outside for a walk—and I'm sure Eddie will be looking down on me. It's good to know that I can find him on my stereo, because he's shining there, too—just where Cupid's arrows can find me, playing out my love for music. Thanks, Eddie—let 'em fly right at me.

Imagine

JOHN LENNON (APPLE/CAPITOL)

(He was a hero to so many of us—and still is. Spokesman for a generation and more, musical legend in his own time, and just as tough in black leather jackets as in a bag or bed-in protest, John was a burning bush of attitude. Dedicated to Doreen (Stelsing) Clifford and Tony Vocile from Elwood, NY.)

As John Winston Lennon has influenced me above many others for pure psychological research value alone (for his and my issues), I therefore get great mileage from this 1971 release. To say that John was plagued by personal demons is an understatement: mother-abandonment, achievement-success recognition, and social adaptability and critical commentary. This extends miles beyond how he expanded my musical-philosophical horizons, and I can think of no other musician whose death personally hit the general public with such a hammer blow to our heart and soul.

I appreciate and admire the way Lennon used his music to mentally transform and rebuild himself, and he laid out his psyche to be scrutinized on this disc. It was John's *other* side that ripped away the curtains of deceit and exposed the fallacies that society hid from our eyes and ears. He pulled no punches, nor did he expect any—but he also handed out some brutal assaults on the parties who had tried to crucify him for their particular issues and vendettas.

Thankfully, the kinder, gentle tunes show the Libra side of John's soul--it's all there and out in the open on the title track: "Imagine" all the people living for today, living life in peace. To borrow from

Yoko's idea on the back cover, try to envision Lennon's piano chords rolling past your mind as you lie on your back watching the clouds on a sunny day. The lyrics may be asking for too much, but in these times of violence as witnessed by today's youth killing each other in schools or worse, the global attacks of car bombs and terrorism unbound--would you turn down this dream? Sounding a bit like a jug band, "Crippled Inside" has a comic edge that was needed to soften Lennon's acidic compositions. Nicky Hopkins adds a great ragtime piano that could come from an old western movie saloon, and that's George Harrison doing the country shuffle on dobro.

Leaving one single rose in a vase as an apology, "Jealous Guy" says what men have wanted to say for all the stupid things we have done to the women in our lives:

> I didn't mean to hurt you
> I'm sorry that I made you cry
> I didn't mean to hurt you
> I'm just a jealous guy

John's vocal is particularly fragile, and this emphasizes his regret—he has only himself to blame. In a Playboy interview in 1980 just before his death, John admitted how much he recognized Yoko as his complementary partner and how insensitive his actions had been toward her. As long as he was putting the cards on the table about his struggles, "It's So Hard" uses an opening blast from King Curtis's sax to clear your head, and John wears a hair shirt of frustration as his gutsy vocal adds to the confession.

The guitars, sax, piano, and strings add a raven-like "Nevermore" confirmation to make it bitter.

Keeping up his pleas for justice, righteousness, and an end to suffering, "I Don't Want To Be a Soldier" grabs the gathered studio assembly (Voorman-Keltner-Curtis-Harrison-Hopkins-Gordon, among others) and marches and chants in protest all the way to the demonstration.

When Lennon was victimized (or set up as a fall guy, depending on who tells it), he could fight back with a verbal ferocity that could startle onlookers and listeners—he virtually used his words as a master plastic surgeon wields a scalpel. In this case, he takes the near punk-like composition of "Gimme Some Truth" and spits venom like an Indian cobra at a portrait of Richard Nixon and his administration's dirty tricks. George Harrison's slide solo flays all accusers who would harm his friend, and Lennon rages as though he's been told to drink hemlock. Down your own throats first, he replies. You just try and tell me that Kurt Cobain didn't admire John.

For all his accusations of Paul McCartney as being a sop in love with his late wife, Linda (and writing music about it), John really did have his own mushy side for Yoko—witness "Oh My Love" and "Oh Yoko!" I don't begrudge the guy the chance to face his faults in the mirror, but these are as weak as anything he ever accused his writing partner of authoring. It's like an Aussie joke about American beer being a lightweight version of sex in a canoe: "It's f*****ing close to water."

Speaking of McCartney, John takes a vicious, lethal swipe at him with "How Do You Sleep," and does an unrelenting character assassination via direct references to *Sergeant Pepper* and "Yesterday." The industry can substantiate that not everything that Paul released deserved long-term airplay (*Ram* and *Wild Life*) come to mind, but I didn't need John's primal scream rages of "Mother" from *John Lennon/Plastic Ono Band*, either. Let he who casts the first stone...

I'll wrap this with "How?" as John looks at the fork in the road and tries to figure his next move. Don't worry--he had plenty of issues left unresolved. I miss you, Mr. Lennon, and the 20th anniversary of that horrible moment in December brought back too many tears and regrets. Thanks for reminding us that we were born with wings—and teaching us again how to fly. As you said to your wife and soul mate, "My love will turn you on." It has—and still does—for all.

Kiln House

Fleetwood Mac (Reprise)

(I will always associate this CD with the dancing slide guitar of "Station Man." Also, Mick Fleetwood really gives a panoramic tutorial on different tones and tunings for drums.)

As a collective group, the original Fleetwood Mac (Peter Green, John McVie, Mick Fleetwood, Jeremy Spencer) had talent to burn. When they added a young kid with roots in Texas blues (Danny Kirwan), it would become an overpowering all-star lineup. Try and find another band with three scorching lead guitar players who were also adept as singers in their own individual right. Regretfully, the price they paid for so much abundance was seen in the reshuffling of their lineup: it seemed like they couldn't stand to be together (on stage or in the studio) for too long. With this literal game of musical chairs, it's amazing that they completed the projects that are their legacy.

When Peter Green split in 1970 due to personal issues, Kirwan and the circus showman-like Spencer remained. It was hard to live up to Green's overwhelming authority and expectations (especially as a blues perfectionist), and there is no doubt that the others felt intimidated by him. Freed of the personality challenges, the result was Kiln House, a disc that is a mother lode of riffs, tributes, and all-out joyfulness.

Jeremy and Danny really led each other to new displays of vibrato magic and chunky chord displays that made it a 'different' sound. More importantly, the vocals (especially Spencer's eclectic identity changes) make this more approachable, and there is background help from a future player, Christine Perfect (McVie).

Spencer's composing skills were rejuvenated with a variety of styles, including his recognized bottleneck work and piano, and the other band members (McVie and Fleetwood) also received credits. The tunes start off with the Elvis-splashed "This is the Rock," a nifty shuffle that reminds us about the heart of the matter of this thing called rock 'n roll. With an off-beat percussion tumbling away, "Station Man" displays the group's superb voices against challenging squawks of slide and lead, and salsa-thick chords that literally chomp away like a hand saw through wood. This was one of my favorite "mystery" songs that I vowed to identify when I first learned about the magic of FM music.

Jeremy always enjoyed displaying a variety of alter egos on stage, and he keeps the engine stoked with a couple of humorous numbers, including the country-western "Blood on the Floor" and the raucous, sneering "Hi Ho Silver," with writing credits to "Fats" Waller and Ed Kirkeby. (I just saw Paul McCartney do "Silver" at a reunion visit broadcast in the Cavern in Liverpool, and it's a crowd-pleaser.) Going back to rock's early influences, he and Danny buzz on guitar as Buddy Holly and the Crickets get a salute with "One Together," and a song kindly credited to Holly's mother, "Buddy's Song." I'm sure the town of Lubbock, Texas, appreciated the acknowledgement of their late native son.

When Danny Kirwan took the microphone to sing, he could be charming and mild, or tough and aggressive. On "Jewel Eyed Judy," he does both, and the guitars sting and burn with pain from a broken heart. His guitar playing was really something to admire, especially with his wah-wah splashes and laser-beam lead lines that offset Spencer's fire on "Tell Me All the Things You Do." Both men show delicate touches on "Earl Gray," and throughout this entire set, Mick Fleetwood toned down the drumming in the more muted style that he would use with the future incarnation of the band in the '80's and '90's. With chimes and a romantic chorus behind him, Spencer sails off with a final Holly-like vocal on "Mission Bell," perhaps indicating the blues and bravado of Fleetwood Mac would soon be transitioning to a more mainstream sound. In fact, his departure was soon to follow.

If you liked the Beatles and <u>Abbey Road</u> for its range of ideas and terrific guitar licks (like "Golden Slumbers"), then <u>Kiln House</u> should be its complement. All bands face a transition phase, and these guys made it safely to the other shore with this set. With the turmoil(s) that this band faced, they only could have done this once in their careers; thankfully, it has kept its listening appeal.

Satisfied

Mr. Lucky (MRL Records)

After I laid this out for a listen, I am more convinced than ever that there is a kind of natural affinity of the coordinates of points South that creates material this good. A kind of a home-grown, musical Fertile Crescent has been nurtured for all these years for the industry--it must be the soil, or perhaps just good karma, but the talent is just getting better each year. There has always been good news available on the circuit from Nashville (which these men call home), Memphis to Muscle Shoals and over two steps to Georgia, but now it's more exciting as new artists are taking themselves into distribution. With that in mind, these guys will melt the winter freeze in your home, and keep you in a groove that's so deep it's subterranean. "Satisfied" ain't the word—I'm celebratin'!

Just dive right in to this mix, because it's a split deck: either a hot, sweaty trek across a barren blues wasteland of pain and misery, or aged-in-the-wood vintage rhythm and boogie. Rick Moore's grainy, hoarse vocals sound like a made-to-order mesh between Dr. John's gravel and Gregg Allman's soulfulness to lead the way, and Sam Stafford comes up with incredible, lion-sized claws of flesh-tearing lead and slide guitars or deliberate, muted runs.

There's stormy-nights-in-the-woods anguish that follows like a bad dream from Joe Warner's B-3, only to shimmer like a rainbow when the clouds are gone; the pounding hammers of Tim Hinkley's piano fall and jump like a gymnast's routine, and the rhythm section of Nick Buda on drums, Jerry "Snake" King on bass, and Will

Rhodarmor on harp send down some dangerous rockslides without any warning.

Some special friends are also here: Jimmy Hall hoots briefly on sax and meets Doug Moffit's horn and Wayne Jackson's trumpet and arrangements, Jack Pearson lends a hand with lead licks on a tune, and Jimmy Nalls takes time for rhythm guitar on some cuts.

I always look for mojo to get things into circulation, and I found a heaping supply (on my favorite tracks): "Dark Before Daylight" has that slow burn that I crave, "Memphis Stripper" and "She's Allright" are gonna be banned from my wife's ears before she gets the wrong idea (and spoils my fantasies) about Southern women, and "Sell My Monkey" whips a slide guitar (disguised as a cat-o-nine-tails beating) behind a cruisin' shuffle.

However, the devil's gonnagetcha when Albert King's "I Wanta Get Funky" comes through and claims your soul. There is also some great gospel here with "Hello Darkness," a New Orleans stroll with a "Good Man Gone Bad," and the best suggestion I've heard in years: "Take It Down to Memphis." Just tell 'em Mr. Lucky sent you—your ticket has been waiting at the gate.

Make yourself a New Year's promise: you *will* make all efforts, superhuman or otherwise necessary, to see these guys play, and while you're at it, insist that this CD is included in the show. I'll tell my missus that I'm working late that night, and we can celebrate together afterwards. Guaranteed we'll be "Satisfied"!

Catch-All

SWAG (YEP 2023)

(I don't care how many good ratings this has: I'd still have locked the doors of the studio—from the inside—before Swag came to record. I'm sure they would have improved their results in order to get into the facility.)

These guys are starting to make me nervous. Each time I try to listen to this CD, I get uncomfortable for the wrong reason: in this line of work, I don't want to keep reaching for a Q-Tip. I've heard of music described as ear candy, but this isn't the place to be foppishly cute, especially when I hear "doodle-dee-doo-dwee-dee-diddle-doo-doo" repeated on the intro lyrics to "Lone." I am sure there were folks who thought the Bay City Rollers were fun, too—along with the likes of the Partridge Family and the Archies.

Oh, yes, the music is full of well-knit hooks and the tunes have been specially crafted for the current popular audience—but I'm gritting my teeth at the same time and not over the whole set. I can't fault Swag's lineup for trying to run these patterns (they were helped by Cheap Trick's Tom Petersson)--but Squeeze overall did this a lot better. Yes, these guys did listen to a healthy measure of The Beatles, Elvis Costello, Small Faces, and The Kinks; I recognize that. It's the best part of the songs, but the sales pitch seems to be for middle school kids—I assume.

Some good solid bites: "I'll Get By" and "Please Don't Tell"; however, there's a 'heavy-on the schmaltz' (that's chicken fat to those who don't know—it's used like grease) sound to "Lone" and "When She Awoke" that would please an 11-year old—if that was Swag's intention to have such a young audience. Jerry Dale's vocal sounds like a lost third member of Air Supply on "Louise," and just tell the engineer to drop that moronic phone conversation he recorded—it's blatantly mindless. I'm convinced that there was too much sugar in someone's coffee in the studio. And while someone's looking for the light switch, please explain the presence of the strings.

I don't mean to keep this up, but please stop Scotty Huff from singing on "Different Girl" until his voice decides to stop hitting those flat notes—they're out of his range. There's a follow-up bridge that skewers an attempt to sound like the Beach Boys and the background vocals are as useful as a vacation in the desert. Look here, guys, you put this tune out, not me, and no one hears me in my car or the shower.

I still think there are listeners who will say there are some other good songs on this CD; I'm sure, but you can evaluate it yourself. I know that this gets a lot of hits for downloads and Swag has a great website promotional package as well as touring. I just wish their music backed up their effort. Well, I'm going to give this to my dentist. I think it's an even trade.

Trouble

E.G. Kight (Blue South Records)

Hey, guys, is 13 a lucky number, a dangerous one—or both? How about thirteen burned-to-a-crisp songs from a woman who sizzles right from the start with comments like this:

> "I put the wild in the Wild Wild West
> I'm trouble
> the devil's scared to death of me
> I'm a handful of woman
> And I'm Trouble with a capital T."

Never has an album been more appropriately titled, because E.G. Kight means what she sings: she's as sassy, classy, and brassy as they come, and this lady has the angles covered like a champion pool player. A smoky voice that can ignite a fireplace on command isn't her only gift; she snarls like an angry cougar when her man does her wrong—so that means, men, that we pay attention here, and don't even dream of trying to compromise her. They say the best man for the job is a woman—and E.G. is here to prove it. Yes, she can be as sweet as honey—but baby, you can get stung to death if you step out of line.

She's also got a royal court to attend her: Koko Taylor, The Queen bee herself, joins her in a scorching duet as they hammer out the truth about how "A Woman Can Tell" when her man's been cheating. We're talking tenaciously tough here; there's no way to argue against either of these ladies. That kind of "I-know-what-I-want" confidence is both sexy and defiant in the hands (and words) of E.G., and that means a woman can wait for the best.

You know this kind of confidence means she's holding her ground and declaring independence ("Better Off With the Blues"; and "It Takes a Mighty Good Man" with special guest Kim Forester) when it's time to cut loose a bad relationship, putting her marker on a "got my eye on you!" fellow like Chris Hicks on "Your Love Looks Good on Me" or the swingin' finger-snapping jazz-jive "First in Line." This is a woman who says "I want to be first in line when you lose that gal you've got!" That's Paul Hornsby on piano, sweating for her attention—and with that red and black cover photo, you can't blame Paul (or any other man) for wanting to curry favors from this firecracker. Earn it or burn it, she says! I smell smoke—and I think it's because E.G.'s got me on the grill. Wow—and they say that Hades is hot? Not even close when she's doing the cooking and you're on the menu!

A woman with this much passion feels her losses in ways that words can't show, and when the time is right, "Let the Healing Begin." Don't rush it…let the moment linger, because closeness is the cure. However, sometimes things just can't be mended, and that unfaithful fool gets the axe in the neck in "The Rooster Song." Hey, E.G. could have whipped out a pocketknife and…would rather settle for a chance to whittle down time in "Blue Dawn" and just let her lesson soak into her aching soul. You still can't catch her off guard, because she wraps up her testimony with a marrow-shaking version of "When a Man Loves a Woman."

What we have here is a no-nonsense shoot-you-with-deadly-arrows Cleopatra—this is like having the bull beat the matador each time. By the way, E.G. does have a gentle side: she can pick guitar like a summer shower ("Better Off With the Blues") and she has a 17-year-old marksman on electric lead and slide in Michael Pierce. Just remember that her mirror on the wall sees into your soul—so keep her as the only picture in your heart—or else. (I've thrown her mine already.) Give your respects and devotion and get her other CDs. It's the wisest—and most sensible thing to do to please a woman like E.G. At least, for a start.

You Call That A Mountain?

B. J. Thomas (Kardina Records)

(When I got this assignment from Buffalo Smith, I protested, "I don't want to write it! There's something unnatural about it!" I gave this CD to my mother to keep. It made sense for her to have it.)

    Athletes and musicians have a common trait: they often stay on the playing field long after they should have retired—or at least, moved to a management position. It's a tough transition being long in the tooth and trying to recapture the charm and vitality of years gone by, but it's a theme that's been told for—a few thousand years?

    With that in mind, I am sitting at my PC, trying to shake off the thought that a nice guy like B. J. Thomas has returned to the studio—and has found himself trying for a Gloria Swanson-like "Sunset Boulevard" release. It's not that he's lost his voice—that's just as honey-smooth as ever—it's just that he's gone retrograde on some songs and it looks like knee-high black socks worn with Bermuda shorts.

    Don't misunderstand me—B. J. is a good fellow, and there is a clear market for him—he would go over great with a better selection, especially something more in line with the crowd from Nashville or on a cruise liner heading for the Caribbean. He starts off with the title song and it's a good tune—it would certainly do well at any respectable Saturday night dance or even at a social prom—but the rest of the set just has to be left from where they came—in better days. "What's Forever For" may not even get to next week, let alone eternity—unless B. J. wants to cheer up some elderly women in a senior's home. However, he <u>does</u> come back quickly on track three, "Somebody's Gonna Lose," and thank heavens he still has the strength and honest sincerity that has been his trademark. As I said, with the right material, a good tune and a nice backup vocalist behind him, he's an old friend who makes you feel like lighting the logs in the fireplace. "Most of All" generically gets the job done, and "I'm So Lonesome I Could Cry" is an acoustic-and-piano slow dance that would work at a romantic restaurant setting, especially when he reaches at the refrain for still-pure high notes. However, he unearths "Another Done Somebody Wrong Song," and I am seeing ladies with blue hair gently waving their heads. If this was his intention, then all right for them and him, too.

"I Lost Me" trembles like a bird with a broken wing, and gee, didn't this genre get taken to new levels of pastiche with Barry Manilow? Lord, no--it's time to trouble Brian Wilson, a guy who has paid his dues with enough dysfunctional family problems to earn someone a Ph.D for analysis, as B. J. tries to milk "Don't Worry Baby." Sorry, B. J., that's the cat you're trying to milk—not the cow. He's not getting the hint, because he's put the bucket down for "I'm Going Home." As little Spanky McFarland said to the rest of the Rascals, "It's *spoiled!*" Even a play on a title doesn't get a break: "Raindrops Keep Falling My Head" just makes me think that Paul Newman is now in his 70s, Robert Redford has lines in his face, and Katherine Ross is probably a grandmother. B. J., your social security check is ready for direct deposit.

Do I call this a mountain? No—this is more like a sand bunker, and someone ought to let him call for a mulligan. At least he's got a chance to play on the senior circuit, and if Jack, Arnie, and Lee can use a fourth man, then maybe he'll find a place at the 19th hole—they can swap stories and sing about the good ol' days at the same time.

Action Packed – The Best of the Capitol Years

RICHARD THOMPSON (CAPITOL)

One of the best acts on tour this summer is a musical mystery man to the general audience—but a veteran legend to his all-knowing fans. However, thanks to a terrific packaging effort by Capitol Records on this new release, Mr. Richard Thompson is ready to step from the shadows and into the spotlight. When the marketing team at EMI called this crackerjack set "Action Packed..." they ought to have been nominated for a first-place trophy for concept and song selection.

These songs are loaded with the brooding, riveting power that Thompson projects with his dark baritone voice and lyrics, and his guitar playing is a complex blend of slashing, tornado rhythms and dancing acoustic nimbleness. I'm strongly reminded of Mark Knopfler's touch, or The Band's Robbie Robertson—these guys would make a terrific showing as a trio on a mixed bill. His imagery captures the boldness and adventure of his rugged ancestry (he hails from the south country of England)—try and imagine a Celtic Warren Zevon's wild ways with a raging fire at his back, calling up all the spirits and magic that lurk in the legacies of Britain.

Additionally, Thompson also rides the razor's edge of the human psyche with obsessive power struggle memories from relationships that tore out his heart. His love songs stay clear of the mainstream "happy days" or "my love is gone"; instead, they prowl through intense dangerous alleys of jealousy, lust, and aloofness, and tell of bad men's renegade adventures: arrogant, proud, and tough. When Richard literally explodes with adrenalin macho swagger ("Fully Qualified to be Your Man"), he's the primal bull elk with the biggest rack.

The incredible thought, however, is that Thompson is a sensitive guy who can turn on the charm, and when he does, his music is as fragile as a soap bubble and as full of colorful images as a stained glass church window. This kind of dual identity is yet another reason that he remains a mesmerizing character.

Wrap all these amazing facets around his scorching lyrics (and he can pen some battery-acid specials), as well as satin-and-lace ballads that would cast him as a hero if he lived three centuries ago—this is a complex man who has a hypnotic power through his music. I dare you to listen to it once and walk away. In fact, I can testify that he has stopped a business meeting when it came up in the CD player—everyone just froze at the same time and asked to see the liner notes.

The best yet: can this guy and his players rock and swing! They also know how to get the most from their instruments, and that especially goes for the double bass and the various drummers and guests, including the folk instruments and the background vocals. My favorite song is…wait, I have too many. It just goes from better to great and onward.

For starters, I have to praise "I Feel So Good," with an amazing sound that comes from magical woodwinds, blowtorch organ, explosive percussion, and Thompson's raging abandonment on vocals and guitar. Anyone who can help me visualize the unrepentant social rebel who has "a suitcase full of 50-pound notes, and a half-naked woman with her tongue down my throat" makes me want to punch a hole in the sky with my fist. Go for it! I'd follow that with "I Can't Wake Up to Save My Life," as it careens like crazy with harpsichord-like keyboards, Star Wars sound effects, and blustery vocals that take wing over Richard's paranoid lyrics.

When was the last time you heard a loved one's appearance referred to as being half-missing and a hairstyle of reptiles hissing? Thompson also knows how to change his time signatures: witness the undulating, slinky rhythm of "Bathsheba Smiles" and a show that should not be missed—and don't overlook those earthy lyrics and rippling, muscular guitars. The same thing for "Mr. Rebound," which sounds like it came from a smoky café in Morocco.

I did say that Thompson has a respectful, gentlemanly air—when he's in the mood—and just follow his fingertips as they dance over the strings and through the summer sun on "Beeswing," one of his most popular requests. It's absolutely brilliant, evoking every memory of those who sailed from Great Britain to this country in centuries past with a king's court of fiddle, flute, concertina, mandolin, and Northumbrian pipes.

Richard has the same awareness of national character and the social classes as Robbie Robertson—they both know how to capture distinctive murals of the common folk and the intricacies of their popular appeal. A song that I just adore is "Waltzing's For Dreamers," with its lonely vocals and a 4/4 pace that is backed up with a sad fiddle and a finger-picking tune that could inspire someone to learn to play guitar. Thompson keeps the same quaintness on "King of Bohemia," with a mournful ballad that has a near-spiritual feel.

The tip of the hat absolutely goes to "Persuasion," which features a duet with son Teddy—and he's a great singer and guitarist in his own right. Teddy sounds as smooth as James Taylor mixed with Jackson Browne—as this was previously unreleased, it's the icing on the cake.

The entire package is perfect as is—and I didn't mean to leave out any other songs. If you have to ask what I have in mind to lead off the "Best of 2001," take a ticket and punch this one as first in line. Thompson is playing near me this fall at a local university, and I can't wait. I recommend dropping in at http://www.richardthompson-music.com to see more of his work—and I'm speaking as someone who only heard of him by name until now. I am a lucky guy to have had this CD sent to me—and I bought an extra one for a friend. Be dangerous and get one, too—you can handle the power of a motorcycle, right? I mean a "1952 Vincent Black Lightning," and just ask for Richard. He's got the keys--and every one of 'em fit the ignition to fire him up.

All Things Must Pass

GEORGE HARRISON (GN RECORDS/CAPITAL)

(I was driving to work as a teacher when I heard the news about George Harrison's death on November 29th. I called from my cell phone to the New York classic rock station, 104.3, and expressed my condolences in behalf of two men who had told me much about their time with George, Delaney Bramlett and Bobby Whitlock. Bobby's keyboards and vocals are stitched throughout this recording, and Delaney taught George how to play slide.)

Typical Lopate family dynamics @ 1970: my mother gives my younger (middle) brother a $20 and instructions to go to a local department store to buy a household item; instead, he follows an inner impulsive command, ignores her shopping list--*and returns with George Harrison's new solo album*. I naturally wait for the axe to fall—but little brother is treated like a hero. Why? The Beatles fascinated Mom.

History repeats itself in 2001, as I discover the reissue of this two-disc family heirloom. It still remains an epic achievement by the mutual efforts of George and his producer, Phil Spector. Yes, the trademark Spectorian "Wall of Sound" is here, but if you take a closer listen, it's apparent that it's not just electric guitars and overdubbed vocals that make this production so "large."

George borrowed from the cast and players of Friends from Delaney and Bonnie's entourage, as well as John Lennon's Plastic Ono Band. With the addition of stalwarts like Beatles session man Billy Preston, D&B Friend Bobby Whitlock, Gary Brooker

(ProcolHarum) and Gary Wright (Spooky Tooth) on keyboards, Carl Radle and Klaus Voorman on bass, Pete Drake's steel pedal, an old pal named Ringo on drums working alongside Alan White, and the spectacular fret board work of Eric Clapton and Dave Mason, the stars above were indeed hearing and seeing glorious works below on Earth.

Many tracks are layered like a multi-tiered wedding cake with rich, chunky rhythm guitars, thanks to support from the Beatles-sponsored group Badfinger, and the vocal arrangements have been embellished to provide depth where necessary. Even the horns (two favorite session men, Bobby Keys and Jim Price) and an orchestra help fill this canvas.

However, it's apparent that there are several musical phases of George (and friends) at work. Like a multi-limbed Hindu deity, Harrison takes on a variety of tasks: George as a country-style performer; the hard-driving rocker; and the motivated, inspirational spiritual poet. It was obvious from the song selections that George was very heavily expressing his Eastern philosophical and religious awakenings, and his writing reflected his search for Truth and inner guidance. As a result, this compilation is more like an artistically melodious biblical ziggurat from ancient Babylon, trying earnestly to reach the heavens.

Thanks to engineering improvements (and some additional updates from George), this is a 28-track bargain for Baby Boomers and Gen-X'ers alike, as five new arrivals make the package. For a real glimpse into this recording, I personally recommend the Beatles Anthology 3 release, which features an early workup of the title song, highlighting George's chord changes and the stark simplicity of his lyrics. It's a preview of what would happen when everyone else followed him in the studio and went about the business of making music.

Go ahead on disc two and see what it became: the rhythm guitars are as sturdy as ever, and mortar-and-brick strength comes from deliberate piano chords, fateful horn statements, and a ploddingly effective percussion. Pete Drake's steel guitar oscillates through octave changes like a banner rippling in the wind, and George's voice is laced with contemplation and reflection.

Harrison's vocals were never known for their power, and he gives me the image of a despondent waif or a young student at an English boarding school who had to watch older, more effective role models. Still, his vulnerability makes the desperation in his singing stand out in contrast (when needed) against the incredible guitar work that must have been done by Eric Clapton. Giving credit where possible, I have to assume that Slowhand is working the wah-wah pedal and creating those incredible yowls—I'm referring to "Tales of Brave Ulysses" and other Cream epics as my sources. He also turns in, as I hear it, some magnificent leads without any special effects on other tunes.

Here we go: "I'd Have You Anytime" has a slow, gentle rhythmic opening with a swaying, exotic lead guitar (I credit Clapton) that is almost Polynesian-like in touch and sound—am I right in saying that Duane Allman used this idea with a bottleneck on *Layla's* "I Am Yours" love poem? I can just see the peacock feather fans being waved by obedient servants in the sultan's palace for his beloved favored concubine. Aww, so everyone—including George—knew he took the Chiffon's "He's So Fine" and retooled it into "My Sweet Lord." Isn't that 12-string just perfect?

Harrison also displays his unique laptop bottleneck style, and the choir raises their voices in thanks for the glory of Universal Love. I remember having this as a single .45 disc. At the opening signal, "Wah-Wah" bolts from its starting blocks—I'm betting for Clapton on the foot control pedal, and I can't tell who else is fighting him for position on lead.

That must be Clapton and not Dave Mason on slide, ringing out like a trombone (yes, Mason was an original member of the fledgling Derek and the Dominos, but left in the middle of the timeframe with Harrison. He also played the lead slide on "Coming Home" with *Delaney and Bonnie & Friends On Tour with Eric Clapton*), and don't forget the horns sounding their fanfare. Pick up on that great background vocal mix, as everyone in the building seems to lend their voice. Like a high-speed machine factory at work, this collaboration can and *does* mean better production and higher efficiency!

I always liked "Isn't it a Pity" for its honesty and sensitivity, and there are compositional references to George's Beatles roots, aided by Ringo's percussion and the orchestra's arrangements. George again provides his unique slide, and the backup vocals sadly chime in their dismay. The driving lead and horns ignite "What is Life," and Spector's mixing truly lends a stadium-sized reservoir of space that is filled by the busy hands at work.

Another pal named Bob shows up here with writing credits—you folk singers know and recognize "If Not For You," don'tcha? There's a great meeting of minds between piano and organ, George provides some delicate slide, and a harmonica blows bubbles in the breeze. The country feeling continues with "Behind That Locked Door," buoyed up nicely by Drake's steel guitar and a keyboard duo of organ and piano. This would be better served and performed by one of the ladies on the Nashville circuit—Dolly Parton comes to mind as a sure bet--as George's voice just sounds too frail to be convincing.

Calamity! The first 27 seconds of "Let it Down" convinced me that a forest fire had just begun from a lightning strike. Bobby W. sends gusts of smoke up the chimney on B-3, George vividly calls for more wood to be sacrificed, and the percussion and horns keep chopping and sawing to meet the supply. With a tricky time signature and a call for global peace, "Run of the Mill" would have fit handily on *Magical Mystery Tour* as an "All You Need is Love" complement.

I mentioned something extra in the package, and it comes in the newly provided "I Live For You," as Pete Drake's steel pedal glides through a perfectly designed solo—this has the potential to be a very happy sponsorship theme for any self-help/improvement meeting. I do like the arrival of the acoustic version "Beware of Darkness," just to hear George's chord work, backed up with an undiluted vocal with moments of frustration. He repeats the formula effectively with "Let it Down."

Let me be perfectly clear, Nixon-style: even though the "rough mix" of "What is Life" has added piccolo, trumpet and oboe parts, it's the karaoke version, folks—buried below the huge instrumental display (but not deep enough in certain spots, if you listen carefully) *are vocals!* Ya didn't quite wipe them off, George!—but it's a good option. I give the man a chance, because "My Sweet Lord" for 2001 has a tantalizing sitar intro, sinewy lead, and the vocals are better and a bit more "sweet." Let the courts (and the Chiffons) take a bow, but Harrison owns this one.

On disc two, "Beware of Darkness" comes slowly out of its cave to speak wisely to the gathered masses, gaining strength from the assistance of four strong arms on piano and guitar. I can't find the credit in the liner notes, but that's George sneezing with joyful abandon and zest on harmonica and enthusiastic acoustic guitar, as well as his and Badfinger's vocal overdubs on "Apple Scruffs," my personal favorite. The name refers to Harrison's dedicated fans, who must again be delighted to hear George pay them tribute. (On a bootleg version called *The Making of All Things Must Pass,* George's discomfort at playing harmonica and guitar is heard as he laments to Phil Spector that the device is getting caught in his mustache and beard and tearing out his hair.)

There's an Olde English nuance to the "Ballad of Sir Frankie Crisp (Let it Roll)" that has me seeing thatched roofs of cottages and those rolling green hills of Britain—I really expected this to come from Jethro Tull's Ian Anderson. *Everyone* heads for the penthouse party of "Awaiting on You All," as Spector takes the mixing board and goes as far horizontally as he can manage. The percussion and slide are echoed to be as "fat" as possible, and tell me again if Whitlock and Clapton's backup vocal chorus didn't appear in the last phrases of "ease my worried mind" from *Layla*'s title track. "I Dig Love" sounds like a cheerleader's chant with that boomy sound again on drums and piano, and the B-3 just curls vapor trails. Eric rules the world on wah-wah with his intro and lead on "Art of Dying," and Jim Gordon thumps heartily on his drums like a physical trainer to keep everyone in shape.

The alternative version of "Isn't It a Pity" clears out the studio, leaving room for the organ to act as a lighthouse fog beacon, with guitar, piano, and strings to steer by to find a safe harbor. Will Mankind ever learn? George offers his prayer to be delivered by the wings of a dove, as "Hear Me Lord" is as dynamic and meaningful as anything on the Christian music stations today.

There were some other goings-on, I suspect, after Phil Spector left the building—I offer as testimony "It's Johnny's Birthday," which sounds like kids were running the control panel and playing with the dials and knobs for 49 seconds. Four sets of extended jams follow, beginning with "Plug Me In," comprised of the nucleus of the original Derek and the Dominos (with Dave Mason), as it's time to rip this joint and play some boogie. "I Remember Jeep" has Ginger Baker, Klaus Voorman, and Billy Preston swapping roles with their counter-parts. This comes across like a soundtrack for a teenager on his first driving lesson: all over the road, but don't forget, it was only a jam for fun.

I am more convinced than ever that Spector had his back turned, because "Thanks for the Pepperoni" has to offer some kind of hint as to what was coming in through the door—and Chuck Berry must have been the one who sent the pizza. Go, go, Little Queenie, go! The session wrapped up with "Out of the Blue," with a moderate jazz-like bashing that features Bobby Keys on sax and some interesting guitar rips.

So, it's been 30 years since I first heard this music, and now I can look back and see from whence it has come and to where it will be going. George Harrison's songwriting and singing are still an important part of my life—it's even better to have this CD, knowing that I don't have to worry about hitting on my mother for a $20. Just let your Beatles fan-friends know that George has released this, and maybe they'll tell their moms, too. I did—but I'm keeping this one for myself. I'll let my brother get her a copy—it's only fair, right?

Soulsville – Souled out 'n Sanctified

Danny Brooks & the Rockin' Revelators

(One of the sweetest, kindest, and sincere musicians I have ever had the luck to meet: Mr. Danny Brooks. His heart is filled with love for God and the faith that brought him from the edge of death into salvation.

At this time, he is working on a dynamic project with Johnny Sandlin, Bonnie Bramlett, Scott Boyer, and Carla Thomas. After staying at my farm home one night, I gave him a huge selection of blues CDs to help with his new-found love for playing dobro.)

You recognize it when it comes through the speakers: it's another musician who has their own version of The Voice. The Voice: that special mix of power, rhythm and blues, heartfelt truth, and majesty. It's a southern thing mostly—a blend of a soul food diet (Gregg Allman), a childhood in the Arkansas Delta (Levon Helm), knowing the Creator as guidance (Solomon Burke), or being born to play the blues (Bobby Whitlock).

It's a voice that growls with a passion, rumbles from deep in the belly like a tiger's purr, and scrapes against the vocal cords like it was gravel going down a chute. And Lord have mercy, You know the children who bring it to fulfillment. They're out there making His music—and one of them is Danny Brooks.

Some strong conviction, people: He sings, "I wasn't born down in Memphis, but Memphis lives in my soul." You can fill your plate with that and never go hungry again, because Danny is every inch and pound a man of "Soulsville" hospitality. Who wrote this song: Johnny Cash? Too soon did we lose you, John—you'd have loved this one. The same chugging pressure is there.

Give a listen to Brooks and the Revelators and you'll be yearning for warm Tennessee nights on the back porch with a dobro, sweet tea, black-eyed peas, cornbread and gravy, and gospel breakfast meetings. You've been Souled Out 'n Sanctified. But keep an eye on your map coordinates: Danny's from Ontario. A Canadian with the earthiest feel for the Word and the good folks down yonder.

Don't ask why—it's one of those mysteries in life, and "Nobody Knows You Like the Lord." Nominated for an award this year, Danny bares his spiritual strength in simple terms—and with beautiful support from friends from the NorthernBlues Gospel All-Stars in this slow, steady song of praise. Just the basics of what you'd expect to find in a good Southern church on Sunday—but that gritty tension from Danny's voice just keeps your hands raised a little higher.

And that's the beauty of what follows: "Fence Me In" is a prayer of dedication to lead a life of service and honesty. Let the tempo move a bit ("Glory Hallelujah") and listen to the clapping in your ears alongside Richard Bell's saintly organ—this is testimony of the highest kind. And if you just want to wiggle a bit in your seat for joy but show respect (while trying to follow the preacher's words), Colin Linden's mandolin will hear those thoughts to "Lift Me Up." Dennis Pinhorn's upright bass adds the warmest assurance needed—an electric 4-string would never have made it this sweet.

Young and old, brothers and sisters, we're "Soul Satisfied," and that's why it's okay to follow the urge to whistle the melody. If your chest is swelling with happiness and love is in your heart, this is a chance to offer praise alongside Danny and friends and feel terrific. If the Spirit moves you, then let it groove you, and "Standing On the Rock" is the best place to be seen. Don't stop counting the remaining songs—you'll fill your satchel with riches each time you reach out and touch them. Finally! when it's all said and done, you're "Souled Out 'n Sanctified." And the satisfaction that washes throughout is from a well that has no bottom. Just let a Messenger with the Voice, Mr. Danny Brooks, sing it to you.

In Concert (Polydor)
Live at the Fillmore (Polydor)

DEREK & THE DOMINOS

(If there has been anyone who carried the Olympic Flame of Guitar Heroes, Eric Clapton would have to be considered. He has matured as a musician who truly brings smiles to everyone onstage with him. Thank you, old friend, for these fireworks displays.)

These packages are really fraternal twins of the same concert: two performances a night on October 23rd and 24th, 1970, at Bill Graham's Fillmore East. If you love Eric Clapton (and not liking this phase of his career is like finding fault with a sunrise), then it's a treat to own both CD's, even though they carry the bulk of the same material on each set. However, the subtle nuances and slight alterations of Eric's serpentine lead guitar and the athletic backup show of the Dominos (Bobby Whitlock on organ and piano; Jim Gordon on drums; Carl Radle on bass) make this a musical "would you prefer blondes, brunettes or redheads" type of opportunity! Just dig in and enjoy.

It always takes just one tune to make me reach for the *In Concert* disc, and that's "Why Does Love Got to be So Sad?" Beginning with a loose exchange between Clapton's wah-wah musings and Gordon's ride cymbal/percussion prodding, the song shakes itself awake like a rearing stallion as Whitlock takes his cue on Hammond B-3 and starts to breathe fire. The band catches the momentum and everyone is cooking, and it's especially interesting to catch Carl Radle's fluidity if you use headphones. Underestimated as a bass player, he keeps himself nimble enough to make his partners give that little extra bit.

Okay, I'm a sucker for rock 'n roll, so just juice it up with a "Bottle of Red Wine." Eric and Bobby just have the time of their lives, and Clapton's vocals and playing are pure enthusiasm, keeping tandem with Whitlock's exhilarating background vocals and laser-beam organ lines. The guitar solo is crisp and punchy, and if your feet aren't nailed to the floor, then you've probably moved the furniture and grabbed your favorite dancing partner. I'd leave things as they are: next up is a raunch 'n roll, and someone needs to "Roll It Over."—you can figure out that some groupie somewhere is patting herself on the back (literally) for the memories from this complement. The lyrics are bawdy and earthy, and Eric's guitar reaches straight for the heavens like a beacon looking for an airplane at night.

There's still room for a party, and Eric shows the way: he's got "Blues Power." Whitlock plays piano like a true percussion instrument, raining down chords to keep pace with Clapton's voracious attack, and the ever-steady Gordon runs on nuclear fuel. One tune that appears as a before-and-after is a favorite of many from the *Layla* album: "Tell The Truth." Stripped bare of the slide work of Duane Allman, this song has two incarnations, and each shows why this was a mandatory part of the set: the anguished, grievous singing of Clapton and Whitlock work like barbed wire to keep a sharp boundary marker that lets Clapton kick up his heels on Stratocaster like a scared rabbit trying to double back on its tracks, urged on by anvil choruses of piano and cymbal smashes. However, on *Fillmore*, Eric throws a nod to Skydog's influence as he slips a bottleneck on his finger and whines and buzzes like an industrial saw on the jobsite.

A special serving of *Layla* tunes makes *Fillmore* a welcomed addition to your collection: "Key to the Highway, Nobody Knows You When You're Down and Out," and "Little Wing." Clapton kicks off "Key" with a clarion blast of notes, then swings down on his chariot as Whitlock rocks him slowly. The lyrics are textured with a barroom smoky feeling, and Eric dreamily loses himself for a few brief moments, only to crack the whip again on his strings. Everyone successfully repeats this format for "Nobody Knows You…", and Eric's vocals stand as testimony to the original author's shame and self-pity, and he puts out his best Freddie King tribute. With a touch of controlled lead mixed with wah-wah and steamy organ, Jimi Hendrix is saluted with the fireworks display of "Little Wing" as Eric pours out notes of 24-karat gold.

If there's such a thing as British gospel, "Presence of the Lord" fits the bill. Eric's voice is strained and fragile, but the melody is initially supported on the strong shoulders of Whitlock's piano and backup vocals. Clapton gets his sea legs under himself—then he fills the sails with a mighty flurry, mixing string-bending with wah-wah effects. With optimism and recovery of sorts in mind, maybe it's time to check out "Got to Get Better in a Little While." Ominously direct and to-the-point with comments about Clapton's battle with heroin ("Sniffing things that ain't good for me"), Whitlock helps build a wall of driving piano with his mates to lay a foundation under Eric's panoramic phrases. In songs like this, the rhythmic coordination of Radle and Gordon as counter-weights really shows why this team was so stabilizing in allowing Clapton his freedom to soar.

As a human dynamo, Jim Gordon kept a relentless pace on drums in a live set (ala Butch and Jaimoe), and he is turned loose halfway through "Let it Rain" to unleash a barrage of percussive fundamentals in his solo. Using a simple but effective kit, he pulls every inch of available space from his tom-toms, using their deep resonance to pull some bottom against the snare's pistol crack and cymbal hiss and splashes. Whitlock's Hammond shudders with fury, and Clapton again leaps for the upper atmosphere. When the others finally rejoin Gordon's frantic pace (I have personal testimony that the boys were indulging right behind Jim, ignoring his warranted annoyance and "get up here and let's play!" prodding), guitar and B-3 sprint home against him for the checkered flag, and Radle keeps them honest. On the *Fillmore* version, Clapton's outburst at this point leaves the solar system at the speed of light.

So, maybe it's time to slow things down—a whole lot. "Have You Ever Loved A Woman" lets everyone move like it's 95 degrees in the shade…and the heat makes all the difference. His vocals rip apart his torment and Eric's searing fingers perform open-heart surgery with a razor-sharp cutting edge. This is why they call it the blues—but this is really indigo-deep and to the core. With that in mind, turn back to *Fillmore* and let Robert Johnson's "Crossroads" remind you of who caught Eric's ear and soul with his own legendary bargain. Deliberate and crisp, everyone runs their routine like a gym boxing workout. For those of you who own the *Crossroads* compilation, this is the same version.

It really comes down to paying dues, and Derek & the Dominos put enough credit in their account to break the bank. As much as can be said about the excesses and emotional upheavals that were the detonating device and/or destroyer of their efforts, we can be thankful that they were so willing to live in this musical lake of fire. Clapton had the best team of commandos that ever strapped on, picked up, or plugged in during this timeframe, and for those who were lucky enough to have been there, seeing was believing. Hearing it again just validates what once was…magic…of the highest order from a man and his friends.

6-and-12-string Guitar

LEO KOTTKE (RHINO)

(The Holy Grail of Finger picking. Although he's not doing the "fast" style any longer, this was the doorway for many of us who are still fascinated by his effortless technique.)

It all starts here: anyone who plays knows that; for the sheer reckless abandonment that ultimately cost Leo his speed by way of carpal tunnel; for the articulate melodies and delightful possibilities; for the "what does THAT mean?" bewilderment over his liner notes that fueled our fuzzy minds. (Getting loaded on anything and listening to this was like going aloft like a kite.)

This is what sets Kottke (and later, the late Michael Hedges) apart: they truly understand the guitar as a percussive instrument. By the way, for those lucky to have seen Kottke concerts or found rare CDs of shows, his wandering comments onstage about song titles are often about the ingredients and inceptions of his work: hilarious monologues.

The tunes individually have unique personalities of energy, tones, and presentation: an auditory garden of flowers. Such technique and dexterity! Clarity! And fast--try doing the hop-scotch dance of harmonics that dazzles "The Driving of the Year Nail."

It's his touch also--almost maddening for those who had been practicing (or wishing to play) and wondering how he made it sound so effortless and natural. "The Last of the Arkansas Greyhounds" rolls and bounces with a perpetual motion machine behind it (and alerting us to Leo's fetish for titles); "Ojo" is clean and bright, and

I see images of an old grandmother-type with a shawl rocking an infant in a cradle over "Crow River Waltz." Leo's slide virtuosity is also introduced here on "The Sailor's Grave on the Prairie," and "Vaseline Machine Gun," an undulating gyration of leaping bottleneck instrumental tribute to a navy submariner buddy of Leo's that kicks off with a brief burst of "Taps."

"Jack Fig" is a treat to understand at this slow pace (it's a buzz saw in concert on <u>My Feet are Smiling</u>), but just as spectacular to see on video for his complex chording and picking. A close cousin is "Watermelon," and Leo's slide squawks show how well suited he is with a 12-string's tunings.

Just to show he's done his studying, Bach's "Jesu, Joy of Man's Desiring" is showcased for its pristine timeliness--you almost want to bow in tribute. "The Fisherman," a gorgeous tune by its simplicity, just bounds along like a happy puppy out for a walk, but "The Tennessee Toad" (Leo's sly dig at his father-in-law), oozes with molasses-like whining slide.

But "Busted Bicycle" saves the day--and recharges everything/one. Inspired by a wayward car and a friend's chained-to-the-lamppost 2-wheeler, Leo works in an old blues riff (hey--the Stones used it on the <u>Beggars Banquet</u> LP) around a banjo picking style with a 12-string explosion. (Check it out live; it's a fireworks display.)

More Dali-like titles ahead: "The Brain of the Purple Mountain" and "Coolidge Rising," but they're both full of fast and clean picking that just reminds you to hit the repeat button when it's all over.

This is something to share because the guy is making the art of guitar playing sound magical--like it's a universal talent for us all to try. Just call this inspiration at its highest.

My Feet Are Smiling

Leo Kottke (BGO)

Remember those great Looney Tunes cartoons where the angry swarm of bees would chase some goofy person/creature who had foolishly given the hive some grief? The bees would morph into great shapes of assault: a descending bomb; scissors; a sledgehammer. In 1972, Mike Michel, a high school classmate who later became my best friend casually dropped the needle of his turntable onto a Leo Kottke LP (*My Feet Are Smiling*.) I wasn't impressed. The first song had some guy who flubbed a song ("The Tennessee Toad" was Leo's intention), but instead, ends up groaning a vocal as he played a thick morass of churning acoustic guitar. So what gives? I asked.

Enter the swarm of angry bees, who took as their target my unsuspecting ears. Leo had finished tune #1 and unleashed "Busted Bicycle," a banjo-styled frenzy on 12-string that had me reeling in shock. A bass line percolated like crazy behind the frantic buzz-saw resonance of the melody—or whatever represented one. How many fingers did this man have? Twenty?

I was hooked—or stung, depending on how it manifested. "Louise" is a mournful eulogy for a woman of loose virtue and easy access, "Blue Dot" has some painful-for-the-fingers dual-string bending, and the more sedate studio version of "Stealing" is cranked with a V-10 engine. "Living in the Country" (which appears on Leo's out-of-print *Circle 'Round the Sun* LP, available from sellers on EBay) follows, as does the mischievous "June Bug" and "Standing in My Shoes" with Leo on slide.

Right after "Egg Tooth" (which is nearly impossible to follow: like an opening break on a pool table when the balls scatter like crazy), the clincher is what Leo calls a "medley," starting off with the gorgeous "Crow River Waltz," sounding for all the world like a lovely lullaby, J.S. Bach's classical "Jesu, Joy of Man's Desiring," and the absolute pedal-to-the-floorboard "Jack Fig." With 26+ CDs to his credit, my head hasn't stopped humming since. And Leo's been "in the zone" since he picked up his first guitar. This is doing what you love for work.

With his earthy baritone voice, Kottke sounds more like a distant cousin of James Earl Jones, and amazingly, he sings well with it (aside from his youthful days of doubt and legendary claims that he vocalized more like "geese farts on a muggy day"). Leo has a…unique sense of humor too; it's part of his performance.

Any distraction, observation, flash-in-the-dark thought, or other perusal will bring a deluge of stream-of-consciousness remarks that remarkably fit in behind his tuning warm-ups, and the laughter that wafts from the audience only inspires him to further mental mischief. Maybe it's because he now has to hear "9/11" associated with his birthday. Leo never seems to do things low-key anyway. Go try and decipher his existentialist Einstein-meets-Salvador Dali-like essays on his website if you want to see how Gomez Addams would have written, go to Leo's site at (http://www.leokottke.com) and excuse it as a quirk of fate.

But Leo likes the macabre (let him tell the audience about dissecting a horse in high school, or working in a morgue), and somehow, the bees that he generates from his fingertips aren't quite so angry; in fact, they're…*excited*! Leo, you're my man!

Sell My Jewelry

Barbara Blue (Big Blue Records)

(Friends said to me, "Do you know what you sound you'd like doing to her?" Damn right I do—but Barbara was very pleased with this. She told me so. Yes she did...very pleased. I know which side of the bread the butter goes: the side that doesn't land on the ground when it drops from your fingers 'cause it's too hot from the toaster...)

The most impressive thing to see when you're in Memphis is... the Mississippi River, right? Not even close—the tides and currents, they say, slow down, when Barbara Blue is on stage and doing a number. The lady may sing the blues, and some wicked funk, too; be warned, though, because she's more infrared, and liable to make the Greenhouse Effect look like an afterthought on the thermometer. Barbara may say she's blue, but I don't know if there's a measurement yet for this musical heat on the spectrum.

This is a new voice—one that would make that ol' river go back for a second look—she commands, <u>demands</u>, and gets attention. It's the kind of effect a vixen named Circe did for twelve months to a wandering sailor named Ulysses. She wove some potent spells, that woman.

In another similar way, if friend and heartbreak E.G. Kight has the pipes of a brass horn, then Barbara is alongside with an alto saxophone for vocal cords, and you <u>will</u> follow her beckon and call. Why? Same as E.G. did: here's another one who's ' "Trouble with a Capital 'T'.". Oh, Lord, this should have been a signal that I was about to beg for mercy, and Mike Finnegan's chilling B-3 acts as Barbara's high priest to draw you to your knees. That's the Texacali Horns who weave and sway behind her (Joe Sublett and Darrell Leonard), and there's no choice but to obey Barbara's wishes. Joe sneers and jeers at your fate, but Barbara holds the power to be pleased: you can't get away, and she's also "Back by Popular Demand." Those three snake charmers who serve their mistress so effectively are Larry Fulcher on bass, working alongside Tony Braunagal's rhythmic drumming, and Johnny Lee Schell's weaving guitar.

What would she bid you to do? She has the "Tool Box Blues," (although I think she's not worried about it). 'Just stick around, baby, you've got something in your tool box (that turns her love light on) and you might come in handy some time.' No need to guess what her workbench is, brother, and you're gonna be changing more than oil. Yes, that's the grease gun in your hands, but not from the hardware store.

But see here: as I said, the woman knows what she wants; she's for real and down-to-earth, and the diamond solitaire on this disc comes from the sweetest chords you can find when Barbara and her men roll out the carpet for "Don't Lead Me On." This is what it's all about: she's got a heart of 24-carat, and that's worth a royal ransom. Power and beauty <u>do</u> have a match, and despite all the worries and fears of losing herself, staying true (and blue) to Barbara could be the finest thing a man could find.

So now you're committed and hooked, and there is something sweeter than sugar coming when Barbara gets over her "Road Blues." You can sway and grind because she's got you in that magic spell, and John "Juke" Logan's harmonica wails like a pet songbird that has just seen the light of a new dawn in the window. Maybe that's <u>you</u> on the perch, looking for favors, and if Barbara's going places, so is her main squeeze, because she "Can't Get Your Lovin' Off My Mind." Accessories are one thing, but love is a commodity, and the self-titled Memphis Queen has her expectations—and fulfillment is a noble priority. There are more dangerous things to do than disappoint her (with a CD like this, honoring her sensuous decrees will become the next Olympic Extreme Sport event).

Barbara has some spiritual musical guardians watching over her, and you don't mess with the vamp and sermon of John Lee Hooker, who must be smiling down on this earthly messenger. Taking a mosaic look at the Hook's titles in a throbbing molten lecture, "From the Delta to the Golden Gates" drills deep into the heart of the blues master's soul in tribute and love. She's also more than capable of handling any tomcattin,' and I pity the fool who instigated the angry manhunt and threats from "Cheatin' Blues." You need some serious insurance to double-down in love on a woman with more tattoos on her arm than you have.

She's still a romantic in spite of all the wounds, and there's a "Drunken Angel" in the picture. Staggering, twisting organ and a gorgeous ballad tune are the medicine Barbara needs. So, since she's feeling alive again, it's because she's been "Brought Together By the Blues," and Honey and Rod Piazza have penned a magical recipe for her. Just in case that doesn't keep 'em crawling back for more, Godmother Janis Joplin will cast down the judgment of "Turtle Blues," and Barbara won't turn the other cheek. If anything, she's ready to sock you on the jaw.

So when they say, what are the great sights out west, there are monuments, statues, natural resources, and other wonders—but none of them sing. And none of them are as magnificent as this woman, who deserves, earns, and offers a package of value that has a price tag worn in her heart. Just think: she would sell her jewels for your love--and she's one helluva glittering gem herself. She'll wear you with pride, too, and that's why blue is going to be your favorite color. Barbara's gonna tell you so.

The Allman Brothers Band; Idewild South; At the Fillmore East; Eat a Peach; The Fillmore Concerts

THE ALLMAN BROTHERS BAND

(On my left bicep is the first of my four tattoos: The Eat a Peach truck, which I had done at Rose's Tattoo Parlor in Hong Kong as a sailor in 1980. To me, this band's name and legacy says, "All Man and Woman Brothers and Sisters." No one—but no one—could and still can hold down a jam like the Allman Brothers Band. From a melding of jazz, blues, country, and rock, they made the South rise again.)

The Allman Brothers Band

"Don't Want You No More" starts out with the searing, up-front statement that would characterize the band's future work. The twin guitar leads roar out a dramatic opening, and are followed by blazing organ, crashing drum/cymbals. Then it's Duane's turn: he steps up to belt out a dynamic riff. The band regroups again for another pass at the opening theme, Dickey then hammers a reply to Duane, and everyone simmers down into "It's Not My Cross to Bear." Gregg's vocals are steamed raw, and his torment and despair are left standing bare and alone as Duane wraps another solo around the framework of Gregg's vocals.

"Black Hearted Woman" rocks along with Gregg's angry lyrics and guitar solos that skip boisterously ahead of the rest of the band. "Trouble No More," their studio version of Muddy Waters's song, shuffles and hesitates while Duane shows his slide guitar call-and-reply style against Gregg's vocals. "Every Hungry Woman" opens with a gust of guitar and B-3 Hammond organ layering the track, and Gregg's accusing comments and voice are painted with cynicism and contempt.

"Dreams" is one of the band's masterpieces, as Duane mixes slide and lead guitar. The drummers coil and release with refrained shots of snare drum and cymbal rides, and Gregg's organ takes the song to a hazy, etheric state. His grievous, intense singing provides the setting for Duane's soaring, spiraling solo. Skydog's mid-way switch to bottleneck lifts the piece right out of the stratosphere, and sets up the infamous, earth-shattering "Whipping Post." Berry starts off with dark and frightening warfare bass lines, the band reaches a frenzy behind Gregg's confrontation of his misery, and the guitars ring out their defiance. Duane and Dickey embrace the pain with their solos, and the band walks on coals to a scorching crescendo. Gregg has never sounded more wretched in his plight when he sings the chorus line.

Idewild South

"Revival," written by Dickey Betts, shows a hippie, peace-and-love side of the band, with cheerful acoustic guitar and family vocals helping underscore the country sound of twin lead guitars and upbeat measure. "Don't Keep Me Wonderin'" offers stinging slide by Duane, highlighted by octave sweeps as he rides up the fret board on his solo. Special guest Thom Doucette also fills in handsomely with harmonica whoops.

"Midnight Rider" is Gregg's offering of a country-rock ballad, with dusty trails fading in the sunset. "In Memory of Elizabeth Reed," Dickey's instrumental wizardy, features a panoramic, Carribean-like intro, and a race course workout for both guitar solos. Berry paints

"Hoochie Coochie Man" with voodoo vocals and threats, and Duane and Dickey pick the flesh off the bones with their solos. Everything is forgiven in Gregg's mind as he laments on piano during "Please Call Home," and Duane plays his heart out beside him, sadly reflecting on his brother's pleas for reconciliation. James Brown would be pleased with "Leave My Blues At Home," a scruffy, bumpy shuffle. These albums were re-released as *Beginnings*.

The Allman Brothers Band at Fillmore East

The Brothers outdid themselves at this home-away-from-home venue, and the legacy of this album is worth every second of the recording. "Statesboro Blues," the Taj Mahal tune that inspired Duane to take up slide, is paraded and heralded here as a show-stopping opener that makes the set jump from the start. His slide intro and lead riffs seem to snicker, joke and flare up his presence on stage, and the rhythm section churns and thumps like the circus coming to town. Dickey's single-note sustained solo has the best phrasing this side of B.B. King; his ability to hold on for a few bars is an understated gem.

"Done Somebody Wrong" shows Gregg again on swaggering, aloof vocals, but Duane steals the show. I call this his "sawtooth slide," because his ending solo sounds like a file or steak knife is rasping away at the strings. Elmore James would have needed sandpaper to get Duane's tone, much less Skydog's skittering style. Special guest Thom Doucette again blows impressively on mouth harp.

"Stormy Monday" lets Gregg slur his weary vocals, but the guitars are crystal-clear with resigned blues sweetness. "You Don't Love Me" lets Dickey and Duane volley against each other in the spotlight for some of their most creative, talented solos. Jaimoe and Butch do a rollicking shuffle that pushes Dickey along, and Duane ends by spraying "Joy to the World" over the audience. "Hot 'Lanta" is an instrumental with jazz roots. Everyone smokes their instruments, and the band jumps a "Fee-Fi-Fo-Fum" hurdle after the drum solo. The ending comes in a swirling cloud of sound: a proverbial, angry genie-of-the-lamp who rises and then vanishes in the climax of organ, stormy bass, cymbal washes, and tympani thunder. The audience must have fallen back breathless in their seats when this song ended.

"In Memory Of Elizabeth Reed" was immortalized during this show, although it's really a mix of two sets. Dickey opens with delicate volume control to raise and drop swells of notes like heaving ocean waves, and the opening twin guitar statement is displayed on an invisible curtain of melody. His solo is heavy again with sustained bars, and then Gregg rips the keys off his B-3 while the drummers snap back their answers. The studio version had Jaimoe on congas, but this set gave him space to lay down barrages on his kit to offset Butch. Their timing and synchronicity were magnificent. Duane picks up the cue from Dickey and hurls a torrent of notes into the air, with phrases that are imbedded with jazz motifs. He ends with an explosion that sounds like an Atlantic hurricane hitting the beach. "Whipping Post" shows the band stretching to its mighty outer limits, while Gregg gets mileage from his weary vocals. The band plays with their hearts on the line, and it completes a 22-plus minute marathon.

The Fillmore Concerts

These are the Fillmore East sets with some variations, such as a restored, missing harmonica solo on "Stormy Monday." However, the notorious audience calls for "Whipping Post" were wiped off, as well as Gregg's enthusiastic request for handclaps on "One Way Out." Other mixes show alternative sides, but I don't quite find the addition of Rudolph "Juicy" Carter on saxophone to justify replacing "Hot 'Lanta." Berry's up-front, prominent bass has been shoved aside to feature the drums, but this does allow Elvin Bishop to crow on "Drunken Hearted Boy," featuring Steven Miller on piano and mischievous slide by Duane, with additional closing announcements. However, it is an easier way to get more music for the dollar, as it makes room for "Mountain Jam," the cornerstone of Eat A Peach.

Eat A Peach

This album chronologically starts with the afore-mentioned "Mountain Jam," which can be heard opening up as "Whipping Post" fades off on the Fillmore East set. It is a stunning, tremendous thought that the Brothers followed the powerful beauty of long song with another, more intricate piece that runs 33 minutes.

The journey starts off with Duane and Dickey trading off each other's lead, then the band takes the theme from a boiling cauldron of layered jazz. Berry shows his prime by rumbling behind the two guitarists, and Duane grabs a short, direct solo, opening the way for Gregg to run for daylight. Berry casts out fountains of hot bass lava, and the drummers fill in with flourishes and ruffs to sheetrock the room with sound and action. Dickey follows with a truly explosive solo that just blows the lid off, and Berry burns everything in his path.

The demolition team of Jaimoe and Butch then take over, with Butch on first solo, slugging and pounding out a furious snare and tom-tom pattern. Jaimoe takes a compact ride on snare and kick drum, and the stage is set for Berry's twisting solo. Oakley thunders out lead bass lines, takes the "Mountain" theme for some jagged runs, and the drummers prod him along like a jockey passing the clubhouse turn. The band then follows Duane's signal, and everyone hangs on while he takes the most meaningful, inspired solo of his too-brief career. His poetic slide swoops and hovers like an ocean bird, and the rest of the band gathers to watch and listen.

It ends (momentarily) as everyone rides their chords over the waterfall's edge of sound. Duane then prophetically leads the band through "Will the Circle Be Unbroken," the "Mountain" theme is recaptured and brought out again, and the band again feasts joyfully. At the song's dynamic ending, a complete recapitulation is offered, and a celebration is unleashed. Duane salutes his band with a breathless announcement of thanks, and it's time to go home.

"One Way Out" reappears here, and the Brothers turned this piece inside-out with hustle and snap. Dickey starts the show off with a quick flourish, hastened by an off-beat drum riff, and the others join in, with Duane playing harp-like phrases. Dickey's solo burns bright, and then Duane and he trade off against each other with muscular statements. Duane ignites some of his trademark "sawtooth slide," and squeals away, high on the fret board. Gregg plays up this display with haughty arrogance and without remorse at his plight.

"Trouble No More" is spiced up over the studio version, with Butch and Jaimoe picking up the tempo and propelling the rhythm. Their ride cymbals smack out like windshield wipers during a hard downpour, Duane throws down squawks of protest against Gregg's matter-of-fact "told you so" singing, and everyone stays on top of the beat.

"Stand Back" features Duane in rare form: his slide brays like a brass instrument. Gregg's vocals and lyrics are earthy and bitter, especially his lament, "Thirty minutes after I set sail, she put up a sign and my house began to wail." Berry gets writing credits, and his bass stomps up and down like boot heels on a tile floor. Dickey showcases his high tenor on "Blue Sky," and the song gently kicks off with electric piano and acoustic guitar supporting the melodious solos. "Little Martha," a lovely tune, blends together dobro, acoustic guitar and bass (on the Dreams box set), showing the gentle, romantic side that dwelt within Duane.

The "new" band, continued after Duane's tragic loss, picks up with "Ain't Wastin' Time No More," Gregg's courageous but losing effort to face up to life without his brother. Dickey ran off brilliant electric slide licks here, and although it was not intentional, Duane's presence shines through his partner's notes. Gregg's lyrics and vocals are challenging and confrontational, and it almost sounds as though he could have overcome the struggles that lay ahead of him.

"Les Brers in A Minor," Dickey's instrumental, dips into international waters as everyone lays down a tale of symphonic intrigue and suspense. The band totally overwhelmed the genre of soundtrack writing with this charismatic masterpiece. "Melissa" was written years earlier by Gregg, but now it sounds like a eulogy for Duane, with references to a musical gypsy with "sunbeams in his hair." Gregg's acoustic guitar leaves space for Dickey's trembling refrains, and the sorrow of the band is brought out for all to hear.

Weed and Water

Paul Marshall (SCO 119901)

(What an easy-going feeling it is to hear Paul Marshall--just like warm clothes fresh out of the dryer. And his songwriting is just as cozy. From acid rocker days with the Strawberry Alarm Clock to country bass and vocals...still the gentleman, too.)

One of the best things about being an editor-writer and getting to review music is the opportunity to sample releases that are keepers for collectors like me. When Paul Marshall sent me a copy of his new CD, I felt like I had a new painting to hang on the wall.

This country singing and playing makes me take a fresh new look at the genre—these songs are good clean fun and respect. With some very skilled fieldhands behind him, his band knows just when to push hard and get the action stirring, as well as melt your heart with a lump of solid gold sincerity that carries calmness and assurance. I'm also going to credit Steve Pouliot with a fine job of handling the engineering board—sir, you have a fine touch and ear.

The great thing in Paul's songwriting is that he has an excellent feel for the range of styles in his playing, and the presentation covers rockabilly, ballads, Cajun kicking, slow romance, traditional Nashville twangin', and a trip back in time to the days of cowboy/girl duets like Roy Rogers and Dale Evans. In a voice that is as smooth as chamois, Paul's vocals provide comfort and peace—and how great that is in times like these! However, he's got more than a fair share of Saturday evening fun to spread around, but it's the kind you could share with the whole family and feel proud to do so.

Just follow his bouncing bass and see which you prefer. In my case, I'm quick to jump on something with a slight jalapeño twist, and "Sifting Through the Ashes" gets my immediate interest. Talking about the aftermath of a love affair gone wrong (okay, that's always good for an idea in country circles), Rick Solem gets his piano right up front where it belongs and makes the keys jump like they were bare feet on a hot pavement, and you can't overlook the second verse's "Like Sherman's march when he torched Atlanta…" Whoa, lemme hear this one again, please!

Just a hop and a jump away is the probable cause of that broken heart, as "Lucy Anna" flirts with a fiddle, accordion, and all the fellas down New Orleans way. Darlin', you've got the magic that turned my head, even if I cry all the way home back to Tennessee. But you know those country singers: there's always chores to be done, and "Work to Do" lets Billy Watts and Cary Park earn their pay on guitar as Shawn Nourse keeps the time clock on drums alongside Rick's rambling, cascading keyboard.

Okay, I've got to be more serious—country music always has that sober side, I've been told--and Paul starts off with "If I had You," which says it straight and true. The title song has an allegorical theme that is nurtured with care behind the sensible, honest vocal arrangement, and there's a faithful, loyal pedal steel in the background. With a twist on a title, "Cowboy Jazz" salutes images of the sunset, a warm pot of coffee, and the open range. If you need a slow dance with that special person nestled in your embrace, then set this on repeat play and give each other a hug when it's finished.

You get another view of the scenery, but this time, it's from the audience who came for the music, the sportin' adventure of romance, and the bands at venues like "The Blackboard in Bakersfield and The Palomino." Considering the lineup that's saluted:

> Buck and Merle and young Emmylou
> Loretta and Kitty and Charlie Pride too
> …Hank Thompson, Wynn Stewart and the Killer, Jerry Lee…

ya know, I've got to believe the man could have sold me a ticket, too.

The soul of this set is Paul's moving eulogy for a beloved parent (in this case, his father-in-law), and "Our Father" is a song worth sharing with anyone who wishes he or she could say how special that man was for raising a family to adulthood. Paul's strength is his gentleness and phrasing, and I'll guarantee this will be heard in all 50 states when that special, private ceremony comes due for reckoning. It's followed by "Going Places Together," which has a '50s "better days" sense of nostalgia.

Aw, go on and admit you thought it's a pretty song, and there's every reason to say so, especially with Teresa James's picture-perfect backup vocals. Three-for-three: "Truth is You Lied" is another slow one, but when the man knows what works, you have to smile and sigh with respect. There's a grand slam home run pitch waiting, as "Stay Little Longer" finishes the set with another picture for the mantelpiece and those warm memories.

Hey, after having the time to listen to this yet one more time again, I think I'm getting to like this country stuff. Maybe all I needed was someone like Paul Marshall to be a guide, because these songs sound better with each spin. I may not go out and buy a Stetson and I've already found I can't handle wearing the boots, but I'm willing to keep trying.

As long as there's a man like this making country music, I just might kick in for some of those names he mentioned…'cause they surely helped give Paul his style. And thankful am I for it too.

In Memorium 1946-1971

Duane Allman

(Bugs Bunny was known to say, "If I dood it, I get a whuppin'. Okay, I dood it!" So "I dood it" too, and, let the whuppin' begin, because this is a bootleg release. But Duane played for the love of music—and that's why I wrote it.)

They say the best tribute of a musician's legacy is the test of time. How does/did an artist compare against his or her peers? What influences did he or she contribute that still manifest today? And most important and vital: does the music hold up with the same fire, charisma, charm, and devotion that made us listen in the first place?

It is therefore a privilege, an honor, and with the strongest affection I bring as a dedicated and inspired fan that I acknowledge the 30 years this past October since Duane Allman left us with a chance to say how much he touched our lives with music. That's quite a statement, but there is a wonderful reason to rejoice: an assignment like this marks a sacred anniversary. With three decades behind a loss as powerful as Duane, it is an effort of love and joy to write this in behalf of so many fans and musicians who played with or listen to him.

What more treasured a way to add a tribute and inaugurate our group effort in music publication than to give center stage to a rebel who embodied a musician's visions in so many classic ways? With Duane, it seems afresh that he truly brought out the best of others in his studio and stage contributions, whether it was in blues, rock 'n roll, jazz, or country influences. In deepest thanks and acknowledgement, this has now been enhanced due to the double-CD I recently added to my collection of Duane's work: *Duane Allman – In Memorium*.

As a new collection of Skydog Allman at his uncanny brightest, I'm lighting this one first. Besides, it has six funny photos in one small convenient place of that red-haired free spirit: Duane with Berry from the Ludlow Garage CD; Duane deep into his solo in the studio; playing an acoustic with total glee radiating in his face; defiant and proud with arms crossed; a marvelous side profile of those elegant chops; and outdoors at Piedmont Park.

Take it back to Muscle Shoals, back to 1969-70, and let the Hawk, Ronnie Hawkins, step up to the podium for a few cuts of testimony. Ronnie is "Down in the Alley," and Duane starts off with a chainsaw screech on bottleneck that captures the slow molasses pace of this song. It sounds like he double-tracked his slide solo, but when you're playing alongside Roger Hood, Barry Beckett, Eddie Hinton, Roger Hawkins, and King Biscuit Boy, Duane had the company to strut his stuff. And off they go, as "Red Rooster" parties all night long behind Ronnie's deluxe boogie, and you can hear him twice call out for Duane on cue to lay down that electricity.

Duane could also drop down solos with a sheer ferociousness that could make a mediocre song sound good. He does so with wild abandon on the next two tunes, buttressing up the Soul Survivors's "Darkness," and then Sam Samudio's (Sam the Sham and the Pharaohs, y'all) "Relativity." When that special ingredient was needed, Duane could season up anything and make it tasty. But for himself—that's where Duane doesn't get the support from his fellow musicians, and it's not because he wasn't trying. Vocally, Duane just didn't have the range to comfortably front a song for an entire album's worth of work, as shown by "Steal Away," a psychedelic wailing cut from a project that was mercifully better left abandoned. Duane redeems his poor singing on "Dimples," but that's on *Volume II*.

And when it came to singing, outtakes from the first Allman Brothers release shows why Gregg was the natural choice for a song like "Trouble No More," which shows up here in a version that was found in a tape on Momma A's kitchen shelf. Duane's stinging treble slide really gets in tasty comments, and it's also worth noting that Gregg really threw his heart and throat into his delivery. The brothers, at age19 and 18 years old respectively, knew their roots. The same goes for "Don't Keep Me Wonderin'" and "Revival," which can also be found on the bootleg CD *Second Coming*.

However, it was also with his extended family of friends that Duane found companionship, and DB and Friends had a party when King Curtis and Duane played in August 1971 in New York City at a radio-sponsored show. Showcasing the talents of their intimate close connection, the self-proclaimed "Three M'skeeters" added in Little Feat's Sam Clayton and Kenny Gradney to party hearty on "12 Bar Blues" (aka "Don't Want Me Round Here {No More}." Delaney does stand-up comedy bits, Curtis blows golden smoke rings, and Duane preens like a peacock with trademark slide guitar comic comments, chuckles, laughs, and quips that literally speak in a special language of his love for playing.

And for all you roasted and toasted freaks, Bobby Weir and the rest of the Grateful Dead were thrilled to have Duane come onstage to join them in April 1971 (just after the legendary Fillmore Concerts shows) to fill in on second lead for "Sugar Magnolia." The visual impact of so many wild and crazy personalities must have been worth the price of an acid tab. This song is worth hearing if only to have a second opinion as to who had more jazz influences: Phil Lesh or Berry Oakley.

The CD ends with two early versions of the Brothers themselves onstage in 1970, taking a spin on "Elizabeth Reed" (at the Warehouse in New Orleans, March 19th) and "Stormy Monday" (at Swarthmore College, on May 2nd). The recordings don't do justice to the band's performance, although they have been cleaned up from sonic distortion, hiss, and crackles, and that's only because the Brothers hadn't really explored the possibilities that these tunes would eventually become a year later on "Fillmore."

But it's Duane's commentaries about the audience ("There's a pervert down here…if any of you young ladies would like to pick up on one…") that would make a fan blush. This is not to ignore or overlook his lusty, leering introduction to Dickey's epic composition: "I've Got Peanut Butter Caught In My Pubic Hair…Crunchy Peanut Butter!" What else can you do when the leader of your band has the *cojones*--and talent--(and love as a leader from his mates)--to make Eric Clapton ask for guitar lick ideas and support on a masterpiece compilation like *Layla and Other Love Songs*?

On side two, though, is when Duane really shows why he was the unparalleled master of both slide and lead in a style that continues to be learned today. "Statesboro Blues" and "Whipping Post" (from a 4th of July, 1970 show) are as colorfully artistic as the liquid light displays that the band used, and even in a shorter version, the latter is still breath-taking and loaded with opportunities.

But come on back to the Warehouse in September 1971, with a fated few short weeks of time left in that remarkable life, when Duane blazed like a comet on "Blue Sky," and elsewhere on an incorrectly dated "Dreams." The recording quality is lacking, but they are the two most vital songs on the package. On the former, Berry finds his wings behind Duane's songbird-in-spring outpouring, following his and Dickey's lead notes like a trio of soaring eagles. This takes the studio version to a magical realm that only the Allmans could have imagined in their creative capacities.

It is on the latter song, though, where Duane's abstract jazz themes traveled to new dimensions. In his solos on previous recordings, he always floated as effortlessly as the out-of-body night trips we have of flying, but on this recording, he dove to the bottom of the deepest ocean to prepare for his ascent. If you want to track it on the sonar scope, the missile he fired broke the surface with that incredible liquid bronze fuel-powered sound on slide approximately 12-and-a-half minutes into the song. (This song is now officially released on the *Warehouse 9/19/71* CD available on Amazon.com.)

Duane must have been as hard to control offstage as he was daring in concert, so Dave Herman (host of the WPLJ-FM show in August) of WABC-FM in New York had to verbally wrestle with his guest's quicksilver outbursts that scurried like the surface of a pond with water bugs. The closest man I can think of as a similar uncontrolled terror to interview must have been the late Keith Moon. I'll argue with my credentials as a middle/elementary schoolteacher that

Duane was as hyperactive as any student I ever tried to control—and we label 'em as ADHD these days.

That doesn't take away from the potential and enthusiasm that goes with that. But coming in drunk on Jack Daniels didn't make Duane any less inhibited--if anything, he was ready to raise holy hell, and there was nothing holding him back. Most likely it was because Brother Gregg had just celebrated a birthday the day before.

This also included an endorsement to the audience to take off their clothes, which Duane cheerfully detailed in testimony for album covers, his views on the raw seething power of Dickey Betts as an unheralded musician, insights on the making of "Layla," and nearly blurting out the private phone number for friend Johnny Sandlin. Oh, and he also encouraged a phone-in caller to meet him (obviously a female) for a potential X-rated rendezvous: "Say any dirty words you want…10:00 at your hotel…I'll bring the whips and masks!" Dallas Taylor, drummer for Crosby, Stills, Nash, and Young, also present at the taping, must have been ready to dive for the fire escape to reach safety, as Duane was wired and ready to explode.

To close the CD, Duane and his beloved band are back at the Fillmore for his gorgeous brief solo ending on the *Eat A Peach* and *Concerts* CDs, as "Will the Circle Be Unbroken?" gathers in the flock to safety. This song in its entirety ("Mountain Jam") would be my vote for the last music I would wish to hear in my final moments on Earth, as it is a magnum opus of jazz, rock, blues, and gospel, built around a pop ballad.

As he was founder and inspirational father of the Allman Brothers Band, consider here that Duane inaugurated what I call the Allman Cousins (Berry, Scott Boyer, Tommy Talton, Pete Carr, Paul Hornsby, and Johnny Sandlin).

They were more than just an extended family group, because they had been making music with him through so many precious moments, and deserve honoring their own category. Delaney Bramlett told me about how Duane and King Curtis and he were so closely bonded; I also saw fellow Domino Bobby Whitlock moved to tears when he finally viewed the photos of Duane's gravesite. There is no denying that many men and women still grieve for their long-gone friend's presence and spirit, and the years will continue to fall aside.

As new generations of musicians and audiences explore the archives, and they will surely find themselves captivated by Duane's extensive collaborations. With luck and personal negotiation, more material may yet surface. It would certainly be his way of spreading the joy of the music he loved, and in turn, our ways of giving it back. God bless you, Duane, for making it sound so beautiful and magnificent. Dedicated to a Brother.

Shot From the Saddle

THE DECOYS (MUSCLE SHOALS RECORDS)

As I recall, a 'decoy' is meant to be something to draw attention away from a main interest, or to act as a distraction. This terrific little package of spliced-and-diced R&B cuts has the opposite effect: grab your hat and keep focused, because these guys have a serious "Men at Work" sign in the road. It's like a club sandwich, with layers of good fixin's and straight-to-the-point delivery when you want the real thing.

The Decoys show that the sum of the whole is indeed supported by the parts (or players). It's nice to have Johnny Sandlin as the commander of this brigade, because he's got some stable. Here's a four-corner framework of painful, soulful vocals (Scott Boyer of Cowboy, part of the Allman Brothers Band extended family), short-but-sweet guitar licks (Kelvin Holly of Little Richard's band); David Hood's slunky, funky bass, as thick as tar as he stays right on top of every bass drum kick; a turnstile of tormented keyboard (NC Thurman), and a muscular rhythm section, supplemented by a cast of local heroes and rogues. Spooner Oldham, Donnie Fritts, Bobby Whitlock, The Muscle Shoals Horns, Brian Wheeler, James Hooker—there's enough guys here to field a damn good softball game, too, as long as the barbecue is kept up (and no duck on the menu, mind you—and that goes double from the Sandlin home).

The Decoys work from afar and close, so when there's a gig, the paycheck beckons. However, friends also count, and when there's room to play and the time clock is off, let's cook!

And do they! The title song immediately shows Scott's growl is a dangerous thing, especially when he's caught on that another man has been prowling around his den.

Well, if "Nadine" from New Orleans was the source of his loss, it sounds like she could melt steel with her charms, and it's no wonder why his imagination is on overdrive. This has a very strong vibe like Mr. Lucky's "Memphis Stripper," so the ceiling sprinkler system may ignite any minute. Yagotta just love those clean lines that Kelvin slices—he's got such a simple but effective approach. Service notice on Steve Cropper that there's a helluva reason to hook up with Kelvin for a duet.

Hats off to Scott for his delivery on Eddie Hinton's "Down in Texas," because the sweat is fresh on Boyer's work clothes with honest toil. His portrayal of Eddie's zest makes you want to hug yourself with his memory, and you make sure you notice the fast-setting cement of the horn section.

Walt Aldridge is a busy author with four tunes featured, and his "Bits and Pieces" gets a man's sorrowful view on an old flame (my Georgia Songbird friend E.G. Kight does a separate version of this for the ladies on *Come Into the Blues*); but rejoice, because Scott's singing from the rooftop about his new main squeeze on "24-7-365," and those measurements are the ones he loves best.

But there's got to be some kind of action that's getting a lot of attention, because "Neighbor, Neighbor" has been snooping too close for comfort. Credit Scott again with taking the gentleness of a song (here it's Gregg Allman's "Melissa"), adding subtle changes (a finger-picking intro versus strumming), and giving it a new set of wings. Kelvin, too, rides the ocean currents on guitar.

When these guys want to have fun, "Get Down" is more than an order—it's a call for comradeship and musical joy, and that's what these guys do best. Getting back to those sad times just won't be avoided, though, and "Good Days, Bad Days" is testimony why depression is a serious condition. Get Scott to a love doctor, because he's gotta get cured, y'all. Kelvin's sinewy guitar offers some remedy on "What's Up with That," 'cause it's getting time to trade in on that woman again. For sure, it's because "Her Mind is Gone," and don't be the last man out the door. But do these guys learn their lesson? They don't call it the blues for nothing, especially when "Desire" is knocking—or swaying, I should say…and Lord, is <u>she</u> calling my name?

Maybe the Decoys were right: the road sign might have said 'Dangerous Curves ahead,' and I have to pull over and have another look—or listen. Just remember that a good pickup in a dark smokey place also refers to more than a truck or a guitar accessory. Sounds like there's some bad-is-good company to find on this disc—and I've got mine in mind. You should get some too, before the Decoys beat you to her.

It's About Time

BOBBY WHITLOCK (GRAPEVINE RECORDS)

Give it up and welcome back a star scholar of musical chops: Bobby Whitlock. Showing off all his vocal and instrumental talents, "It's About Time" has the depth of experience and access of interest to please folks from all ages. This package comes from a man who is blessed with a voice that richly carries a rainbow of intensive expression and ideas that cut across generations. Best of all, the always-soulful "Bobby Dubs" wears his heart on his sleeve throughout every song in this tasty collection of new and old material.

Bobby has always been known as a magician on a Hammond B-3, a sparkplug on piano, and a rocker and R&B specialist with grit and gospel in his blood and songs. The years have been good to him: he has gained a depth of passion and maturity to his singing-a sense of rich warmth and strength that only can be achieved as a gift earned through hard work and Time's patience. Even better, Bobby showcases two marvelous assets: his slide guitar, and his friendship and collaboration with two instrumental wizards: Steve Cropper on guitar and the appropriately-named Jim Horn on saxophones. Credit should also be given to the late Duane Allman for the wisdom to show this good friend the technique and merits of a bottleneck-and Bobby has obviously been practicing Skydog's recommendations.

"There She Goes" would easily pass as a ballad for a lost, departing sweetheart, but Bobby throws us something extra with this wistful lament: it's not about a broken love affair--it's about his daughter's journey to find truth and meaning in her life. Bobby literally leaves us in the doorway of parenthood memories as he watches his now-grown child embark on her search. A lush string arrangement by producer Paddy Prendergast frames a thick carpet of B-3 and piano refrain, and the slow pace captures Whitlock's distress and pleading.

Bobby snaps back on track two with an old favorite from his Layla days: "Why Does Love Got to Be So Sad," but this time, Bobby has a chance to take the reins where Eric Clapton once held court. Cranked along by Darryl Johnson's bass and Horn's saxophone lineup, Bobby swoops and wails new life and energy into this piece. The title song makes it clear why this man's writing skills have been in demand by a collage of fellow musicians, as Bobby heralds a rallying cry for the world to account for a global reckoning of brother-and-sisterhood. This is followed by "Wing & A Prayer," clearly displaying Bobby's contemplative moments and spiritual growth that comes from listening and participating for hours in gospel church services. Jim Horn, on tenor sax, confidently stands beside his friend

There's a tiger by the tail when Bobby picks up a slide (he uses a 5/8 or 11/16 socket when possible), and the lady who inspired "Sold Me Down the River" surely must have realized that this man can bare his claws. This has the texture and substance of pure Bonnie Raitt aggressiveness, and Ashley Whitlock's sassy backup chorus vocal does her daddy justice. Jim Horn's soprano sax kicks off "It's Only Midnite" with a poet's voice, and Bobby's piano and gutsy, gritty vocals chase after his buddy like two colts on a romp. Bobby brings out his favorite six and 12-string acoustic guitars on "Standin' in the Rain," reminding us why Tom Dowd wisely selected "Thorn Tree" as the last cut for Layla.

Drummer Brady Blade and Jim Horn take turns cooking like popcorn in a microwave on "Born to Sing the Blues," and Bobby's Memphis days are boogied to a golden brown. Of all the apropos statements this man has ever crafted, he was and is, indeed, able to claim this as a personal and righteous honor.

Whitlock's voice paints a gorgeous pastel arrangement for his (now-ex) on "High On You," and Jim Horn again comes in as best man at this renewal of vows. Love definitely keeps the fireplace warm and glowing in the Whitlock household. Subtle, muted guitar by "Colonel" Cropper adds to the sincere arrangement. "Bell Bottom

Blues" was Eric's need to display his angst over Patti Harrison thirty years ago, but Bobby has showcased his keyboards and Leslie amps to properly reveal that an older man can still grieve. Beau Whitlock remarkably haunts the background vocals with a voice that could only have come from his father's pipes-the younger man is now capably filling the notes his father sang on the original.

"Ghost Driver" (and the inside-liner photo of Bobby's trashed Ferarri Daytona) clearly displays the thrill-seeking rocker that runs through his veins (at least, until he traded in his last fast car for the slow-and-easy Cadillac). Barry Swain's guitar bursts and Horn's sax chants serve as the pace car on this speedway course, followed closely by the always-dangerous B-3 and Bobby's wind-whipped stormy vocals. Everyone in the studio comes back for a celebratory hug and reunion at the end for "I Love You," and Bobby and Buddy Miller laugh and dance on an electric mandoline and 12-string exchange between vocals. It's a perfect, cheery way to wrap up a wonderful gathering of happy, caring artists who love their work and are glad to show it. Jim Horn plays the court jester with sax squeals, Beau adds in an acoustic finale, and it's time to make sure the "continuous play" button is engaged on the CD player.

This release is a perfect gift for anyone who needs that "hard-to-please" present for the friend or loved one in their life, as well as a riverbed of golden nuggets for the coffeehouse and cover musicians who want to flex their muscle and show some quiet strength at the same time. Get the tool box out and ready when Bobby comes to visit-he's expecting that socket to be available for some good music. Better yet, hop, skip or bounce on down the road to grab this item: as Bobby would say, "It's about time" you had some Whitlock in your life!

Pain

LUCK BROTHERS

Aside from "this is a sample of Philly {Philadelphia} soul," how else do I describe something from two guys (Art Austin and Tim Gleeson), aka Luck Brothers--when this is something that seems to have vanished in the mysteries of "artist{s} who never got a break"?

The Luck Brothers, a black/white duo who specialized in the small gigs around the City of Brotherly Love, caught my attention in '04 at the Tin Angel when they opened for Rory Block, the legendary blues award-winning lady who can play the old acoustic style so hard her fingers have bled onstage.

The release of *Pain* was one I endorsed to various outlets and magazines--and I kept up contact with Tim in an effort to try and get them better management as well as a more aggressive label. With the help of a few friends, the Luck Brothers have left behind something that is fun, simple in its arrangements, and even a bit wistful. Staying close with each other (Austin plays percussion and does lead vocals; Gleeson adds in guitar, keyboards, and backup vocals), along with a bassist and some b/g vocals too, this is sweet stuff that would have lit up any good party.

The title song brought a lot of laughter, especially from the women in the audience, as Art easily played up "pain in the...as I know it" as his way of complementing his lady. "Boom Bottom" (one that our man DC should enjoy) makes it really clear which part of the female anatomy gets Art's attention--and I love the opening lick Tim hits on guitar.

But a two-part serenade on the classic "You Don't Know Me/ Come Live With Me" puts a more sincere light on the two guys: Tim takes the first part in a cocktail bar-style vocal and jazz guitar/piano background, with Art chiming in. They switch roles as Art takes over with his heart in his hand and one knee on the ground as he proposes to his sweetheart on the second half, and Tim adds in agreements. Finally, the CD wraps up as "I Can Never Win" tells of rejected love and perhaps the fate of the Luck Brothers: they just could not "ever win," no matter how much we tried. It was something we sure had put down for the odds in their favor. Tim wrote me recently to ask for a review of his new CD, which I gladly did, and it's there on his site at http://www.timgleeson.com. I hope he brought a rabbit's foot and maybe a four-leaf clover, because I wish him ALL the luck in the world!

Judi Jetsunn

THE WORLD ACCORDING TO JUDI JETSUNN (CD BABY)

(I have never been a big fan or listener of hip-hop—until my brother Barry, who has produced music, slid a CD promo of this woman into the car's player. My ears immediately began to sting)

Dig this: my family thinks I'm whacked because I believe in aliens.

Yeah, I grew up on *Star Trek*; my family also says my ears are pointed. Check out my pictures as a kid to see it's true. Now hear me out: I'm an astrologer with an undergraduate degree from Rutgers in psychology, and I've done graduate school too. I know there are people out there who feel like they've been abducted. So where does a cosmic kid like me find a chick? Men are from Mars—and so is Judi, or somewhere out there near the fired-up asteroid belt—and she's Red Planet Angry too. Prepare for assault on your deviant ways.

Meet Ms bad-to-her-Wolverine-Adamantium-bones Judi Jetsunn. She slams down a script with a snake's tuning fork of a tongue: pulsar bombs from Darth Vader's home ship laser-locked on my ass. I am stunted, hunted, *blunted*, and been punted: Judi has the Attitude; giving me the latitude, won't stand for my platitude. I'm being called Liable; she's solar-system Tribal, and my lust is justifiable.

Catch her Grinding and Gnashing, J-Jetti dashing; funky down Tenacious; torn-down hellacious; the woman's outrageous: "Damned (if I do, damned if I don't)." What's her grief? Family put her down for not being "catalogued" in a social stereotype: black is White and White is black. They're Cutting Down her boyfriend; blame it on the Almighty Boob Tube and Stupid music videos. Words spin like pinwheeling galaxies past my ears. She's a galactic live-jive box of Good 'n Plenty Candy, but the sweetness is a jaw-breaker.

Judi's husky growl reminds me why Siberian tigers are the largest of the species and throwbacks to their cold weather origin. Thick as a foggy morning—except Judi's got her High Beams clear 'cause she's been jacked: "Shoulda Known Better." Creep, your dung's too deep, and she's gonna stick your head in it for ripping off Ms J.

Caught in the act, it's your turn for the rack, and Judi's ready to throw that whip right between the legs; ain't no use to beg. When you play Jetsunn's game, prepare to pay the stakes; own up the dues that you make: these are rules for men who are fools who mess with Judi's jewels. That's your head she's gonna buff with a grinding stone when you up and leave her all alone. A migraine for a lame-brain who's nothing but a dead-end train.

You know a Queen Alien like this would pop a baby girl—but do you know how a female praying mantis mates? Your lesson comes too late: she cannibalizes—right in the middle of getting plugged. Check out a two-legged kind that eats her mate and "Think About It"—for leaving her to handle the bundle of joy. Rip your liver out first, brother. Judi cracks skulls to put down men who need to know it straight and clear why a back door exit is a bullshit excuse for being a father. So what gets her juices jamming? "Glasses," 'cause real men aren't into just silicone tits and big asses. Get your education, spread it 'cross the United Nations, men make passes at chicks with the glasses.

So are you safe with this Wild Woman-Being of the Worlds Beyond? Absolutely not—she's more Klingon than anything; probably has tentacles hidden behind her back like Doc Oc, and maybe one of those lizard tongues too, that tastes your fear. Wait a minute--Prepare me. I want to be spliced, diced, and sacrificed, Aztec captive-style. Baby, I think I'm in Love with You.

(Just a few friends who deserve High Honors and Mention)

In 1968, when Sly and the Family Stone hit the scene by way of San Francisco, their music was magically potent: an adrenalin rush of soul, rock, gospel, and volcanic R & B. They were more than racially blended: here was a collaboration of hip cats and strikingly sharp foxes.

The F.S. could blow your doors off with vocals that bounced off walls like Spiderman and a sense of groove that dug a new cellar in your house because your feet had pounded that hard. "Dance to the Music" in concerts started out with a slow tease by Sly on organ and enticing whispers, as beautiful as the studio version that shook the shingles of the roof. It's audio motivation in a righteous way!

Their performances were as much a tribute to the power and energy of a movement that began in Motown--but I would credit the Temptations for Family Stone high voltage show. ("The Temps?") Hell, yes: go back and dig up "Ball of Confusion" and "Cloud Nine" and listen to the challenges and counter-points of their vocals alone--and you'll see some of the paternal heritage of Sly and the Family Stone. In his own right as well, Sly has been a heavy influence on everyone from Living Color to George Clinton's success with Parliament/Funkadelic, as well as Prince.

Sadly, Sly had issues: personal and professional. Politely said, he could not keep his nose clean, and a 1971 Rolling Stone interview--or an attempt at such--by Timothy Crouse is as much a testimony as well as transcript of how much snow and blow had drifted into Sly's yard. The attempted comeback(s) never quite materialized; his manager admitted that there were two personalities controlling Sly's artistry and willpower. Nevertheless: Bill Graham knew how to set up a show, and that's what Sly and the Family Stone could do. The next year, Woodstock showed the rest of the country that he and the band were a sight to behold and hear.

    This is about testimony, people, and you will <u>not</u> turn your back and say, "That's not my problem." It's about legacies…of violence, pain, hate, suffering…in the name of heritage; in the name of raw apathy…in the name of ignorance. In Otis Taylor's big hands, plucking and strumming on an electric banjo, mandolin, or acoustic guitar, it's a way to cry out for justice—and mercy and forgiveness.

    They don't make prophets like this anymore—they did once upon a time, but that was back in biblical days. If there was a reason to listen to this man's songs, it's because he wears the dust of history on his physical body and within his heart, and along with that, the crimes of passion that have been done in the name of righteous intention.

    These CDs are about commitment: a way to remind us that we have choices to make in our lives, both individually and as a social unit. The actions that we make can come back with a sword or an olive branch—and thankfully, Otis has a gentle way with his power, especially from a man who can stare into your soul from the cover photo of *White African.*

    His companions are right beside him like avenging angels: Kenny Passarelli's thudding, plodding bass, holding the chains and shackles of generations, daughter Cassie Taylor's ghostly backup vocals that moan through the leaves on the trees on a hot moonless night, and Eddie Turner's tortured slide and lead guitar. Yes, the obvious comparison is to John Lee Hooker—but Otis's strength is that he's doing it his way. You'll feel it too, once Otis lays his music on you.

Roadwork
Edgar Winter's White Trash

As a rock 'n roll/R & B line-up, Edgar Winter's White Trash could melt the competition with the "scorch-and-torch" blistering vocals of Winter and especially, the rumble and growl of Jerry LaCroix. They first take it through the roof on the gospel-influenced "Save the Planet": both men compete in a lengthy "Lord (Lawd) knows!" sandpaper throaty duel, then LaCroix enthusiastically bounces back behind the horns and Bobby Ramirez's cymbal smashes to pull the crowd along and "Jive JiveJive." That's followed by the sweaty, ballsy, and heartfelt urgency of Otis Redding's classic "I Can't Turn You Loose," and Jerry's pleading is as much from lust as love for that special woman.

Not to be upstaged, Rick Derringer pounds away to show that he's "Still Alive and Well," and turns Chuck Berry inside-out while flailing away on "Back in the U.S.A." What has become a personal family joke ("Where's your brother?") in the Winter family is unleashed as Johnny steps up to churn through a potent "Rock and Roll, Hoochie Koo," a song originally best known by Derringer's former group, the McCoys. And then Edgar takes over--and absolutely broils the stage with "Tobacco Road," complete with scat vocals, demented hoots and shrieks, and a raging electric piano/guitar duel.

To end this, the band relocates to the Apollo Theater in Harlem, where I recall reading that the black audience initially turned and began to walk out when the band came out, fronted by the whitest man they could ever imagine (an albino) doing some funk--but "Cool Fool" proved immediately that Edgar was the former and any doubters were the second. Follow that with Stevie Wonder's "Do Yourself a Favor," some smoking horns, a hot wah-wah pedal guitar, and finally, Jerry urges everyone to "Turn On Your Lovelight" and makes it glow. Count this as one of the best live gigs of the '70s; a White Trash show was as valuable as a bagful of diamonds--and they could shine as bright.

I'm Every Woman
Rory Block

Praise the heavens, this woman can soar with a vocal range that must hit at least--three octaves?—and she can unleash a blues explosion on acoustic guitar with a slide for the fuse. The title song has enough shakin' and bakin' to burn those extra calories, but it's her stunning voice that gives you a workout through a fire walk on 2000-degree coals with blistering gospel numbers like "Ain't No Grave Can Hold My Body Down." Love has found a maiden as strong as steel when someone has to take a stand and be the backbone of R&B tradition, or as delicate as silk when Rory's got the testifying need to be "Talkin' 'Bout My Man."

Blues for Chloe
John Lisi

Tom Waits should wish he had the chance to sound this rough and be this smooth—and play with piranha lust bottleneck on 12-string acoustic, lead, and dobro. This is chunky, funky, and slunky, and when the "Little Red Rooster" sees the light of day, you're gonna wish you had slept in late and not stayed out all night. Seems like ol' John has done some woodsheddin' with some friends down in Baton Rouge—raw and raspy, and pass that likker jug while you're at it.

The instrumental title song (dedicated to his new-born daughter) is a downpour of sadness that brings images of empty arms and lonely beds. There's also room to cut the rug with your toes for a knife when "Skat" rips it loose in fine boogie-woogie fashion, and his leading lady's name is "Caldonia." Woman, why *is* your big head so hard? Never mind, "Little Schoolgirl," you've got John to help carry your books—for starters.

Saved!
Northernblues Gospel Allstars

I'm having problems with my compass—the harder I try, the more it keeps pointing in the wrong direction (not South). It's made a beeline for Canada! Well, they call Toronto "Memphis North," and when Danny Brooks rolls out that gravel-and-glory voice on "Still Standing Tall" and the title song, every day is Sunday and the sun is shining through the chapel. Mr. Hiram Joseph takes you by the hand, children, to show you "A Place Called Home," and the lovely Miss Amoy Levy walks on a cloud toward "Higher Ground."

With arms outstretched wide enough to embrace all Man and Womankind, John Finley's gentle rendition of the classic anthem "A Change is Gonna Come" offers shelter for the world. No matter what your background is, people, this is as open a celebration of faith as they make. Share it with a friend—when they hear this kind of vocal beauty, they'll want to get *Saved!*

From Clarksdale to Heaven – Remembering John Lee Hooker

Various Artists -

From a child of his body and the children of his music, this is a chance to pay respects to the man who made his guitar a blacksmith's anvil and pounded out rhythms of sorrow.

Look for Jack Bruce's Ozzy Osbourne-like sneer on "I'm in the Mood," along with Gary Moore's Godzilla footsteps on guitar. That's Jeff Beck playing robot-metallic notes on "Will the Circle Be Unbroken" and "Hobo Blues," and Peter Green's vocal sounds like a decaying zombie obeying his master on "Crawling King Snake."

John Lee himself paints a "Red House" with something other than crimson pigment, and I've got to credit Robert Hunter's composition, "The Business," by Greggs Eggs vocalist Suzanne Sterling for giving the old man that special smile with a posthumous kiss.

Somhelgisfel
Joe Richardson Express

Keep the doors and windows unlocked when you hear this--a handy exit is the best thing for survival instincts when you feel your flesh crawl. This is what a Rottweiler would sound like if it could play music, and Joe looks like that evil wizard Saruman in "Lord of the Rings."

If you want to conjure up some powerful spirits, don't expect anything that will be easy to handle when the Express summons them-or else. This is primal, raging, and aboriginal in nature, and if you find the hair standing up on the back of your neck, just be glad your head is still attached to feel it.

Joe and his buddies can crack your back as well, just trying to move to those on-the-torture-rack rhythms. Lenny Kravitz gets a thumbs-up for "The Gospel," and Jimi and Stevie Ray sent "Cry" and "Mother Rain" down from the Heaven's Hall of Guitar Heroes. Watch out for the "Black Sheep of the Blues": you're gonna be the one who gets skinned for your hide.

Not safe yet? There's a touch of dobro mojo when you reach "Virginia," but "Witch Cat" will boil you alive in a Louisiana bayou cauldron with a voodoo chant. Dig this--J.S. Bach gets soul too: Joe blows a "Mass in Delta Minor" on harmonica. Salvation comes with the morning light, and pray for mercy.

Return of a Legend
Jody Williams

You don't need to teach an old dog new tricks—it's the other way around for all those young pups out there who think they know their roots. That includes special guitar guests Sean Costello and Tinsley Ellis. Class starts on with track #1, students, and never mind that the professor has been on sabbatical for 30 years—start taking notes right now.

Wise and Otherwise; *Dog My Cat*
Harry Manx

If you spliced Jackson Browne and James Taylor together and did a blood transfusion with Ganges River water, you'd create Harry Manx. Playing a unique 20-string Indian guitar called a *Mohan Veena* (in honor of its creator), lap slide guitar, and harmonica, Harry plays flawless, exotic ballads that stretch across the Asian continent from Japan to Bombay.

If that's not rich enough, there's some Muddy Waters blues ("Can't Be Satisfied"; "Baby Please Don't Go"), some Jimmy Reed ("Shame Shame Shame"), and unless you're stone-cold comatose, a version of "Foxy Lady" that ought to be dedicated to Halle Berry. Jimi would be thrilled and chilled at the idea—and opportunity.

Live at Carnegie Hall 1972
Bill Withers

For a man who came from West Virginia, Bill Withers has probably touched the souls of more men from the inner cities of America than most. He could sing as though he had walked alongside the people who were the subjects of his songs--as though he watched them try to overcome odds that were too big to handle. Aside from the personal view of his experiences, he made us feel like we were friends--and in some cases, brothers united against a struggle.

As a black man, he was a voice --especially for those from Detroit, Newark, New York, and Chicago--where the male population found that only certain doors would open for a way out of the cycle of poverty, drugs, and death. The military was one avenue--but during Vietnam, too many veterans came back with what is now being diagnosed as PTSD (Post Traumatic Stress Disorder). Even worse…some came back crippled in body as well as mind. Bill sang about this in a song that still shakes with the anger and pain of Korea…'Nam…Iraq…Afghanistan…and other battlefields: "I Can't Write Left-Handed," about a vet who is lamenting his disability for a fight that he had no reason to be involved with in the first place. Considering the status of today's veterans, when played for someone who has never heard it, this is a song that says that nothing has changed--no matter where the combat takes place and for what reason a soldier is told.

Aside from the cold reality look-in-the-mirror, Withers is more about a view of life that few of us appreciate: "Grandma's Hands" starts out with a long tale of his memories of his mother's mother and how she cared and protected her grandson, and how spiritual she was in her beliefs, especially shown through her love of gospel music. The laughs that come from a knowing Harlem-based audience reflect this. Bill also sings of the pain of relationships from the view of a man--not a woman--who is facing an angry and reluctant potential thirty-something-year-old mate in "Let Me In Your Life." I'm not the one who broke your heart and did you wrong, he sings. Give me a chance to prove myself. We're both older and wiser--and I'm not 'him.'

This is a classic performance of hope, belief, anguish, and more--it's a collage of emotions that comes through in an urgent manner. Recorded during a rainy night at Thanksgiving time, his performance is recognized as a snapshot of the '70s and the aftermath of the questions that followed the deaths of John and Bobby Kennedy, and Dr. King. He knew the idealism that was cut short for a nation that had been promised so much. And that was how and why Bill Withers made hits: he made us feel like he knew us personally and could relate to our issues--how we viewed them--and how much betrayal we felt when they were torn apart by life.

Cryin' and Screamin'
John Ussery (and the Full-Tilt Blues Band)

The first five seconds on track one ought to convince you—it's the quiet guys whom you have to watch. John's the Roy Hobbs (see the movie *The Natural*, with Robert Redford) of guitar, having taken

20 years (!) off from playing after he had a dispute with a friend in the studio.

But the touch was still there—and when Ussery took up where he left off, he must have gained The Three Kings (Albert, B.B., and Freddie) as guardian angels during those lost years. It shows—they were John's inspiration, and as the title says, this man lets his guitar bleed his heart with the blues.

Imagine how Lyle Lovett would sound if the worm in the tequila bottle turned into a live rattlesnake when you got to the bottom, and that's Ussery on vocals: a tough side that swaggers and struts. The brass/horn/harp section of the FTBB smokes like a bad forest fire, especially during John's Delbert McClinton-like "I Been Pickin' 'Em Up" (and layin' 'em down).

This is the return of a bad—a **very** bad man, and thank God for that. Sheriff Ussery is back in town, y'all, and he's here to lay down the law—as judge, jury, and jailer. Pay attention and get it straight with John, or you'll be "cryin' and screamin.'"

Essays and Reflections

Jam for Duane 2005

OCTOBER 27-29
2ND STREET MUSIC HALL
GADSDEN, AL

(My dear friend, mentor, and "Wise Woman" Ann Sandlin, wife of Johnny, brought to my attention the annual Jam for Duane Allman, hosted again by Carl Weaver at his music venue in Gadsden. I was thrilled to again see Scott Boyer, and to meet Tommy Talton, Paul Hornsby, Bill Stewart, and Lee Roy Parnell. From this gig also came a dream that almost came true: to write Allman Brothers Band roadie Kim Payne's autobiography, requested by Kim himself. With luck, I was living near Gadsden in 2007: these people were the most sincere and kindest folks I've met in years. And when the music and stories are this good, there was no stopping us. Thanks again to Carl for all his hospitality and enthusiasm.

Unfortunately, at this 2012 update, events have caught up with Mr. Weaver, and he is in prison for murder. They don't say you've sold your soul at the crossroads for nothing.)

It comes down to the more important values of life that make the difference: family, friendship, and love. When memories are counted, it's the legacies that we leave behind that matter—and in honor of those who gave them to us but are no longer here to present them, it matters how we cherish their gifts.

It has been said so many times, "The Road Goes on Forever." From October 27-29th in Gadsden, Alabama, the Road does go on forever, but so does a tribute to a man's legacy. Some call it Southern

Rock; others know it as the Allman Brotherhood, founded by a man's vision—the late Duane Allman--that incorporated those three qualities: All Man and Woman Brothers and Sisters in music. It took a small sleepy Georgia town named Macon to generate a musical movement. And light up the wires, because another movement in the same way is starting to shake.

This is an anniversary gathering that was conceived more than 22 years ago by Brent Sibley, but is now manifesting in a bustling busy hall in Gadsden that has the makings for a new awakening for this lovely city down by the Coosa River. It's the Jam for Duane celebration, marking the day this special man died, and letting his mission carry forward. The three-day event is hosted by Carl Weaver, owner, manager, and soul-shine director of the 2nd Street Music Hall.

Take it in like the top of a tall tree down to the thick trunk: the Allman Brothers Family and its extended offshoot branches are but one of the parts. To Duane, his friends were family as much as the close-knit ties he had to his brother and mother. The Allman friendship was extended to band members, roadies, and colleagues—and part of the joy of this festival is a reunion of Duane's mates. "God Bless Duane Allman" was heard more than once from the microphones—and Johnny Sandlin made sure Brother Berry Oakley had mention too. The faces are grizzled, gray, and with some wrinkles and lines that only come by a musician's renegade ways—but they're worn with the pride and joy that comes with the lifestyle. Four men have put aside differences, delays, commitments, and such ("They've been tryin' to get us all in the same room for a long time!"} to come and play for their friend, and just seeing the likes of Scott Boyer, Tommy Talton—key members of Cowboy—joined by Johnny Sandlin and Bill Stewart—who comprised the short-lived Sandlin-Stewart-Talton trio during the mid-70s—make spectators bring out vintage, rare LPs for autographs, but also to bring handshakes and thanks. Toss in for good measure (and keyboards) the fingers of Paul Hornsby, and along with Sandlin again, we have two members of the embryonic Hourglass—the band that gave Duane the room to explore his blues chops before the studio days at Fame and Muscle Shoals.

These friends have not truly played together as a committed unit for a good 30+ years—but this gig is for their friend; their brother Duane and his inspiration. They now call themselves the Capricorn Rhythm Section, recognizing Johnny's production wizardry at the Macon facility for Phil Walden. Standing in on guitar is another six-string ace: Lee Roy Parnell, who knew his life would change and lead him out of the small Texas town to his own future after hearing Duane. Others are here too, who didn't play, but handled the gear and were paid and recognized as much: Kim Payne and Mike Callahan.

Another fallen friend is also honored, but he has his parents (and comrades) to carry his banner: Eddie Hinton, the Muscle Shoals gravel-voiced singer and guitar session man from Decatur who was in the competitive Five Minutes (Hornsby and Sandlin were in an earlier version) on the circuit when Duane and brother Gregg were learning the trade. Eddie died a few years ago, but his parents are attendees here to watch his friends tell of the energy, inspiration, and spirit their son brought. And as anyone knows, Duane followed Eddie's role as lead player after putting in his own dues for Rick Hall at Fame Studios. The bonds are also there on disc: "Going Up the Country," featuring The Duck (Sandlin), The Dog (Allman), and the Bear (Hinton). Eddie's songs, "Down in Texas" (done again by Boyer's collaboration with The Decoys) and "300 Pounds of Hongry" swing with affection and humor under the fond guidance of the CRS, as did "Everybody Needs Love" (from <u>Letters From Mississippi</u>.)

The event is as much a story about Carl Weaver's efforts to revive and resuscitate this charming building with the statues of the Blues Brothers standing guard outside. A shorter, beefier version of actor Brian Denehy, Weaver's heart and love for the blues and good passionate music covers the walls and floors—from the ornate carved mahogany center command station that he imported from England, to the rich wainscoating carvings, elaborate mouldings, and trim work that frame the back wall and archway and side bar railing, to the intricate wrought-iron railing, to the fieldstone enclosures of the main floor sound booth, as well as the recording studio in the back. There are tall outdoor streetlight fixtures bolted to the floor, too:

this is the French Quarter done 'Bama-style. And the sports bar that is being completed in the back portion of the building will boast a 50-year-old scoreboard. But if the music has made your mouth water, just step across the big parking lot to Cooter Brown's and feast on those juicy BBQ ribs and steaks. Musicians, be sure to wipe your fingers or you'll get new meaning to the words "slide guitar."

Tunefully, the warm-ups made their best deals too, with tunes from Otis Rush ("You Reap What You Sow"), to Jackson Browne's "These Days." Various covers of "Statesboro Blues" were lit up, first by the Zillionaires (who also gave a hot "Born in Chicago") and then a left hand slide-right hand bottleneck sparring by Lefty Collins and his gold Les Paul, along with the No Mercy Band. Speakin' of feastin', the last three days have been edible for ears and eyes: a packed Friday-night "glad you could make it!" was standing-room-only. Folks as far away as Indiana and as nearby as Florida have filled the seats, and yes, look twice: (former) Allman tour mystic Kirk West was up close, and that was (the late) *HTN* editor Bill Ector on guitar during the final day jam. Chris Musgrave, touring assistance and production reconnaissance in behalf of Dickey Betts & Great Southern is also here.

The best credits go to the sets themselves: two apiece for the CRS and then the all-afternoon jam on Saturday. Paul Hornsby's B-3 peered through the instrumental "Evergreen" with that Booker T. and the MG's feeling, and the band glided into Cowboy's "Time Will Tell" with Tommy Talton's Glenn Frey-like pleasant vocal, and Boyer then took over for a raspy "Down in Texas." Scott's voice, once innocent and youthful, has thankfully seasoned into a stronger Willie Nelson "molasses-and-red pepper" spice: sweet when it needs to be soft, but surprisingly hot. The audience viewed the ensemble and from the seats came a call: "How many Gibsons?" Came the answer, met with laughter, "Only takes one!"

That's the truth—and if Duane could only see his friends handle the chore! Of course, we had the days of Duane and Dickey, and of course, the current Allman line-up has Derek and Warren, but when Lee Roy's "Goldie" squawked with those unique slide tones that Duane pioneered, Tommy had as much to declare, especially on "Where Can You Go?" Both men eyed each other in a case of combat-turning-collaborative, and Talton brought his slide down to the sonic end of the fretboard for those birdcall screeches. ("I tried near forever to learn bottleneck, and then one day, it just happened!" he said.)

Golden nuggets from Gregg Allman's <u>Laid Back</u> release were also resurrected: the sad-but-true "Queen of Hearts" and "These Days" strolled slowly by, along with "Midnight Rider" and "All My Friends." Scott snarled defiantly, "Don't Hurt Me No More," authored with N.C. Thurmond, and LeeRoy agreed, answering with his own vocal on "There Ought To Be A Law" but with thoughts of Skydog to help lesson the pain, "Please Be With Me" made things better. And believe it or not, The Marshall Tucker Band made their presence felt with a terrific version of "This Ol' Cowboy," with Lee Roy and Tommy filling in for Toy and Charlie Daniels on fiddle. Even the next generation has their chops waiting: Scott Boyer III got up there on Night #2 for a snapping good electric time that had his daddy proud. Oh, yes, *of course* they kicked in "Shout Bamalama!"

This was a session of love, too—but let me explain. A white-haired man and lady—Eddie Hinton's parents--who sat at the back table alongside Ann Sandlin and me—where I watched an older gentleman named Tony Lempkin—or maybe it's Lumpkin--come up to the lady and introduce himself as the lead singer of the Bleus, a band that was trying to make their mark on the R&B airwaves with a few recordings they had made back in the days of Muscle Shoals. I watched and listened as the man got on his knees to take Mamma Hinton's hands in his and tell her how much her son had impacted his life in a positive way: that he had been a 17-year-old-wanna-be singer who had turned to Eddie for guidance.

However, in that young inexperienced way that we all seem bent on learning from, he had let immaturity have a stronger turn, and he showed up drunk on beer for a recording session. Eddie sized up the boy and led him out back by the Tennessee River—and pushed him in to sober up. Upon making it back to safety, Eddie delivered a tongue-lashing directive to decide what was more important: music or foolishness. It inspired him, Tony told her, so much so that he totally committed himself to learning to sing—and to be a sincere person in his adulthood.

He achieved all that and more, now being financially secure enough to provide for his grandchildren in a career that had nothing to do with entertainment—but he had learned his lesson from Eddie's words. At that moment, over Carl's PA system, "Everybody Needs Love" came through—the Bleus's version, with Tony on vocals. It was obvious that he put his integrity where his future would be and followed Eddie's tutorship.

So this gig is a collaboration of those who knew Duane--and other friends--personally and professionally, and are here to let his—and their—music tell of their respects. The talk floats around the tables and from the stage in small bursts, but the same words; "…he loved playing…wonderful guitar player…so much inspiration and so gifted…changed {my} life when I heard him play…What more can we say than a humble "thank you" to these folks and the man who brought them to us and each other? It seems so simple—but maybe that's all Duane would have asked. He surely would have enjoyed sharing the music. God bless you, Skydog: the Circle will Never Be Broken either. And the Road truly Goes on Forever in your memory.

Buddy Guy (Acoustic)

THE COUNT BASIE THEATRE
RED BANK, NJ
MARCH 18, 2004

Buddy took the audience to school—at least, he makes up his own curriculum. And the main coursework is the art of seduction. This was a very scary lesson to watch and hear—'cause Buddy was not taking anything less than 100% for results.)

"The man is after your dinner and you ain't getting close to the dessert menu, Junior. The platter has been licked clean—I'm not talking about your fine china, son--and you didn't have a bite." Mitch Lopate regarding Buddy Guy after the show.

You know about Johnny B. Goode. Now meet his cousin—or better yet, leave town if you love your woman, 'cause Buddy B. Up-to-No-Goode. Buddy, The Old Goat/Sly Fox was out tonight, howling and crying the blues. The trick is that it's his mating call—not a death knell—and it worked like lightnin'—all the fine ladies lit up for him. And the men were cheering him on! Go, Buddy, do your mojo smoke—even if she loves you for 60 minutes tonight, I get to take her home (I hope). But those guys are gonna be praying and paying the blues because the Old Goat/Sly Fox just might be top dog in her mind when the passion is rising.

Go away from my door, Buddy No-Goode; I love my woman as she is, and all that weeping and sighing is pitiful. It's pitiful 'cause you do it in ways she likes and I can't—don't show me up no more.

Those Young Turks calling out "Viagra!" and "Levitra!"; those aren't song titles that Buddy needs to hear. He has his own wavelength, and it's like a bee going for the honey. Hey, what did I just say?...not fair, Buddy, and stop sharpening those antlers. Ramble on down near some other man's pasture and leave my flock alone. You'll find your doe in another fellow's woods, I'm sure of that.

So Buddy Guy has gone acoustic—a big gorgeous Gibson--but no matter, 'cause his idea of being unplugged ain't quite gonna match your qualifications with your lady—and that's your loss, Jack, if she gets to feeling Buddy's hum. Fluid restrained shivers and skitters run off his fingers, and he's "Done Got Old" with a throbbing pace that reminded me of John Lee Hooker's "My Dreams." Woe, woe, but what you don't know is that the sap runs strong in that old oak; don't let your woman climb in his branches!

And he yowls like a black cat moan. Get away, I say, Buddy! Leave me in peace and stay back from my fence. What do you say to a man who wails, "I had one leg in the East and another in the West; I was in the middle, tryin' to do my best!" Mr. Hoochie Coochie Man, be gone, I'm begging you.

No, no, this is like giving a pyromaniac a box of matches as a present; the audience is caught in his trap. Young fools, the Sly Fox is after your women; stop cheering him on like that! Gonna be dues to pay, and you're not watching the merchandise! And Buddy knows what's hot and worth shopping for too. He has his Buddy-Bag of Blues tricks: the Masters are calling his name from Heaven. I heard 'em as clear as rolling thunder: Muddy, John Lee, Lightning Hopkins; Marvin Gaye ("Ain't That Peculiar"), Jimi, Stevie Ray; there's even a lecture on the discography of the European scene in the late '50s when jazz was synonymous with blues and a performer had to hold his chops in both styles.

Yessir, this is the time of the old Lion; hear him roar. Just keep clear with that lioness, or you may not be holding your cub. Buddy may be perched up on that stool without an electric guitar, but he's still got plenty of voltage.

And when his polka-dot guitar comes out, here he comes, one hand tapping out lead lines as neatly as anyone else uses two—that's because the other has a drumstick for a slide. It's too late, Jim: Buddy's out with that cordless guitar and off the stage...and you know he's coming into the audience, so give her up with a proper presentation; he's been looking at her grinding all this time. That acoustic magic was just to get you hypnotized, sucker.

So here's what I recommend: definitely see him when he's in town; the man is driven by compulsions and needs that demand resolution. Need a date? Go by a retirement home and find a nice lady who would like to feel young again. And let the acoustic blues drive her wild. Consider it a righteous thing and don't worry about all those fine legs you know are in town—you want them to stay away. Buddy will get them by himself, don't worry. Ever see how they find truffles? You ought to see how music does the same thing, Buddy Goat-Guy style.

I'm sufferin' for it. And he's laying out just fine with the blues.

"Women Who Cook"

FEATURING KOKO TAYLOR, JANIVA MAGNESS,
DEANNA BOGART, AND JENNIFER WRIGHT
THE COUNT BASIE THEATRE
RED BANK, NJ
JUNE 5, 2004

(The ladies ruled here. And for what it was worth, Deanna Bogart spun my head and heart like a roulette wheel. There's a picture of her daughter, Alix, on one of her CDs—and when I saw it, even my friends were bewildered: Alix looked just like me as a young boy. "How are you going to explain THAT to her?" a friend asked me. I only wish the ball fell where I had placed my chips, but Mama Deanna is better off with her drummer man, Mike...)

They had this gig mis-labeled. It should have been billed as "Women Who Sizzle." Thank God it was a cool evening, or else the sprinkler system would have been activated. There was one regret: due to competitive scheduling by the Jersey Shore Jazz & Blues Foundation, an outdoor venue had just concluded with an outstanding performance—so it was hard to be in two places at once. For what it was worth, and that meant everything to those of us at the Basie, we more than got our fair share of the value.

Now I know why the baseball fantasy league had such a field day when A-Rod joined the Yankees: the lineup potential was too good to overlook for a guaranteed win. Just look! An all-time W. C. Handy Award winner (Koko), a 2004 nominee (Janiva), a two-fisted dynamo on keyboards, sax, and vocals (Deanna), and an R&B

belter (Jennifer). This is another reason why Red Bank made the May 2004 edition of *Smithsonian Magazine* as "one of the hippest places to visit" in the U.S.

We dearly love our music here, and the Count Basie has more than its namesake on the marquee to show it. If you're an artist in the music industry, you bring the very best in your portfolio—nothing less accepted. Ladies, not only did you pull our musical heartstrings, we heard your deep passion for your craft. And that's what made it special—each one took her own turn and style in portraying what she felt as her inspiration; her muse. And oboy, did it make us jump!

These shows are rare, but more than a typical night out for entertainment. It was something like watching (and listening) to the on-stage equivalent of the U.S. Women's Olympic 440-relay team: right from the start, each lady burned past anyone and anything standing in her respective way, then passed the baton (microphone) to the next runner (performer) and onward to victory and an ultimate celebration of joy. In the end, the winners were both the musicians and the audience—and everyone in the theatre seats felt as though they too had been rocketing down the track lanes to the finish line and gold medal ceremony. I had the luck and support of the management to be there for the sound check, and it was great to see the camaraderie, plenty of jokes, laughs, and good connections.

Besides, the best place to get a terrific meal at a bargain price is right across the street: The Eurasian Eatery gave Deanna, Janiva, and me the corner table, and these gals are working friends from 20+ years ago. Catching up on their childhood and family memories that mixed and matched was just the right framework to set up the evening's display of support and partnerships.

Taking the first turn as a local girl and Red Bank favorite daughter, Jennifer and her band, Terraplane Blues, jumped out with "Amazing Grace," putting everyone in an open mood, and moved into Robert Johnson's "Walking Blues, fleshed out by rich chunks of slide guitar. A stormy sax made everything come clean for "Dirty Laundry" while Jennifer growled and prowled before us, and the intensity rose when she modified the Etta James classic, "I'd Rather Go Blind" by changing the tempo. The pleas and begging of

"Momma, He Treats Your Daughter Mean, supported by Deanna B. on fiery sax, brought on a wave of applause and howls of pleasure.

Speaking of Ms Bogart in more formal terms, her opening boogie-woogie rampage on the piano totally caught some people off-guard with the assortment of fluid mad dashes, aerial assaults, double-reverse moves, and sprints. Hey, guys, remember how Detroit Lions running back Barry Sanders used to throw those "I-moved-in-two- places-at-once" splits at the defense? Imagine that visual instead with two hands jitter-jabbing back and forth in a wild display of body English.

Deanna's a Detroit native, so it must be something that's a Motor City special. Jerry Lee Lewis wouldn't cover as much territory sitting before the black-and-whites as she does—but her style is really more Chuck Leavell, tutored by George Gershwin. A polished veteran on the East Coast circuit as well as a premier guest around the country, Deanna simply has the everything going her way, including a potential gold mine discography that demands ownership, a riveted-tight band, smoky, husky vocals that Fleetwood Mac's Christine McVie would wish to achieve, and a beautifully tarnished vintage saxophone that really resonates when she lets loose those scorching notes.

You may have not felt the flames as this one passed the competition in the race, but there was smoke under someone's feet. This is a <u>natural </u>keyboard player—you can hear it in her style (well, at least *someone* made use of lessons, it seems!), and she easily can pull the sorrow from a Wurlitzer organ, a choir of angels from an electric piano, or rolling fog from a synthesizer. If this was the second act, it was worth the show alone, and I would hold this as a standard measure for others from her.

You're an R&B fan, you surely know that Janiva Magness was a Handy Award nominee for this year's Best Contemporary Female Blues Artist. The third lane, and there was no doubt, was clearly marked by the lady in the form-fitting leopard-print dress.

That was obviously the way she liked it, as "I'm Not Ashamed" (from 2003's wonderful <u>Use What You've Got </u>CD) made her intentions known that she wasn't letting up the pace. (I would have died for that title song, as it has enough movement from the hips on down behind a thunderous beat to make a skeleton wish for muscles.) Janiva has a unique rub-board in her repertoire: it has a second potential as body armor with a *bustier* for a woman's figure, and Lord, I don't want to tell you how much those utensils she held are loving their job. "Work With Me, Baby," she urged, and that's what we all wanted to do if we could be up there making music.

Just for the fun of it, look at her cover photo of Blues Ain't Pretty: see that clenched fist and the snarl on her lips? Do not even attempt to consider trying to tame this big Cat. And as long as you're on it, check out the unmerciful torment from Kid Ramos's lead guitar on "St. Gabriel." I watched Janiva run through the warm-ups, and there's risky business with a big payout in everything she does. Donald Trump, here's someone who should run your "Apprentice" show. And all this from a woman who coos "Act Right" as if love is something special on the Atkins Diet.

Koko. She can carry her name in one hand—the one that holds the microphone is all that's needed. With her band, the Blues Machine (led by her son on guitar), she absolutely ruled, justifying her reputation as "The Queen of the Blues." It was the last lap, getting near midnight, but this lady saw everything as clear as day. "Let The Good Times Roll," she commanded. They did—and so did we, overwhelmed by the throaty hurricane's beckoning. "Tell Mama" and "Somebody Bring Me Some Water" were showcased in between a boisterous round of applause for the first three acts (yes, it surely must have been hot up there).

Koko occasionally found the need to sit and rest her bones, gathering up strength to rise again and get it down, telling us, "We're goin' down in the basement!" for some deep Chicago blues, Muddy Waters-style. Roaring with passion as only she can do, "Hoochie Coochie Woman" put a raw ingredient into the altered words: "I'm a wo-man!" I saw Buddy Guy do this to the ladies, but Koko wasn't taking anything else for an answer from the men. "Jump for Joy" was the response, and everyone joined in for a exhilarating "Wang Dang Doodle," including her insistence to "Get 'Speedy' up here—where's that little girl who played that piano?" The band played on in an extended jam while Koko recuperated backstage, and then it was another group encore for "Sweet Home Chicago."

Therefore, men, when the woman in your life says, "It's 'Ladies Night Out,' and I want to be entertained," just know that she has a reason in this blues season to be expecting a show like this. Either plan on a vacation that makes this tour available, or just head on up to Red Bank and wait for the next gig, because it could be better to be blue than black-and-blue by those who can sing them as well as deliver them too.

Roy Buchanan

– A LIFE-AND-DEATH GRIP ON GUITAR

(And this guy didn't like publicity! Sorry, Roy, your legacy is still too big to hide. I don't think Eddie Van Halen could have carried Roy's guitar case, let alone play his axe.)

Think for a moment about the anaconda snake of South America and the incredible crushing power it gets from its tremendous size. Now transfer the thought of that powerful grasp to human hand strength, and then wrap it around the neck of a 1953 yellow-blonde Telecaster, courtesy of the late Roy Buchanan. Nearly 300 pounds thick, Roy had the mass of an Amazon constrictor, too, but he could virtually squeeze atoms of electrical energy from an amplifier through his fingers.

When I listen to Roy, I am overwhelmed at the prehistoric reptilian danger signals, supersonic siren alarms, incendiary explosions, tortured screams and shrieks, and cosmic laser blasts that he would rip from his guitar. He had an Alexandrian Library of sounds to draw upon: some moaned like an anguished, tormented soul in Hades, and others yowled and wailed like a cat in heat--ghastly, ghostly sounds, and probably reflected more of Roy's darker brooding thoughts than he realized. Don't forget: this is the man who said he wanted to marry a nun and, with those deep-set eyes ablaze with intensity, confided to Robbie Robertson he was part werewolf.

Buchanan was also the absolute master of the volume control knob—listen to the intro and the ending solo of "Five String Blues" from *Second Album* and tell me it sounds like the agonized cry of someone in mourning. Or try the pealing quivers from the opening notes to "Man on the Floor"—it shudders with intensity. It's not something you want to spread, unless you know the deep pain of the blues. Perhaps you should listen to "The Messiah Will Come Again," which appeared on both *A Street Called Straight* and *Guitar on Fire – Roy Buchanan – The Atlantic Sessions* (Rhino). Roy clearly knew how to bare his inner grief as though he was being eaten alive from within the pit of his soul. And Buchanan had his share of demons, including heavy substance abuse with pills, marijuana, and alcohol.

Only two other men, in my opinion, deserve such exalted status as pyrotechnical wizards, and Jimi Hendrix is one; Jeff Beck, the other. Therefore, it's obvious why Roy paid homage to both men on *Guitar on Fire*. In fact, it was Beck who really opened the door for me on Roy: his cover of Stevie Wonder's "'Cause We've Ended as Lovers" on *Blow by Blow* mentioned Roy as a dedication, and the grieving intro volume swells were clearly a Buchanan inspiration. Roy also did "If Six was Nine" on *Guitar...*—but even if he hadn't covered Jimi with that song, there's no doubt in my mind that Hendrix would have felt at home alongside Roy on stage or in the studio.

Steve Cropper certainly did: he fights beside Roy on several of the Atlanticpieces, including the MG's "Green Onions" in a duel with Roy that would make your eyes water, too. Roy brought out every piece of heavy artillery he could bring to the field during his solos with Cropper—check out the first song, "Ramon's Blues," to see which man was more ferocious—and Buchanan ripped on "Onions" as though he was paring and peeling his strings with a jackknife blade to get those sounds.

Some of Roy's songs stand out in my mind for pure tonality. One gets me for sheer animal power: Willie Dixon's "My Baby Is Sweeter" from *Malaguena,* which has two versions, both of which feature one of the most searing, serrated tones to be wrenched from the depths of darkness. There's also Roy's cover of Joe Walsh's "Turn to Stone," which lashes out with an abrasive solo.

He also played tricks with a slide, but shed the elaborate phrases that characterize the style. Instead, he chose to use his dexterity and quick fingers to run cartoon-like statements on "Hawaiian Punch" from *When a Guitar Sings the Blues* (Alligator), one of his personal favorite albums, or the country-picking twists and turns of "Okay" (from *Guitar on Fire*. On the latter, Roy sounds like a mad fiddler who can't make up his mind, there is a great organ solo that jumps the scales like they were train tracks, and a great octave-changing ending. Don't miss it).

To help decipher some of Buchanan's occult skill, I contacted Ellwood Brown, who produced *Malaguena*, and a man who knew personally knew Roy for years as a friend. He states,

"Roy frequently stated that the reason for the high action was to get a cleaner sound. In all probability, the guitars that he had access to early in his career could have suffered from warped necks or just plain poor quality and would have fret 'buzz.' The cure would be to raise the action a little, but sometimes that wasn't enough, so you just had to live with it. Because of the unusual limberness of his joints, he would be able to deal with a higher action than someone with normal limitations. He was what we call 'double-jointed' and could touch his wrist with his thumb either forward or backward.

"So, to go on, he soon discovered a couple of things: a clean sound, better sustain, and curiously enough, with a raised action and nut, the string is actually easier to bend than with low action; less friction with the fret board, for one thing. Of course, this led to the necessity of larger Gibson type frets. I'm sure, knowing Roy's sense of humor, that it must have tickled him to watch someone else try to play his instrument at a jam session or while sitting in.

"If you're not a guitar player, you are wondering by now, 'Well, why doesn't everyone have high action if it's so good?' The reason is that beyond a certain point it goes from extremely difficult to impossible to make chord changes. Single notes are one thing, but for chords you would need hands capable of coming down on the strings at a 90-degree angle with 100% certainty. Roy also stated that the high action kept him from getting sloppy. It requires precise technique of which few are capable.

"Later in life, he did lower the action considerably with no apparent change in the quality of his technique. He said his hands just couldn't take the all-out playing at concerts for three hours or more. When he was a band member, he didn't have to put out 60 seconds of every minute. Most of the time he was playing rhythm or fills, but later in life, on tour, fans expected something every second and even Roy couldn't turn back the biological clock. Hence, the lighter gauge strings he used in the later years. This is one of those questions that can be answered to a guitar player and to someone totally unfamiliar with the instrument--the second is much more difficult. I hope that I have sort of split the difference and given you an adequate answer."

Yes, sir, you did, and a whole lot more.

Roy's life came to a mysterious, tragic end in August 1988, in a jail cell in Fairfax County, Virginia. I would rather avoid the stories about what happened on that night because I can't say for sure. Depression and loneliness obviously had caught up with him, and he had fought against them for years.

I would rather think that as tragic as his death has been to those who knew him, he found a way to tell us what he really needed to say in one final effort. By just listening to his vocals—he had a deep baritone deadpan, flat delivery—I gather Roy didn't talk much. Instead, the message came through his fingers—and he made sure every possible bit of the range of human hearing would know it, too.

Roy's incredible strength is probably at work in a higher dimension—I figure if Heaven's angels can teach him to play the harp, then just consider those incredible summer thunder-and-lightning storms as Roy trying out his technique on a new stringed instrument. Besides, how can you beat the potential atmospheric amplification? He surely is plugged in to the Supreme Power supply—and we can shake hands and agree on that. Just don't squeeze so hard, please—I've gotta practice on my guitar—with low fret action, mind you. But you can bet I'd leave alone the strong-arm fretting technique in respect to Roy's memory—and abilities.

Robert Randolph & The Family Band

THE STONE PONY, ASBURY PARK
JULY 2, 2004

(My man Robert and the Family Band are a Supreme Dream! If you've read the stories about him, Randolph is the new Prophet of Strings—and 13 of 'em on the steel pedal. Prepare your ears to be twisted around your head.)

Robert Randolph & The Family Band gigged last night down at the Stone Pony in Asbury Park last night behind a partially hidden orange full moon. But no one was looking up in the sky to see the heat lightning flashing behind us—there was too much energy possible to believe onstage. Some shows need to be seen to be appreciated; others to be heard. Go see this man play, because Robert and the Band need to be <u>felt</u>—and the action totally enveloped the audience from our toes on up. Give those calf muscles a workout!

If you can grasp it, an instrumental of Michael Jackson's "Billie Jean" absolutely slithered like it had no backbone, teasing us with wah-wah effects on pedal steel. Randolph's style has two forms: a percussive and the traditional pedal-style gliding (he can smack the bar in his left hand down on the strings as though it's leaping). But watch him bend down low, head cocked to one side, and see how intimate he gets to the instrument—and then tease a sensuous waterfall torrent of notes. He also coaxes an ultrasonic rainbow of brass squeals, air horn blasts, siren warnings, and bull elephant challenges from those fingers.

But he's just as much a pure physical contact player, football-style: the man just pummels the guitar. At one point, caught up in a frenzy of gloried passion, he jumped up and pinwheeled his chair away with a stomp that appeared to have torn it to pieces.

What did he want? "I Need More Love," and so did we, giving it back behind bassist Danyel Morgan's vocals. Imagine Smoky Robinson mixed with a feline in heat, but Morgan has a different kind of cat scratch fever—and your ears will love it.

Danyel, by the way, is the locomotive force behind the Family band, punching/popping out a stampede of notes that keep a dominant chunky glue with lead guitar overtones, much like Victor Wooten (from Bela Fleck's Flecktones). Think that was tough to follow? Try an instrumental "Voodoo Chile," complete with *chocka-chocka* riffs that echoed both Jimi and Stevie Ray—but from a pedal steel? You just paid with your soul to hear these men play! At least 35 women from the audience climbed onstage for "Shake Your Hips," and moving that and everything else they had, nearly completely hiding the band, and Robert's sister Lenesha came on for the lead vocals to help her brother for "Smile" (from the new *Unclassified* CD).

The band also showcased a routine that begs to be put on your wide-screen: they switch instruments in the middle of a gig. A monster beater on drums, cousin Marcus Randolph jumped out and traded places with Robert—and if you can believe it, there was no telling the difference in pure technique on that 13-string pedal, right down to the leap-frog hopping left hand. It's in the genes, man. It's a true Family Band.

And if that's not bad enough, Danyel turned over his bass to Robert and moved to a Stratocaster. You've seen fast hands, I'm sure, but he's just a blur. And back and forth they went: a solid-body to keyboard player Jason Crosby (who also traded it back to Robert). While we were treated to a morale-boosting tour bus tune, "The Happy Song," Jason broke out on electric violin, inserting "Axel's Theme" from *Beverly Hills Cop,* and there was a huge serving of

"Pressing My Way" and "I Don't Know What You Come to Do" (from *Live at the Wetlands*).

The answer is obvious: Robert Randolph & The Family Band have come to provide the answer to our energy needs. To hell with the oil companies and the high price of gasoline. It's an old cliché, but let OPEC pump the last drop they can: The Family Band plays with pure musical power.

Jackie Greene

(Opening for Buddy Guy)
The Count Basie Theatre, Red Bank, NJ
March 18, 2004

I normally do my show reviews with the usual emphasis on the main act; it's obviously whom the crowd has paid to see, myself included. However, this time, let me give word about the opening act—because this kid not only kept Buddy Guy at bay for a while with one heck of a performance, but he got himself a standing ovation—and in a place with the rich cast of performers gone before, that's an admirable thing to see.

Yes, I got in a few minutes late, fiddled with the playbill and occasionally looked up at the young man on stage—and then I found myself listening and watching with interest. Blowing a tasty blues harmonica and really filling up the space in between with fluid and rich chords, Jackie Greene sang and played his way into the hearts and ears of the audience. Confidence—that's one thing he had, and his voice carried it strongly with the homespun lyrics that he poured out in a sensitive tenor. Maybe another Jackson Browne? The urge to catalogue him was immediate—but not as easy as I wanted. The harmonica was vintage Dylan—and maybe Neil Young.

The same for the guitar: on an acoustic, he looked as though he had been on stage for years, especially with the furious rhythm he set on several songs. Who did something like that…Buddy Holly? Maybe. Where did he get that maturity? Something like Waylon as a young man…and he finger-picks ballads ("Gracie") like Willie did before he went grizzled and gray. But Jackie is skinny—has a mop of dark hair that sits under a porkpie hat—and looks like someone ought to take him home and keep him for a while.

At the 30-minute mark, it was obvious that the auditorium was locked in with him. That's when he pulled out the seat to the keyboard setup and proceeded to ripple as fine a boogie-woogie cabaret piano as Billy Joel would do—and yes, the harp was still clamped and honking. No fooling: this is why those lessons you quit in spite of your parents' pleas were valuable. He's also quite adept at bluegrass banjo, electric guitar, and a Hammond B-3 too, but that's on the CD. That's when I sauntered out to the lobby and looked for the vendors--where and who is this guy? I want what he's playing out there. And yes, he's made Rolling Stone's Top 10.

So why am I so surprised to see good talent like this on the circuit? I shouldn't be if I had been following the news: from the dusty hills of Northern California comes another, steeped in the heritage and traditions of the wandering minstrel. Gone Wanderin' (DIG 106), released in November, 2002, won the **California Music Award** for the "**Best Blues/Roots Album**" in May 2003; he's been on the national Americana Chart for over a year. In 2003, he toured nationally with singer/guitarist Susan Tedeschi, blues master B.B. King and pop icon Huey Lewis, as well as multiple dates with John Hiatt, George Thorogood, and Taj Mahal. In virtually every venue, Greene has set support act house records for CD sales off the bandstand, and played high profile festival dates across the country the summer of 2003, including, the Newport Folk Festival, the Strawberry Music Festival, the Rhythm & Roots Festival and the San Francisco Blues Festival. He's sharing national tour duties with Jonny Lang and of course, Buddy Guy.

And yes, the CD rocks—with good licks and rough-and-ready stuff. "Tell Me Mama, Tell Me Right" just slides ever so gracefully under your shuffling feet, "Mexican Girl" has Jackie torn between love and destiny, "Down in the Valley Woe" goes aloft with a fast-paced crescendo, "Cry Yourself Dry" means you just closed the bar, and "Freeport Boulevard" is where the action's at for a hot night—unless "Judgment Day" means that you've reached Paradise. Or better yet, just follow the kid on tour at **www.jackie-greene.com**. Now, let me get back to the CD; is he a western Van Morrison? Maybe he came from the days of Poco? Just can't help comparing him…and most likely, he's gonna be just fine being himself. He seems to have the stage set with the talent he's showing.

Bobby Whitlock

– The Domino Effect

(So there I am, sitting on the porch of Bobby's house in May 2000—at that time, in Oxford, Mississippi—and I've flown down from NJ to interview him—on my dime. He's sitting there fooling around with a dobro, and all I can do is gawk: "Omigod, this is a real rock star musician! This is the guy on the <u>Layla</u> album!" Some things never change. Years later, I saw Bobby at his home in Tuscumbia, Alabama, after he had come over to the Muscle Shoals Sound Studio on his new Indian motorcycle, and sporting his new tattoos.

    I guess it's a natural thing to say that when you've had a life like mine—especially my early childhood—that "I was born to play the blues." It's the way that I was raised—hard physical work was expected to be done by a child to help make money to help support our family. If that meant bending over in the fields, doing back-breaking work like the other adults, then it was understood that this was my way of contributing. I'm talking about *real* little, like a little bitty boy. Not even eight years old; much smaller. I chopped and picked cotton until my fingers were stiff and sore—cotton's nasty stuff; it can make your skin dry up and bleed if you handle too much of it. I rode the back of bean planters in the countryside out there in Arkansas. The sun would be beating down, the air would be hot and dusty and our throats were parched, but we had to work—there wasn't much else to do and we had to pitch in and help. I hauled all kinds of produce.

    Did you ever hear the phrase "a shotgun house"? Well, we lived in one, down there in Marmaduke, Arkansas. That meant you could fire a shotgun from one side and there wasn't anything like a wall or any other rooms to stop the pellets or buckshot from going anywhere but straight out the door—it was kinda like a three-room, one-house deal. It was also known as a high-water house, because it was sort of built on stilts to keep it dry when the high water rose. You could literally read last year's news through the cracks in the walls because that was the insulation in this house.

Sometimes, it was necessary to scare off—or worse—anything or anyone on two or four legs that might be trying to break into the place. Yes, we knew we were poor—I could tell that by having to sleep head-to-toe in a bed with my grandfather, "Peapaw" Whitlock. For heat, all we had was a pot-bellied stove, and food…well, I remember one time when a rat ate through a loaf of bread that we had saved… it looked like a train had gone through a tunnel from one end to another.

My daddy was a preacher and what you'd call a "professional student," and he felt that this would take the mischief out of me, as well as teach me discipline that was necessary to be a son of a man of the gospel. I took my share of beatings, too: tied up by the wrists and whipped because I wasn't acting serious-like during church services. I'm talking about this happening to me as a young fella of eleven years—not a child any more, either! He took me out back to the barn and trussed me up and used the leader-line of a mule team on me—I'm talking about a seriously thick piece of leather! He kind of had what they call a "Napoleon complex"—I didn't know then he wasn't six feet tall until I grew bigger than he did.

My daddy would drag my mother and me and my sister and brother—they were too young to work--all over, looking for some place to work while he did his preaching. I can still see pictures in my mind of her in a home-made dress and high heels, standing over a hot wood stove and cooking on a Sunday. My mother and I had to go work in the fields to feed ourselves because my father would come home for two days and be gone again. On Sundays and Wednesdays, folks would take the preacher's family into their house and show their hospitality that way. I remember one family—the Turberville's-

-whom I thought were rich because Mr. Ross Turberville had two mules and a tractor.

You would have to meet my kind of kinfolk to understand them--they just did things their own way and nobody had better interfere--what we called "rounders." They would as soon as fight, steal, make moonshine or just get into plain mischief--just imagine how a raccoon would act if they were part-human. It just had to rub off on me, growing up with people like this. I can remember Peapaw Whitlock living with us, whittling and then *spitting* on that stove, and drinking boiling coffee—I never would have believed it in my life, but it was that hot.

He also did something that I learned about when I was on the road as a musician: Peapaw would smoke regular tobacco—Bull Durham was his brand—during the day, but at night…then he'd take something else from another pocket and light up that. When I first smoked marijuana, I knew what it was! I said to myself, "That old sonovabitch, he was smoking pot!" Of course, it was during the '30s and '40s, and people's attitudes were different, and so was the practice of indulging in those kinds of things. Especially for us folks who lived back in the hills and hollows—it was more understood as a way of combining medicine with driving out the pain of making ends meet and getting through the harshness of living.

For example, there was Aunt Berthie and Uncle Elvin--they were my kin from Marked Tree, Arkansas. Aunt Berthie was a great big woman, with hair down to the ground, and Uncle Elvin was my Pea-paw (grandfather) King's brother. Well, you sure can say they were a little bit odd: in their home, they had pigs in the bedroom and chickens roosting on the head of the bed. They ran a store there, a kind of general store where you could buy all kinds of goods. I can see those wooden sidewalks in my mind…but the point is, the government wouldn't let them sell anything out of that store unless it had a lid on it or a wrapper. I would have been hard pressed and double-dealt to buy *anything* from them, but they were kinfolk.

Well, it wasn't too long before Aunt Berthie went into an institution for the mentally handicapped. One day, Uncle Elvin called Pea-paw King and said, "Hey, one of Berthie's relatives has died, and we gotta take her to the funeral." They had a pick-up truck with a chair in the back of it--it was something straight out of "The Beverly Hillbillies." So, they took her out of the side door, which was quite a feat for a woman of her size, and put her up in that chair.

Then they took off, doing about 45 miles an hour down a bumpy gravel road with Berthie perched up there, and rocks zinging from under the tires and smoke flying in the air. Peapaw said, "I felt the truck hit a bump and looked up and everything got real springy under the wheels, as though we had just shucked ourselves of some extra weight." Both men looked in the rear view mirror, and saw Berthie tumbling end-over-end in the gravel behind them. Uncle Elvin said, "Doggone, she's gone and dove out of the back of the truck!" So, both men went and picked her up, dusted her off and put her back in the chair, turned around and drove all the way back to the institution. They hauled her out of the chair, dusted her off and backed the truck up to the side door. Then they went to the front desk and declared, "She ain't quite ready yet!"

Like I said, growing up with these folk can leave a lasting imprint on a young boy's mind--and I was an impressionable child. Being poor was a way of life that was just something that we accepted--so the petty criminal activities in which the family participated was just considered another way to make ends meet--it was a way to survive!

Let me give you another example of how they survived: they were "miners." Oh, no, there was no prospecting for gold or other precious minerals—that was too much hard work for nothing. Their theory was simple: what was once yours is now <u>mine</u>. One time, Peapaw and Uncle Elvin—this must go back about 55 years or so— were out on an "excavating" mission in Mississippi, riding around in an old beat-up car. They were gonna dig up *something* somewhere, but they just weren't sure what it would be. Then they came upon a farmhouse and went out and stole this farmer's chickens—chicken coop and all! They opened up the back of this old car and put the whole thing in there—chickens and coop and all—and drove away in the dead of night.

Well, sure enough, just like Aunt Berthie and the truck, the chicken coop *and* the chickens fell out of the back of the car, and there were chickens running around loose all over the place. My grandpa, Peapaw King, went back to the farmer's house—the guy from whom they'd just stolen the chickens and the chicken coop!!—and knocked on the door. "Could you give us a hand out here?" he asked, "we got ourselves a problem with all these chickens!" The farmer followed him back to the car, helped them round up all those loose birds and tie up the chicken coop, and put it in the back of the car again!

They started up the car and began to drive away—but that's not the King family way of doing things, so they stopped and thought a minute. As a token of their appreciation, they backed the car up alongside the farmer, who was still standing on the side of the road. Uncle Elvin stepped out and handed the farmer a chicken, which the startled man placed under his arm like a loaf of bread. Sure enough, my grandfather and Uncle Elvin drove off and left the poor farmer standing on the side of the road, scratching his head with one hand, holding a hen in the other, and wondering why two men were out in the dead of night with a trunk full of squawking chickens and a coop that looked a lot like his. To tell the truth, a Pentacostal preacher was holding a revival in Lepanto, AR, and he, Pea-paw and Uncle Elvin were in cahoots with this chicken stealing. After he stole the chickens, Pea-paw left a note on the chicken house, "We steal from the rich and give to the poor, we left you six, to raise us some more."

Peapaw King also got himself thrown into the Polk County Farm in Arkansas for stealing a loaf of bread and a quart of milk—don't forget that I'm talking about the times of the Great Depression---and my grandmother, "Big Momma" King got a job working there in the kitchen. It was like a complete scenario from the Paul Newman movie, *Cool Hand Luke:* they bull-whipped him with a cat-o'-nine tails, and "Big Momma" slipped him some red pepper powder to put in his shoes and helped him break out of there. They had the hounds on his trail real quick-like, but that pepper stuffed them up. I saw those scars on his back from when they whipped him.

On the other side, it was the Whitlock's that were trouble. My Peapaw Whitlock was a moonshiner, and he died because of it. I remember him literally lighting that stuff up—if it had a blue flame, it meant it was real, real good! He was going out on a delivery—but of course, he had to sample it a bit to make sure it was of the proper quality and strength—and he got himself drunk.

So, there he was, taking a case of freshly-made brew across a newly-cut cornfield during the night on what must have been the coldest Thanksgiving day on record—I mean, it was *nasty* bitter cold, down near New Albany, MS. He was carrying a pint jug with him on the way back—that was to be expected—but he didn't see or *couldn't* see—depending on his condition—where he was going, and he tripped over a corn stalk. The fall didn't kill him, but he landed on a sharpened cut stalk of corn, and it punctured his chest. He turned over on his back in the middle of the rows and just froze to death. The boy who was running the fence on that farm came out the next day to work and found my grandfather lying there with his arms outstretched to the heavens and a pint of moonshine behind him. Lord knows if he was trying to ask for help to raise himself up or he was trying to reach out first for that lost jug!

The only joy I had was when I would have a few spare moments to hear music at the church, or when I sat with my grandmother, "Big Momma" King, who would play her dobro for me. Thank heaven for those moments—they were the shining light in my life as a three year-old boy! It was a beautiful National dobro, made in the late 1880s, and there were hula dancers on the front and back. Big Momma would sit me down and play gospel-style to me, "Turn your radio on, get in touch with Jesus." I can still hear her now!—and I have that dobro with me. I've gone and had it painted—at one time, a lady named Genya Revan, who played with 10-Wheel Drive, had it and kept it safe for me.

See, it was always with me—the music—it was in my soul and in my spirit. So when I look back at those hard times, I can say I was a singer, and I sang *all* the time! I'd be working out in the fields with the migrant workers and the poor black folk who were sharecroppers, and they'd sing all the way to the fields in the back of rickety, bouncing trucks, and then they'd be singing while they were working, and then on the way back home. I'd be singing right along with them. So, yes, I'd say my roots were always there in gospel, blues and soul music—I was born living the blues, and I learned to sing them to get through those harsh times!

How Blues can You Get?

PETER GREEN AND FLEETWOOD MAC

(Typical "mischief-making" topic: name the five best guitar players ever. Here's my list: Jimi Hendrix, Duane Allman, Eric Clapton, Jeff Beck, and...Peter Green.)

Trivia question for the day: name the late '60s group to simultaneously field a trio of killer guitarists who could each independently rampage the studio and stage with stomach-churning blues and handle the chore of vocals as well. Throw in an overseas heritage as a devoted bar band who just played the basics and were known to party hearty. We're not talking homegrown Delta men, either, who knew the roadhouses, but they honored their forefathers' influences: the Kings (Albert and B.B.); Otis Rush, Robert Johnson, Willie Dixon; and Elmore James. (The last one is a hint.)

Goin' to Chicago, y'all. Still caught off-guard? This premier band lost those three heroes to fame, drugs and drinking, insecurity, and religion. And *then* women came onboard and turned whatever firewater remained into light beer—but not to put down the ladies for their efforts: they ultimately earned them hits on mainstream pop FM radio.

Before Stevie Nicks and her love affairs with Celtic mystique; before Bob Welch and his Robert Palmer-like vanilla ice cream vocals; and the early '70s days of fragile pop stars trying to write tough hooks—ladies and gentlemen, meet Peter Green's Fleetwood Mac. You couldn't ask for a more honest musician than Peter—he literally told John Mayall to take his music and shove it because it wasn't true-blue enough. Remember: B.B. King onstage once credited Peter as a better player with more feeling than Eric Clapton and *George Harrison—and those two gents were directly addressed as members of the audience. (*I've heard options that the other guest was Mike Bloomfield.)

Regardless—if you think that you know your blues chops and players and have left Green off your top five list, then go back and review your color spectrum standards. Peter had the touch that sent shivers down B.B.'s spine—that's what the man said. And just for fun, Pete could saw down the strings with a slide and turn out a spectral 6-string bass solo on the live versions of "The Green Manilishi."

This is the guy who was invited to jam with Jerry Garcia and special guest Duane Allman at a Grateful Dead concert. Carlos Santana knew what treasure he found with Peter's "Black Magic Woman" too. Those are Peter's licks he's playing. The title? That was Peter's girlfriend, practicing a little "not now, honey" celibacy. And she wouldn't "pick up my magic stick." Some parts on a man turn mighty blue when you don't get any. Oh, yeah—Peter could blow blues harmonica too. 'Nuff said?

It doesn't take size to play the blues: Jeremy Spencer stands only 5'3", but he had the largest heart a body could contain for Elmore James (and Homesick James) and slide guitar. When Jeremy bit down with an opening chord that drenched of "Dust My Broom" influence, he'd often snarl out loud with glee. It was his dead-on impersonation of Elmore's material that kept him in check; at the same time, it became a gangrene-like sore that eventually drove Peter Green to distraction because the band had become a parody of its own influences.

Fleetwood Mac had various stage entities, thanks to Spencer's mimicry, including a Buddy Holly tribute, a rock 'n roll party, and Doo Wop/Dion and the Belmont stunts. Green, as the key guitarist (and most proficient) had to banish Spencer off-stage during gigs in order to maintain order. Green's inaugural gathering of Fleetwood Mac embraced Jeremy's raucous enthusiasm, but it was a limited offering: a musician who could shine on material of his own choice but was stubborn and resistant to change.

ROCK 'N' BLUES STEW II

So you're a youngster of 17 with a baby face and blonde hair, and you play a mean Texas-style blues with heavy vibrato—you're in a group called The Boilermakers—and you've caught the eye (and ear) of Peter Green. Hello, boys, meet Danny Kirwan.

In the Mac world of musical genies, Danny offered piercing lead and strong rhythm in support of Green and Spencer—and along with poster boy looks, a tenor voice that gave enough earthiness to warm your bruised heart. Caught between the stunning displays of ego and talent of Spencer and Green, it's amazing that Danny survived as a member for the short duration. Green's skills left Kirwan in awe, but Danny gave Peter the steady bracing needed to make '69-70's *Then Play On* stand out as Green's swan song.

With the need for teamwork once again, Spencer and Kirwan joined ranks in making the follow-up, *Kiln House*, a platform for Jeremy's charismatic displays and Danny's meaty lead licks and instrumental songwriting on cuts like "Earl Gray" and "Tell Me All the Things You Do."

The collapse came before *Bare Trees:* Spencer departed after a religious movement inspired him to renounce his name and lifestyle, and Danny was left to shoulder his Les Paul and responsibilities as the front man, along with Bob Welch's pop-oriented ballads, held together with Christine McVie's piano and vocals. Kirwan continued to contribute notable instrumentals ("Danny's Chant" and "Sunny Side of Heaven"), but the band is remembered more so for Welch's feathery "Sentimental Lady" (done also on his own solo release), as well as 1973's "Hypnotized" (from *Mystery To Me)*. The results were anything but blues; more like the Moody Blues, and that's a sad statement.

With respect, Fleetwood Mac's namesakes were also strong fundamental blues men: bassist John McVie, a co-member with Green in Mayall'sBluesBreakers, walked out when the eclectic leader brought in horns and ordered them to perform in a jazz mode. McVie could bob and weave gracefully, but was more comfortable just pulling the plow behind the others' direction. Mick Fleetwood put all of his skinny 6'6 frame into crushing percussion tricks that could gracefully adapt tone and muffled drum skins and rolling tom-toms along with world-on-my-shoulders drudgery through repetitive 12-bar songs and comic routines.

The blues have left their price (as any musician who plays will tell a listener): Peter Green has returned to the stage and recording studio with The Splinter Group, but he's a shell of what he once was. A once cheerful, vibrant voice that could moan the blues as well as shag it with rock 'n roll vibrancy has eroded into a creaky gasp. Electric shock therapy to help him recover from the LSD he liberally sampled has left him unable to play with the power he did, and his routines are now basic Robert Johnson tributes.

The year 2008 saw Jeremy Spencer reestablished again with *Precious Little*, a solo project that captures his consummate skills as a songwriter and virtuoso slide player. According to an unofficial Danny Kirwan web page, he is allegedly found in various shelters for the homeless and destitute in London, a victim of alcohol abuse and his own fears and worries about competing as a guitar player. No wonder: in the days of Fleetwood Mac's blues, he helped set the standards. John McVie and Mick Fleetwood continue to support and play together…but if there's any blues left in the band, it's baby-blue. And that is why they need to be remembered for what they were: the best band on both sides of the Atlantic that ever played the blues.

Where to start? A serious blues collector will have the aforementioned *Horizon* set (a great price at $40), and I endorse the *Boston Tea Party* three-some. Go for Green's farewell virtuosity on *Play On* (he wrote one helluva classic guitar coordinate on "Oh Well"), and the *Live at the BBC* 2-CD set. Add *The Vaudeville Years of Fleetwood Mac 1968-1970* and *Show-Biz Blues 1968-1970*.

For some tight live blues, try *Shrine '69* and get a "Lemon Squeezer." You'll need *Jumping at Shadows – The Blues Years* double CD, and to end, go for *Peter Green & the Original Fleetwood Mac – Alone with the Blues*. Yawanna get Peter bending strings as neatly as Albert King on "Born Under a Bad Sign," right? And collaborator and friend Duster Bennett did Muddy Waters justice by giving Peter "Trying So Hard to Forget," as well as showcasing Green's tormented blues lead guitar on "Jumping At Shadows."

Finally, *Blues by Green* has a few tunes that are repeated on other discs, but worth carrying. Magnificent in their efforts, Peter Green's Fleetwood Mac deserves a place in the blues Hall of Fame.

David Crosby and CPR; March 2004, at William Paterson University's Shea Center for Performing Arts

(I have a saying: "If it's liver, then tell me. Don't douse it with ketchup and try to tell me it's roast beef." In other words, don't try to cover it and pretend it's not there. I felt the same way about David Crosby's performance: it tasted like something I didn't want to eat.)

Sacred cows are supposed to be honored and treated with respect. In that regard, I tend to look upon my musical heroes of the late '60s-early '70s in the same perspective: earthy in their social outlook, gifted with their talents, and motivating by virtue of charisma. However, like cows, heroes sometimes stray from the herd and have to be brought back home again.

When I heard that David Crosby was playing at WilliamPatersonUniversity, I was mildly amused at the offer to review the performance. His background is not unknown: we're talking about a two-time Rock 'n Roll Hall of Fame inductee. I have the Byrds's box set; CSNY was a part of my growing rebellious phase as a teen, and I very fondly owned several Crosby and Nash LPs.

I've also seen the A&E *Biography* selection on David; his life story and escapades are Herculean in their abuses and indulgences—and there are various blistering comments about him and his bandmates in Bill Graham's excellent autobiography, *Bill Graham Presents*.

However, according to the press release, David has found new momentum with jazz-like touches after uniting with a son, James Raymond, whom he gave up for adoption 30 years ago, and his group, CPR. And of course, I hoped to hear that classic rock zest again.

Perhaps the usher who tried to read my ticket stub in the dark without a flashlight was a clue that something might be amiss—and upon looking out on the stage, David added to that impression at first. Standing there with hands in his pockets and singing, he looked like a shaggy white-haired walrus with no sense of urgency. I came to hear that harmonic voice, and alas—its range has been reduced; almost flat at times, almost breaking elsewhere.

But okay, Time has been collecting fees from the man—and he had a cute way of forgetting the song play list. Jeff Pevar's slide guitar and voice accented a soft ballad, "Through Here Quite Often," about strangers who meet in random all-night diners and other places, and James filled in on a keyboard portfolio with background vocals, accompanied by drums (also adding in background vocals) and Andrew Ford on bass. Next up was "One and All," a vicious-but-honest pop-rock dissection of Ken Lay of Enron and all the other robber baron CEOs who pillaged their company funds.

Crosby seasoned this and other social commentaries throughout the show with his own special brand of humor, and it makes room for good comedy. Pevar showed his dexterity here with a laptop double-neck steel guitar, but continuously struggled with his amps throughout the show. When the band hit their stride on tunes like this, Don Henley comes to mind—but more effectively musical. For what it's worth, there's nothing more annoying that ruins a song's potential than cramming extra words into the lyrics—it throws the rhythm and time signature off.

Onward we went: Statue of Jesus," co-written by Pevar with Crosby's long-time friend and comrade Graham Nash, sprinkled gentle Spanish guitar and electric piano and synth behind a tribute to Rio De Janeiro's famous landmark monument, and a joking introduction to another CSN piece that Nash also penned: "Hot Dogs in

Space." Noted in the remarks was that this song was not meant to be included on the original CD.

Okay, I'm convinced. It wasn't just David's struggles to keep that graceful tenor voice afloat like a kite on a balmy day; sorry to point this out, but on songs like this and "Luck Dragon, as well as others, Mr. Raymond didn't inherit Dad's pipes, either, and those high notes were made for Graham. But a good keyboard man, yes. Social unrest being Crosby's crusade of choice, "Yours and Mine" confronted the senseless acts of conflict that take the lives and innocence of youngsters with AK-47s and other weaponry.

For all those come-and-gone hippies (and there were a lot of graybeards and heads in those seats!), "So You Want to Be a Rock 'N' Roll Star" gave Pevar a good chance to do his Roger McGuinn thing, "Guinevere" floated on mystical currents, and "My Country 'Tis of Thee" also waved proudly, guided by the spirit of late guitarist Michael Hedges. Crosby reminded us again that he is as dedicated a patriot as ever—that we have the right to speak up against our government's improprieties—and that we should cherish the legacy of our national documents of freedom.

Okay, but I would have given anything at that point to hear his anthem of independent identity, "Almost Cut My Hair"—but no luck. Instead, off the new CPR CD, "Ghost Town" (with a Tom Petty & the Heartbreakers rhythm) and a good rocker, "Katy Did." Tag along a potential autobiographical "At the Edge" with that, but the band wisely added in the volume to mask the vocal flaws that kept appearing. Note this: I didn't catch the drummer's name, but David acknowledged him as the best he's worked with, and I didn't think Dallas Taylor or Johnny Barbata were that bad. However, this new guy really made it look easy and sounded terrific (I like the low bottom-sounding tom-toms).

The band cooked up some Brazilian influences at the end, everyone took a random solo (better to do that bass on a 5-string; higher potential), and "Déjà vu," complete with David's scat vocals, brought out smiles and memories. "Ohio" came back for an angry encore, but that was all that mattered.

So what's the moral of the story? Yesterday morning, Saturday, March 6th, David Crosby was arrested in New York City for possession of marijuana and a handgun. Seems he had checked out of the hotel and left behind a carry-on bag, which was found by a clerk and searched to identify the owner. Hey, David, you forgot more than the song list. Better luck next time, old friend. And as Satchel Paige said, "Go easy on the vices. The social ramble ain't restful."

Wildflower Festival

November 13, 2001
The Count Basie Theatre
Red Bank, NJ

(It's great to see the veterans out there on the circuit, working together. I had the good fortune to catch Judy Collins and Janis Ian, along with Roger McGuinn, at a previous performance. I also met Richie at BrookdaleCommunity College, where I taught—and he's a real gentlemen and scholar.)

Collectively and singularly, the Wildflower Festival (Judy Collins, Roger McGuinn, Janis Ian, and Richie Havens) is a scene of (musical) heaven on Earth. Older hippies don't fade away—they spread the word through their instruments and songs, and let me say that Judy Blue Eyes looks and sings like an angel. Janis Ian stole the show back (from McGuinn's nimble-fingered magic) by unveiling a virtuosity on acoustic-amplified guitar that rivals Lindsey Buckingham in technique, and her singing resonates inside you when she lets loose. However, you can't beat Richie in the #4 slot, and his personality has the heartfelt warm sincerity of love for Man and Womankind like the late Chicago Bear, Walter Payton, or the Cubs' Ernie Banks. In fact, that's the other quality that makes this show so good: everyone sings with their own distinct style, and then they make it fit as a quartet.

Happiness, joy, inspiration, and good fellowship abound on this tour, and it shows throughout the show. Everyone takes a few songs at a time, rotating in a round-robin effect that allows the audience to really take in the different flavors of sound. There are great vocals and eye-and-ear popping instrumentals— Janis Ian still has that wafer-thin vocal style ("Jesse" starts off, which is my favorite, but she also sings with a punch when needed).

Additionally, she can play stinging jazz-like phrases within a pop motif off the bass strings that absolutely rivet attention to the stage, and if you can imagine it, she has a display of pedals that let her voice use echo effects that come from beyond this world. For any picker's amusement, Roger's 12-string captures the energy of a huge beehive. If you need a studio guitarist, let me assure you that either of these two can send your sidemen reaching for their stuff—let me assure you that Janis Ian kicks on guitar. Who would think it?—the little waif from the '60s is a brass-knuckle picker with a heavyweight punch.

Their singing can capture a sea of laughs and smiles, with personalities are as much of the show as the music--Richie has a stage presence that radiates like a Merlin, and he's the Master Storyteller— wise beyond years, charmingly witty, and just a treat to speak with backstage with a philosophy that brings facets of Taoism into the 21st century (we met him at a local college last December.) Judy's melodic 12-string and piano were delicate and beautiful, which describes how she appears on stage with her flowing blonde-white long hair. Try matching that thought against Richie Havens' purple robe and ringed fingers, and the place loved it.

Musically, each stepped out with his or her own statement— happiness, sadness, mirth, and innocence, and they truly took all four together and separately. With Judy starting off, the mood was delicacy and fragility, and she honored the memory of fellow balladeer John Denver as "Rocky Mountain High" and "Country Roads" were spliced together in various choruses and testimonies. Roger McGuinn came next, with the chance to show his Dylan influences and J.S. Bach inspiration with "Mr. Tambourine Man" on that marvelous 12-string Rickenbacker. The old favorite Byrd songs were there, including my favorite: "Chestnut Mare," and his humbleness disproves any of the aloofness he had in earlier years with that group.

As a stand-alone, Janis's statement that "I'm here to provide the depressing side of the show" really brings out the tremendous pathos and overwhelming disappointments of her story-songs—as a social commentator, she has her finger on the pulse of broken hearts, wounded spirits, and introversion. She wraps up her set with an assertive swagger on Nancy Sinatra's "These Boots are Made for Walking."

Perhaps the message of this gathering is spiritual: Judy absolutely brought tears to our eyes with a saintly rendition of "Amazing Grace." Considering the grief and suffering that we have felt as a nation and individually since September 11th, the timeliness and poetry of the hymn has new meaning to offer us. In the closing songs, all four members came onstage, inspiring each other and encouraging the energy of the team as a unified entity.

When the final encore ended, we left with a sense of heaven-on-Earth—and perhaps that is a message that is as vital as the music itself. It is wonderful to think that camaraderie can find new levels with friends like these—both for us as an audience and for the players.

Rory Block (special guest: The Luck Brothers)

THE TIN ANGEL, PHILADELPHIA, PA
MARCH 7, 2004

(Such a fragile, gentle lady—and such a voice and technique! Her portfolio of music is worth collecting to hear her playing and singing. I especially enjoyed her story of rescuing a lost stray dog in minus-20 degree weather one winter in upstate NY; the song "Mama's Stray Baby" from her <u>Last Fair Deal</u> CD is that testimony.)

I've been to shows that made me laugh; some that made me annoyed; others that gave me a modest amount of satisfaction. Call it the routine fan admiration. I was mighty impressed in Chattanooga when I first saw E.G. Kight—now there was a show to remember! But I'm here to say I never ever saw a performer who so scared and overwhelmed me to nearly break down until I saw the woman with the voice and name of Rory Block. Some performers play guitar onstage; in the words of a friend, "Rory *is* the guitar!" And that statement is only a fraction of her electrifying capacity as a singer and performer.

Rory's one of the—if not *the* most dedicated and honest musicians, man or woman—to pay tribute to the old blues masters in a traditional style that can't be forgotten. Hey, Martin Scorsese, go back and check your research! Eric Clapton said that he was frightened by Robert Johnson's recordings, eh? Well, I'll counter-confess the same thing—Robert's falsetto didn't make me shake either—but Rory? A walking library of Johnson, Son House, Willie Brown,

Charlie Patton, Tommy Johnson, and all the others who stood by while Mick, Keith, Brian Jones, Peter Green, John Mayall—and Eric—took the honors.

It's also the power she exudes onstage: a guitar is a percussive instrument, and you'll not see anyone—especially a woman!—kick the ever-loving hell out of the stage floorboards with a sledgehammer beat as Rory. And the *whack! pow! pop!* of her socket wrench slide against the fret board too…keeping time while her fingers claw and snap the bronze strings on her acoustic. *That's* enough body English alone to make you hold onto your chair for self-defense.

But she's a Storyteller…and each song is honored and revered for the friend, colleague, or mentor who guided her with it—even her beloved dogs get their moment. Dedicated she is to Robert Johnson, and from her new CD (*Last Fair Deal*) she respectfully resurrected "Terraplane Blues"; "Traveling Riverside Blues," and the title song. In fact, she's a walking encyclopedia of Johnson's licks: "Hellhound on my Trail"; "Come On In My Kitchen"; "Walkin' Blues" and "If I had Possession over Judgment Day" are in the set. She starts off with "Preachin' Blues," as good a job as I've ever heard Peter Green do—or maybe Peter did it as good as Rory.

From her past and present comes the names and faces…each one gently framed in her hands with memories of the gifts they have brought: Stefan Grossman's travels with her in their teen years as they traveled the South in search of venues and dusty rare forgotten Martin guitars in pawn shops; the minister and choir leader at the AME church where she sings in upstate New York (now *there's* a place for some potentially fantastic recordings if Rory's one of them!) who insists that his troops be cued and ready on their own intuition; the engineering friend and companion she lost to cancer ("Like a Shotgun" from the *Tornado* CD); an old man who regained his value for living after losing his beloved wife ("Two Places at a Table" from her new CD); and the merry chase with publishers to get song titles correct: describing how "County Fair Blues" (also from the new CD) was erroneously converted from the prison known as 'County *Farm*,' as well as the hidden meaning of "SookieSookie." (That comes out as a real good way of saying 'it's just fine as it is.')

But Rory's also a spokesperson for all those other emotions we keep inside: hear her tell how blue a woman can feel when it seems the world has failed her, even in the glory of motherhood of "Mama's Blues" (off the title CD). And if there's any doubt left—and if you possess it, "Ain't No Grave Can Hold My Body Down" (from *I'm Every Woman*) will pummel you with martial-arts *Chi* punches from the most powerful natural musical instrument known: the human voice. Bet you didn't know they moved the huge works at Stonehenge and the Pyramids by sound, did you? That's a little secret from me to you.

I need mention here that Rory's opening act, The Luck Brothers, are as funny and talented a duo as can be heard on the circuit for up-close and intimate "Philly Style" R&B. Arthur "Art" Austin (congas), looking like a smaller, more solid version of George Foreman, happily scooped up chunky chords and subtle wah-wah riffs from tall-and-lean Tim Gleeson, and seasoned them with a gruff, salty voice that reminds me of a mix of Taj Mahal and Ray Charles. From the giggles and chuckles, the women especially were especially delighted with the directness and shrug-it-off attitude of the title song "Pain (in the ass)" from their new CD.

Rory's more than happy to sign copies of CDs after the show. And if you're near Memphis or have the opportunity, she's performing again at the Handy Awards, as well as holding down several nominations. It's gonna be a terrific show—and I hope the stage doesn't collapse under the next person to take it after she's done kicking it. I'm sure, though, it'll be supported by the virtual strength of her act.

E.G. Kight

The Tropicana Billiards Ballroom
Chattanooga, TN, January 2000

(Ever go on a vacation to relax? That's almost what I had in mind—until I heard and saw E.G. Kight play. I ended up dating one of her friends, Ms Sunny Stephens. I was warned and it's true: Gotta watch them Southern women...)

I came to the South...I saw a show...and I was conquered—thanks to the power and persona of The Georgia Songbird, Ms. E.G. Kight, and her band. Hear now, my tale.

With a voice that has the power of a brass horn in the hands of a virtuoso (my guess is the Archangel Gabriel!!), E.G. knocks the daylights out of a range of songs that cross back and forth from tearful blues to steamy sensuality. Do you remember how Dizzy Gillespie looked when he was letting loose those gale force winds through his trumpet's mouthpiece? Well, that sound has taken human form.

It's no secret where she gets her influence: a good friend like Koko Taylor is worth every second of E.G.'s on-stage persona, and this talent is too bright to hide. Her sound is a cross between Phoebe Snow's fragility and Janis Joplin's anguish, but E.G. is really carrying on the work of the blues as her voice shimmers and radiates. If Janis's sound was 'Southern Comfort,' then E.G. is cognac—and her voice is not alcohol-influenced. As I write, "Crossroads" is scorching our ears, and Eric Clapton's vocals could not match this on the Fahrenheit scale.

Onstage, she's absolutely in her element: the quiet, modest country girl is now shaking her hips and singing ala Elvis, and picking away with absolute conviction on a blue-and-mother-of-pearl Fender Stratocaster. This is why she's the consummate musical field general: there's no choice but to follow the burning intensity of the music. Her supporting band is a variation of veteran warhorses and young rising stars (just wait till you see her lead guitar players). Even the audience gets involved: friend and fellow singer/songwriter/guitarist Tom Horner helped out with two ferocious, shaking versions of "Stagger Lee" and "I've Got News For You."

The obvious question is this: how on earth can someone so volcanic be kept in the dark? Yes, E.G. is as sweet off-stage as spun cotton candy, and as refined and respectful as any gentle Southern belle. That brings me back to the first paragraph: if there was ever a reason for a seismographic warning about a pending earthquake, the music world-at-large in this country needs to tie down and brace up for one helluva show when E.G. fires up.

The Richter scale also recognizes little tremblers, and when she's in the mood ("Blue Dawn," co-written with Horner), the only thing that's quivering are the tears in your eyes. She's also a knockout composer in her own right, as testimony will endorse in full measure on her latest release, the incendiary _Trouble_ CD (that carried me away with the first bars of the title song).

E.G.'s country roots are neatly mixed into her set, too—"Angel from Montgomery" is rocked slowly in its cradle, darling, with wavering bottleneck, and Dusty Springfield's hit, "Son of a Preacher Man," leaves you gasping for breath. But it's "Somewhere in Atlanta" that E.G. stakes out as her fortress (co-written with friend/co-manager Sunny Stephens), and there's no doubting why so many bands have honored this wonderful city.

Speaking of places, her encore could level the walls of Jericho: she steals a heart-melting version of "I've Been Loving You Too Long (To Stop Now)" from the immortal Otis Redding. As I recall, the only other woman to righteously take a song from Otis and claim it for her own signature is Aretha Franklin—so I'm sure that E.G. is the one to wave this banner. On her second CD, _Welcome to the_

Blues, she closed with this one, and it demands replay after replay (a half-hour would be a suitable beginning; this one song was worth my trip south on I-75).

That isn't enough: she and her band mates one-upped the Killer, Jerry Lee, with an explosive rendition of "Great Balls of Fire," and the chicken in the fryer never crackled so much as the boogie-jazz of "First in Line." (That's where I am for the next show, and E.G. plays a 3-part, five-hour set! How lucky can I be?)

So this review is really a message in a bottle, but it's okay, I'm not asking to be rescued. It's a lot easier for me this way to see E.G. perform, and if that means that I break the lease and let the landlord chase me, it's okay. Maybe I'll buy him a ticket, and get a full refund for the rent—because I'm staying if E.G.'s playing. Forward my mail!!

(I did forward my mail—as a result of this show, I made more trips to the South to hear and meet bands and musicians...which sparked my eventual relocation to Boaz, Alabama.)

Mike Nesmith

From the Monkees to a millionaire, you can't argue with a man in a wool hat

A music journalist has to be careful when accepting an offer to write an essay about his or her favored musician of choice. In my case, I was caught by my own trap (the term is "hoisted by one's own *petard*"), and I think it was used on an early *Star Trek* episode with Captain Kirk. What simply happened to me is that a blogger buddy from Minnesota named WhiteRay threw the idea back in my lap and asked, "What makes Michael Nesmith more interesting than any of the other country-folk-rock musicians from the same time period in his genre?" It took a few days to let it simmer until I found an answer—or several.

For one, he yodels.

No, not the rolled pastry; the way he sings, of course. He yodels—and that clued me in to some of the Nez magic. It's his way of carrying along the legacy and tradition of those singers who incorporated that method into their work in the country vein of musical bloodlines. Jimmy "the Singing Brakeman" Rodgers, for one—and absolutely, there's a big hunk of Hank Williams, too. They would surely be included—it's part of Nesmith's heritage as a native son of the Republic of Texas; it's that mix of refined/respectable gentleman and hell-raisin' rascal.

But it's also a mix and blend of Nashville, but it comes through other locations and fellow musicians. It goes as far as the Pacific Northwest region where Danny O'Keefe comes from (listen to "I'm Sober Now")—and then you can count in Boz Scaggs down at the

Muscle Shoals studio in 1969, working on "Waiting for a Train." Nez, however, makes it a staple part of his production—and it just fits naturally, as though he knew he was born to yippee and whoop. And no, I already know how much influence folks like Gram Parsons, the Flying Burrito Brothers, and Pure Prairie League had—I mean it's different when Nesmith plays because it's like he was singing about himself and not some distant ideal or goal like a busted romance and how to fix it.

If you really want to hear how far back he made it clear, turn it back to the Monkees's first album and slip on "Papa Gene's Blues." That James Burton-like Nashville lead guitar is, I think, where Mike's heart has been right from the start. Follow that with "Sunny Girlfriend" from the *Headquarters* release, and you've got the next clue. Forget all that foolishness that was part of the group's act: Michael Nesmith was always a serious musician who honored his country roots. And backing that up is the whine of a pedal steel guitar—it's found on almost all his songs ("Mama Nantucket" is a great example—and not the kind of title I'd associate with the instrument).

That's another part of the man's appeal: he had a businessman's approach to writing songs and lyrics in an honest but earnest way that lacks any fancy gimmicks. It was his approach to acting as well; for what it matters, there was no other option with the clowning antics that made the other three Monkees seem so cute. Even the Beatles needed George Harrison to be considered serious at times. Nez, on his part, keeps his production basic and focused—but adds just a tad of mischief. My favorite tune is "Rio," partially because he deliberately rearranges words and images to create a fantasy of escaping to South America for the adventure of it—and the way he playson the title itself when a woman's voice proclaims, "Not *Reno*, dummy! **Rio!** Rio de JIN-ero!"

See? It's not an obvious thing; it's more simple than all the elaborate parts. He sings and plays like a musical collection of old movie stars: he's sort of a singing mix of the best characteristics of Cary Grant and Gary Cooper: polite, firm, and funny, and quiet when it counts. That is, quiet until he writes a song—and then he's out for a good laugh and a good time on the town.

Heck, maybe it's that Mike Nesmith is and always has been a man who knew what he wanted and how to do it—and he lets the music do his walking and talking. Or maybe it's just that confidence that comes from—can I say—"a home on the range"? Any way I try to pin it down, it just comes down to a man who knew what he could do and how to make it fit his needs and his music as well as his life story.

Can't argue that with a man in a wool hat and a millionaire to boot.

Interviews

Bobby Whitlock Talks About Derek & The Dominos, Duane Allman, Gram Parsons, Eric Clapton and more...

(I found Bobby Whitlock through Delaney Bramlett; it was a marathon session talking with Bobby and twice as much fun to look at the story of the man who helped craft "Layla" and many Other Songs of Love. This interview was done just after the first Gulf War campaign. His autobiography is set for release later this year.)

I see you released a new album on the Grapevine label, and it's called <u>It's about Time</u>. Tell me (about) it, Bobby.

BW: Well, it's not a double or a triple, but a quadruple entendre. It's about time I had some product out; it's a song about, it's about time that we changed things and made this world a better place to live. The song speaks for itself. That's pretty much it; you just really have to listen to the song and the lyrics to understand what it's all about, because it is all about "time," and it's gonna be recorded in one century and released in another. So it's a whole time frame - I wrote it the day before we bombed Saddam Hussein, okay?

> "and the children crying in the streets,
> Sons and daughters, dying at
> their mothers' feet,

> *it's about time*
> *to be set free,*
> *it's about time,*
> *it's our destiny.*
> *Sooner or later, we're gonna get along.*
> *Sooner or later, we're gonna sing a song*
> *of peace.*
> *Lovin' your fellow man,*
> *As far as the eye can see.*
> *Hand holding gentle hand,*
> *It's About Time.* So that's the essence of it.

Interesting, because you were talking about being aware of time, as a young man.

BW: *A friend of mine that I was talking to that's a guitar player, Peter Young, that's gonna play with me, just yesterday. I told him, "I've always known, when I was even a little child, what I was gonna do, and about incarnation and reincarnation. I've always been aware of this thing - I've discussed it with my (ex)-wife, Vivian, and everything - I've always known what I--that this was my destiny.*

I've always known this. I've never had any aspirations of being president of the United States, or senator, or anything like that, or owning a shipping company. I've always known this, and I've always known that all the changes that I'm going through and I've gone through, have led up to this point in time in my life. Peter said, "That's pretty amazing!" (laughs).

So you've always known music was your medium.

BW: *Even when I was very small, less than three feet tall. I've always known, and I've always known that I would be in this position, and I've always known this. I've never forced it--it's never been a forced issue. My uncle Troy told me--he's dead now--and he played flat-top guitar and mandolin--he said, "Do it because you want to, not because you have to, and it will make sense," and that whole thing just brought it to light to me. This was when I was real young, because you can't go out and do what I do to make money, because then you won't make money. Money is just the aftermath - it follows you. My whole thing is like I have something to say; there's so many ways to say "I love you."*

There's been--how many times has the song been written? and it's a different song every time, but the same message. But it's kinda like I'm a faucet; a spigot, rather, a water faucet that turns on, and all of these things are in the air, all of these ideas and melodies and messages are in the air. I'm one of these people that are channeled in that area that is attracted to (this).

I have this ability to just say things and sing things and play things that just strike home that are real natural. I don't mean that in any other way - there are people who are destined to be directors of companies and there are people who are destined to be great golfers; I'm destined to be projecting this message and sing the way I do.

One of the songs from the <u>Layla</u> box set that you helped co-write follows this: "Tell the Truth," which is just what you've been saying.

BW: Yeah, that came to me one night. I was at Eric's house; (I) stayed at Eric's for six months and then we got a place in town - we called it "the Domino flat." It was 'hell on wheels,' I'm telling you, we were a terror.

But we were young and out of control. It came to me: the whole world was shaking, and it felt like it. The whole thing came to me, and I made up chords. It was an open 'E' but everything was backwards. Eric helped me on the very last verse, and I just wrote the whole thing that night - it just came to me - "the whole world's shaking, can't you feel it? A new dawn's breaking, I can see it." And there was a new dawn, and it was a new dawn in my life, and there was a new dawn in that it was a new day.

That's great. So you've been very much aware of what's going on in the world and changes we've been coming through--to the millennium.

BW: I think more people are becoming more aware than people are becoming afraid and leery. They understand that there's a humanity that needs to be involved in this whole life process and concept. I believe that more people are becoming more centered, spiritually and moralistically. I believe things are turning around - I know I am. I know that I'm changing, that I'm growing, and that I have grown. I would hate to turn around and suddenly, I'm 92 and never experienced this whole life process.

Back to your early years, when you were younger, and you knew you were going to become a musician: was part of that because you were born in Memphis and you were so much steeped in the Memphis sounds?

BW: (thoughtfully) No. Like, when I was real, real little, it was just a part of me--it was in my soul, and in my spirit. I sang all the time. I always knew it - I'm talking about real little, like a little bitty boy. Not eight (years old), but smaller. I just always knew it! I mean, I chopped cotton and picked cotton, rode the back of bean planters and stuff as I was growin' up out in the country, in Arkansas.

But I always knew that I was goin' to do - it was in my spirit. It was the heart of me. I always knew this. It's nothing I set out to do--like I just didn't suddenly turn 15 years old and decide to play. It's something I've always done: sing and sittin' down and playin', it came as a natural thing to me.

What did you start out (playing) first? Was it guitar or was it keyboards?

BW: It was guitar! My grandmother, "Big Momma" King, used to sit me down on her lap when I was about three or four years old, and had this old National dobro. It had hula dancers on the front and on the back, and she'd sit down and play me (*softly sings gospel-style*) "turn your radio on, get in touch with Jesus." She had long hair down to the ground, and she gave that guitar to me when I was about 14, and I immediately sprayed it black. Then it got lost, over the years.

Then someone, a girl named Genya Revan, who was with 10-Wheel Drive, called me one time, out of the blue, and said, "I have something that belongs to you." I left it with her in New York, because I knew it was going to get lost in the shuffle. As it turns out, I got the guitar back and I restored it. I put her name on top of it, inlaid it--after all those years!-- and I played it on the record (the new release).

Speaking of guitars, I want to skip to a song that you're known for, off the Layla album - it's the last one, "Thorn Tree in the Garden." Who is that about?

BW: No, there's not very many people--I've only told this story--one time. I don't think that anyone would believe me, but I'll tell you: it was about a dog - a little dog that I had. I used to live at the Plantation - remember the song, "Shoot-out at the Plantation" that Leon Russell wrote? There was thirteen of us: Jesse "Indian Head" Davis, Jimmy Karstein; there was a bunch of us living in this house in California. And I had a little puppy that I named after Delaney's daughter, Bekka Bramlett.

So I had a little puppy and a cat, and I was one of thirteen people that was living in this house in the Valley. This guy - I'm not going to give his name because I think that would be inappropriate--said, "You need to get rid of these animals, we can't have--there's too many people in this house at the same time, anyway. There was Chuck Blackwell, who played drums with Taj Mahal; I mean, there was thirteen of us living in this house!

And so I got rid of the cat; I took it out to Delaney's house in Hawthorne, CA, and left that with Delaney and his mom out there. When I got back, I wasn't going to get rid of my dog, Bekka, but I got back and this guy had taken my dog away, and it really upset me. Rather than doing anything physical or anything like that because it really hurt me emotionally, I was thinking, well, 'a snake in the woodpile,' this and that; then I went, no: 'thorn tree in my garden.'

And so I wrote the song, sittin' in my bedroom and the "thorn tree in my garden" was this guy who had disposed of my dog. And the song is about my little dog, and he was the thorn tree in my garden. It's not about a woman or anything; it's about love.

For a favorite pet: that's really nice. Speaking of Delaney Bramlett, how did you two guys meet?

BW: I played all the clubs in Memphis and in the South during the mid-'60s, and everybody came - I was the first white artist signed to Stax records, on their "Hip" label - their so-called "pop" label at that time. I hung out with Steve Cropper, my mentor and a friend to this day; "Duck" Dunn was my first producer. I was there when the StaplesSingers did "Long Walk to D.C." and Albert King did "Crosscut Saw" - I was in the studio.

Every time that Stax was open, you used to go down on McLemore (street) and not worry about being killed - I was there! Every time the doors opened, I was there - it opened at 9:00 a.m.; I was there at 8:30 a.m., and I stayed all day and night.

I watched them do "Hip Hugger" and "Slim Jenkin's Joint" and everything like that. And then I used to go out on the road with Booker T. and the MG's. I went to Lanskey Brothers and got a lime-green suit - the collar went out to my shoulders - and I sang when Isaac Hayes and David Porter quit goin' out on the road with the MG's, I would go out and sing out in front and do all the Otis (Redding) songs and stuff. So, I was hooked up like that. Well, "Duck" Dunn discovered Delaney and Bonnie in a bowling alley in Hawthorne, CA., and he brought them to Memphis.

ROCK 'N' BLUES STEW II

It was the second album--it was the first record--but it turned out to be the second album, done in Memphis. He brought them to one of these clubs I was playin' called the Cabaret Club - now it's a tuxedo shop - but I played all the clubs: The Louisian' Club, Paris Theatre - everything! At the Paradise - I'd go down to the Paradise and I'd be the only white person there. In a sea of black folks, I'd be the only white person at the Paradise, and not afraid or threatened oranything. Everything was copacetic then. It all changed when Martin Luther King, Jr. got killed.

But "Duck" discovered Delaney and Bonnie in this bowling alley and brought 'em to Memphis. They came down-- everybody would come, like Eddie Floyd, and Cropper, and "Duck," and they would all come and sit in with my band. All I did was soul music, and Booker T and the MG's stuff, and I did "Expressway to your Heart," remember? and Young Rascals stuff - that's all I did. If you didn't know how to play "Midnight Hour," I wasn't gonna be bothered with you.

I never had heard Eric Clapton or nothing; I didn't know nothing about no Cream or anything like that. I wasn't interested in all that diddley-diddley stuff, and pink hair and everything; I was like strictly into rhythm and blues. He ("Duck") brought Delaney and Bonnie to hear me one night--it was a Thursday - and they heard me and said,"We're gonna put a band together. Would you like to come to California?" I said, "Yeah!" and I was gone on Saturday. I just packed my doo-wah diddy bag, and I had my Nehru jacket on, and got off the plane in California, and I ain't never been nowhere, except to Macon, GA., with the MG's, flying - that's the first time I ever flew. I wentto California and you know, things changed (chuckles) big time (laughs).

I'll say. I know the album you're talking about; that's the one they called <u>Home</u>.

BW: Yeah, well, it's the second album, but it was really the first one that we recorded. The first album released was <u>Accept No Substitute</u>, and that was on Clive Davis's label, Electra.

You're right, that's full of rhythm and blues and soul.

BW: Yep, that's who was playin' on it - it was the Stax guys. We did it all down at Stax. As a matter of fact, I still got my jacket off that Electra album, I still got that coat. That's the only piece of memorabilia I have, really. It's got Leon Russell--we did "Ghetto"--boy, it's a real, real good record.

It's definitely one of the nicest things I've heard. Jumping ahead: now you're in England with Delaney and Bonnie as part of their Friends, and you're on tour with Eric Clapton. Whose idea was it, on the inside jacket picture, to have you guys walk through the desert carrying all your gear?

BW: Barry Feinstein - the guy who did all the photography. We went out in the desert--you remember a guy--I can't believe I remember--Albert Grossman--he managed The Band--that was his Rolls Royce. And Barry's feet (hanging out the window). We went out to the Joshua Tree. Gram Parsons! He discovered Delaney and Bonnie--we were playing in Snoopy's Opera House; five dollars a night, five nights a week. He's the one who connected us with everybody - really, Gram did.

But that's Barry's feet hangin' out, and Albert Grossman's Rolls Royce. We just went out there and was walkin', and it just happened, it was one of those things - we went out to the Joshua Tree, where that boy--his road guy took him out to the Joshua Tree after he died.

I was wondering, because I noticed everyone's carrying gear but Delaney!

BW: (laughing) Is there a common denominator there or what?

I see Eric's carrying an electric guitar case.

BW: And I'm carrying a guitar--he's got mine, and that one was his.

ROCK 'N' BLUES STEW II

That album is one of the most exciting live albums I ever heard.

BW: (matter-of-factly) We moved fixed stages. You gotta figure we had Jim Gordon, Jim Keltner; both of 'em on drums, we had a guy named Tex (Johnson) on congas, Bobby Keys, Jim Price, Leon Russell, Rita Coolidge, Delaney and Bonnie, myself! Dave Mason!! Eric Clapton, Dave Mason, and George Harrison--I mean, that was one serious, serious band!

We were a tough act to follow--we opened up for Blind Faith in America, and we were shuttin' 'em down. We were getting front-page reviews, and that's where we met Eric. I mean, we were blowin' them away. They were doin' "Can't Find My Way Home"; they had Stevie Winwood in the band, and Ginger (Baker) and Rick Grech.

See, we befriended Eric--he couldn't believe our camaraderie--we always hung out in hotel rooms and stayed up all night, playin' guitars and singin' and raising hell, telling people to go to sleep and quit bangin' on the walls (laughs). But that was our nature--we'd do it on the airplanes, we'd sing on the airplanes and stuff, that was our nature.

Eric really loved that camaraderie, and he wanted to work with us. Delaney--I remember standing outside--we were in MapleLeafGardens, in Toronto, and we played there, and we were lookin' at Blind Faith, because we opened up for them. He said--he was lookin' at Eric--"What do you think about him playin' with us?" I said, "I think it would be great--he's a great guitar player, but he's gonna have to do somethin' about them pink pants!" (laughter). That's kinda how it went.

(laughing)

BW: This is true. And then I went through my tenure with the whole Delaney and Bonnie thing, and we went all over the world - I mean, it was a great band, a great thing that happened, and I learned a lot. I kept my mouth shut, except when I was singin', and my ears and eyes wide open. When it came down to doin' it, I couldn't be with Delaney and Bonnie any more 'cause they were fussin' and fightin' all the time.

Everybody had been goin' through drugs and doing all that shit. I called Steve Cropper - I had married an old girlfriend and we were living across the street from Delaney and Bonnie, and they were fightin' with each other - it was just awful.

I called Steve Cropper and said, "I gotta get out of here; I'm hooked up with a woman who wants me to go back and chop cotton and drive tractors, and I can't do that!" And he said, "Why don't you go over and see Eric?" I said, "I don't have any money!" and so Steve Cropper bought my airplane ticket, and I had $120 in my pocket. I called Eric and I said, "Hey, man, do you mind if I come over and visit for a minute?" He said, "No, come on over, I'm just getting my hair cut."

Little did he know, I showed up the next day, and that's really how it happened. So, (Steve) Cropper gave me the advice to call Eric, and also bought my airplane ticket, and my first wife's ticket back home. I gave him credit on my album (laughs): thanks for the advice. Thanks for the advice and the ticket, Steve! (laughter.)

That's really kind of you. I see by the liner notes off the <u>Laylabox</u> set, that you, with Dave Mason, who was an original member of the early Dominos; you were looking to have a Sam and Dave type of approach to the band.

BW: That was my idea - that's what I figured out how to - I was kind of a fire under Eric's ass as far as it was, vocally, 'cause he wasn't real secure with his vocals. His first album, as a matter of fact - we did the "Eric Clapton" album, with Delaney and Bonnie and Friends - but Delaney sang all the songs and Eric just came up back behind him and sang exactly what Delaney had sang. Delaney put everything, all the vocals down and Eric came back behind and just put 'em down, exactly like (sings softly): "I'm lovin' you, lovin' me, it's all the same!"

Eric was real insecure vocally. He's more secure now, but he ain't Otis Redding, but I mean, he's a good singer. But I put a fire under his ass, and it was an option that I took, just to - our band was open - we didn't want no chicks, and no horn players, we wanted a four-piece rock 'n roll band, and we did it, and I chose to it like Sam and Dave. He'd (Eric) do a verse, I'd do a verse, we'd do one together, we'd do the things together, I was doing harmonies and all that, so that's how that all came to light.

For example, on "Tell the Truth"!

BW: I was doin' my 'John Lennon' low harmonies. That was my John Lennon stuff. John Lennon would do a lower harmony under Paul (McCartney), and I would do that kind of a thing. It was whatever the song called for and dictated, is what went down. Sometimes, the best part is no part at all.

You did it also on that Chuck Willis song,

"It's Too Late"--you came in right behind Eric, also.

BW: That's right. It's just whatever it felt like, whatever it felt was right. That's what went down. We all trusted each other enough - we were professional enough to let each other have room, and space, and I believe that's true, at this point in time in my life: Hey, am I gonna tell Jim Horn what to play? (laughs). Am I gonna tell Steve Cropper what to play? (laughs). No, I'm not! I'm gonnaleave it to their good judgment, 'cause they know - they hear it - they see the 'big picture.' I mean, I see the 'big picture.' If I'm doin' something with someone else, or for someone else, I know what my part is. Just like I said earlier, sometimes your part is no part at all. You can always make up something, but then that 'something' just very well may not be the one that sinks - that goes in the hole. I think, "less is more."

Now we're up to the time period when the Dominos have begun to jell, and you're in the Criteria studio in Florida. I saved the original <u>Layla</u> album jacket from 30 years ago. Inside, there's a picture of a handsome-looking guy wearing a bandana, with his arms folded, a white shirt, hair tucked back over his ears, looking confident, like he owns the world - there you are.

BW: Yeah, I was feeling real confident about everything. I mean, we were in there, doin' it. I told Tom Dowd - I got the idea from him when we did George Harrison's *All Things Must Pass* album - that album is just Derek and the Dominos with George Harrison and sundry guests. We were a constant - we were a mainstay of that whole album. Phil Spector was so funny in the control room; man, they really needed to have the whole thing running in the control room. And, plus, we did the "Apple Jams."

When we got to Miami, I told Ronnie and Howie Albert, and Tom Dowd, "If anybody walks in, it's just tape; just turn it on!" - whether it's Eric by himself, or me and Carl (Radle), or whomever it may be, just turn the tape on. So that's how we wound up with all those jams and everything.

You have four or five long jams on that box set.

BW: (enthusiastically) Oh, big time! When we were doing the band, we would play in 'E,' - just 'E' - (laughing) for hours and hours and hours down at Eric's house, and we had a complaint from a neighbor: Can you guys change the chord? (more laughter). Just change keys, please! (laughter).

That's great! I'm thankful the LP photos are in color, because there's a great color shot of you with your arms around a very special guy: Duane Allman.

BW: Yeah! He was my bro'. His brother (Gregg) had gone to California, and was doing that Hollywood thing. Duane and I, we were close; see, I knew Duane before I knew Eric or anything. Duane and I had been mates for years - we were friends for years.

He also played on *Motel Shot* and *To Bonnie from Delaney* with you, with Delaney!

BW: That's right - so he went back a long ways with us, you see. It was just one of those coincidental things - they (the Allman Brothers

Band) happened to be playing down in Florida. It all evolved - Tom (Dowd) wanted him there, and I wanted him there, and he was excited about this Eric Clapton-thing. Eric had never really heard about the AllmanBrothers, or Duane, or anything, but when he walked in, boy, it just really completed the picture.

We were in the middle of recording at that point in time, and then Duane came in and it was just like - brilliant. He was my - I was his 'little brother,' he'd say, 'cause Gregg was off in Hollywood. But Duane and I, we were - we were <u>womanizers</u>!

(laughter)

BW: I'll put it to you like that (mischievous laughter). I think that's as gentle as I can be with that! (more laughter). We were on the phone, and Macon, Georgia was busy in Miami! (laughs).

You told me that Gregg is godfather to your daughter.

BW: That's a fact! He was there at the hospital.

Tell me about the story.

BW: I had moved to Macon, after the Dominos and all that. I went down and talked to Phil Walden; that's when I started my Capricorn (label) tenure, and I moved down to Macon. When my first child was born - my daughter, Ashley -she has writer's credits on one of the songs, "Born to Play the Blues" - that's another story - and also is singing on the album that's coming out here in the new year - when she was born, my first album with Capricorn came out the day my daughter came out. (laughs) I was in the waiting room and Gregg came walkin' in with a six-pack of Heineken, sits down and says, "I knew you was by yourself," and he sat with me. We heard when my baby was born, and he's my daughter's godfather.

That was <u>One of a Kind</u> (1975); is that correct?

BW: *That would be it. It's one of a kind. She's my only daughter, and she's gorgeous, and sings, and is so talented, and so is my son, Beau, as well as my son, Chris, and my other son, C.J.*

That's wonderful. Thinking back to Duane for a second, there's one of those jams, the last one, #5 - you guys go on for 18 minutes, and Duane does some marvelous sawing away with that bottleneck - I swear he's sawing away at the strings!you guys had a wonderful time on those long ones, those long jams.

BW: *That's what we did. If you listen to that album from front; from the start to the end, everything is exactly where it was and how it came about. There wasn't a positioning of 'this song comes here, and this song is gonna be placed in number five (slot)' - it was exactly how it went down.*

Everything is exactly how it went down. When we went backand we had room for another song, Eric said, "We got room for one more song." I mean, we didn't have enough songs for--we didn't have enough material for one album, much less a double album. I went out and wrote some lyrics in the middle of the whole thing, on "Keep on Growing."

Great song!

BW: *Yeah, we used to do that as a jam. We had another jam that we used to do called the "Airport Shuffle." But "Keep on Growing" was a jam, and we just put it down. They were gonna trash it - I said, "No, gimme a second. Gimme a pen, and 20 minutes." And I went out into the lobby of Criteria and wrote the lyrics and went back in and tried to sing it,and it wasn't for me to sing, but Eric and I could sing it together, perfect - it worked out perfectly. But I wrote all the lyrics in, like, 20 minutes. (sings in a husky voice) "I was standin'!" - you know, that whole thing, it just all came out. I said, "No, we can't trash this song!" And so a lot of that went down as we were there!*

Next thing you know, we were going in and Eric and Tom Dowd said, "We've got room for one more song," and they said, "Bobby, would you like to put something on here?" I said, "Well, this is kind of a 'love' album', and so that's when I said, "How about 'Thorn Tree in the Garden'? Tom Dowd, in Producer magazine--one time, I read an interview, he said that (song) is perfect stereo recording: with the voice, and the bass, and Jim Gordon with the little bell, and the guitars: Duane and Eric, and myself - he said that is the epitome of a perfect stereo recording.

And that comes from the man! - Mr. Dowd - and I felt real proud about that. So, they closed the album with it, 'cause it was the last thing that we did. I'm real proud about all of that; I feel real good about all that I've done, what I've accomplished, maybe the lives that I've touched, and the changes, and maybe a difference, in a little ways, somewhere or another, you know? As a matter of fact, there was a party that was goin' on, and this was in Columbus, OH; it's got that university there.

These people had a party for me after one of my shows. And so I went to the party, and I had to catch a plane, and I said, "I've got to go," and they said, "No, you've got to wait - you need to wait, there's somebody coming to see you." I was getting ready to walk out the door when this man and woman walked up. They said, "We've just got to say 'thank you.'" And I said, "Why is that?" See, I never really knew about what kind of impact that we, as writers and artists and singers and players have on the world. They said, "We've just got to say, thank you." I said, "For what?" They said, "Thorn Tree in the Garden." He said, "I was just getting ready to leave my wife - I walked out the door - I was walking out the door and the song came on the radio. I turned around, and we were arm-in-arm."

I said, "Thank you very much, I'm flattered," and he said, "You don't get it," and he went, "come here, boys!" And there was two curly-haired, red-headed kids come walking up; two boys, they were twins. He said, "Without you writing that song, I would have never been with her and we wouldn't have these children, and we have a good life." Suddenly, I knew that I had a role in this world, and that it was an important thing that I'm doing.

I'm glad to capture that story.

BW: Isn't that a good story? That's the gospel truth. I hope these people read this article and remember it, and contact me. I wish I knew who they were, because they changed my life - they changed - those two people, and those two red-headed curly-haired boys, changed my concept of and my view of my perception of where I am in the scheme of things on this planet.

That's a great tribute, Bobby, I'm glad you got a message like that; that's wonderful. Let me ask you about two of your bandmates who can't participate for a number of reasons. I'm speaking of Jim Gordon and Carl Radle. I was very sorry to read about Jim's illness (author's note: paranoid schizophrenia - he murdered his mother during a psychotic episode and remains under heavy sedation in an institution) during the '80s - he was a marvelous, versatile musician. What's your take on Jim Gordon?

BW: He had the heart of a freight train, and there wasn't nobody at home. He could play like a locomotive, but when you looked in his eyes, there wasn't nobody home. I told him he needed to get help. A long time ago, he said that he heard voices. I told him, "No, that's like, I go to the closet; that's that 'small, still voice,' that's called a conscience.

He said, "No, I hear voices," and that was a long time ago. All the drugs and everything - maybe that part of the brain that assimilates things had gone because of all the heroin and the cocaine, and the morphine, and everything. Maybe he had done too much of it, the serotonin (level).

Maybe he had eliminated his brain of being able to put things together; I don't know, it's just my philosophical thinking. I feel for his family - my heart goes for and to his family, and it's a tragic situation that he's in, but he put himself in there, and it's a choice that he made. He could have stopped doing those drugs and sought help, but he chose not to, and it cost him his life, it cost him the lives of all of his family members, but on top of everything else, it cost his mother her life. It's real, real sad.

I heard he could play non-stop - he just wouldn't stop drumming.

BW: *That's it! Like I've told you: like a locomotive, like a freight train. He's probably one of the most talented people that's in jail for the rest of their entire life for a major atrocity.*

I was amazed that he only played keyboards on some of Delaney's albums - he never touched the drums (on some songs). Of course, he put the coda on "Layla."

BW: *That was him and me. You hear that real big-sounding thing; that was him, and you hear where it's real screwed up, that's me. So, Tom Dowd put both parts together - the piano coda. That's Jim and myself at the end of that thing. (earnestly) As a matter of fact, he did not write that - he did not write that. Jim Horn wrote that. Absolutely true, and that's a fact: I can attest to that. I'm a witness. Jim Horn showed him that - Jim Horn just did my album - and Jim said, "Lemme show you somethin', and I went, "Whoa!" - he did!*

I remember Jim Gordon and Rita Coolidge were livin' together up on some canyon, and I was stayin' in the house down below, and they were upstairs, and they were trying - Jim Gordon played me this thing, and they were trying to put it together, him and Rita. It turns out, Jim Horn actually really wrote that coda. Like I say, I'm tellin' you the truth, I'm a witness.

Another person: was Carl Radle an underrated bass player? I don't think he ever got the credit for what he could do.

BW: *No. He was a downbeat player, and I mean that in a positive way. He wasn't (sings a funky, popping bass shuffle) - he wasn't one of them upbeat, slap-em, back-em kind of a deal. He'd go over there and put his head down and stand in a corner, and just play and do the thing he was supposed to do - he was just right there on the money. I remember one time when we was playin' in Great Britain - it cost them a pound to get in - we didn't charge them anything - and we played this club that was upstairs - jam packed! I looked up at Carl and he had those round John*

Lennon glasses and they were just frosted over. It was steam from everybody that was in there (laughs).

He was wild!.was absolutely wild, but a great player. A silent raver - I never saw him with a woman, never saw him with a man, never saw him with a woman. Then, one time I walked into his hotel room and he had six women in bed with him, and I said, "Awright!" (cackles of laughter). And he's layin' up there with a big shit-eatin' grin on his face! (more wild laughing). He had three on one side and three on the other. (gleeful laughter). (proudly) He had his legs crossed; it was just totally, totally too cool! (peals of laughing) I just opened the door, looked in, smiled, shook my head and closed it, and turned around and walked away.

That's great!

BW: Lots of stuff I never told anybody; nobody knows this insight!

By the way, your songwriting, and people covering you - did you know Buckwheat Zydeco covered "Why Does Love Got to be So Sad?"

BW: Yeah, and he's too cool - that guy can really play a (Hammond) B-3. Vivian, my (ex) wife, got me a Buckwheat Zydeco thing, but it doesn't have "Why Does Love Got to be So Sad?" on it. But I've always wanted to hear that, and I haven't been able to get hold of it yet.

But that guy can really play a B-3, man! I've heard him do that; I heard it back in the late '80s, and it took me a second to realize what he was doing. I recognized the melody; of course, it didn't have the guitar wash that we recognize. He's a real player, man, he knows what to do on a B-3. Not a whole lot of people know what to do on a B-3: I can only say there are four people, like Jimmy Smith, Booker T. Jones, Buckwheat Zydeco, and me. That's the only four people I know that know how to operate a B-3, and I don't mean that egotistically, I mean that as a matter of fact.

Hmm, 'cause I was going to say, Gregg (Allman) plays a B-3.

BW: Yeah, but Gregg has one that's all - he asked me one time, he said, "You get more sound out of one Leslie than I ever heard. Can you fix my organ?" I went in back of his organ and it's all the electric stuff - I mean, he had taken the guts out. I do it real natural. I can tweak it up and everything. Yeah, Gregg's a great B-3 player, don't get me wrong. He's one of my favorite - he's one of the most soulful white guys I know.

That's an interesting point you made about the sound of your organ - listening to the Dominos live CDs that I've got, as well as the studio material - you used to put out a tornado of sound; it literally swirled - it moved, and you could see it moving around - I could, at least.

BW: Yeah, in your mind. On this album I've got coming out, I've got a 1959 Hammond B-3 that's never been played by anyone but myself, with two Leslies. I set one Leslie on one speed and one on the other. And on some songs, I put three organs on, which means there's six Leslies goin', and they're spread out, and you would never know it, unless I told you. It's the most awesome instrument - it's a powerful, powerful instrument. Not loud-like, but it's powerful: it's got a lot of dimension and depth about it. If you'll be gentle with it, it can be huge.

That's what you did. It's kind of like watching a genie pop out of a bottle in slow motion - how the cloud filters up out of the bottle!

BW: Yeah, that's a good synopsis of it. What I do, I go in the back of the organ and work in the back side of it, go into it, and I get the most output out of the power amp, to where you don't overdraw out of the Leslies, and I change the vibrato and the tone sounds, but it's things that are like, personal things. I couldn't tell someone how to do it and they go do it and do it the same way - it would be like someone telling me how to tune a guitar. I wouldn't be able to do it like them. Except, Duane told me, "Just tune it like you play it. If you want an open 'E,' make an 'E' and tune it." (chuckles).

That's how I learned to play slide, from Duane, and his technique. It's a personal thing: no one can get an Eric Clapton sound except Eric Clapton. I can go and get Steve Cropper's guitar and let him turn it on, tune it up, and put it the way he plays it, and I could put it on, and I would not sound like Steve Cropper. There's a touch! it's something that's real elementary! but ever so huge.

Let me ask you about some people who have had the pleasure of working with you - a little name-dropping here: John Prine.

BW: My buddy. "Slow Boat to China," and "Silent Night"; "All Day Long"--I did a bunch of stuff for him.

Yeah, the <u>Great Days: The John Prine Anthology</u>. You also worked with Steven Stills!

BW: Yeah, <u>Down the Road</u>. Yeah, as a matter of fact, he left me that thing - we were at Criteria again, and he left me that to mix - Ronnie and Howie Albert and myself were down there. There was one song, "City Junkies," that was a song that I have, that we were doing, and it wasn't called "City Junkies," it was called something else, and he tookeverything off and rewrote everything.

Ronnie and Howie Albert looked at me and said, "He just ripped the song off, right in your face!" I said, "Yeah, that's okay, I don't mind" (laughs). He wound up leavin' me and those guys to finish all the vocals and mix the whole thing! Then I took it back to Colorado. So I was actually a producer on it, not just a player. Then he went up there, to Colorado, and did the number - changed everything around.

You also worked with Dr. John: <u>Sun, Moon and Herbs</u>; you did the vocals in 1971.

BW: Sure did! Aren't you good! Yeah, it was Eric Clapton, Mick Jagger and myself. I could tell you something else that you don't know: I worked on <u>Exile on Main Street</u>. (sings) "I don't want to talk about Jesus, I just *want to see His face!" Yeah, I did that, but it took them so long in those days - everybody was doin' dope; Keith would come in at 4 o'clock in the morning, and nod out in the middle of a solo - I'm not talking bad about him or anything like that, but I mean, you do things around everyone else's schedule, and Mick and I were sittin' out there, but they neglected to put me down as a credit on the album.*

Jimmy Miller was producin', Andy Johns was the engineer, and when I told Jimmy about it, he went, "Oh, no; man, I forgot!!" I went, "Hey, that's all right, 'cause I know." Bill (Wyman) knows; Charlie (Watts) knows.

You were also on Bonnie Bramlett's <u>Lady's Choice</u>(1976).

Yeah, that was a Capricorn thing - we sang a duet. You done your homework, haven't you?!

Mike Nesmith covered you—and George Jones!

BW: He did "Bell Bottom Blues," didn't he? Cher did "Bell Bottom Blues." George Jones, Tom Jones, Glen Frey! Sheryl Crow! Johnny Rodriguez!

Did you work with Jeff Healy? A very interesting guitar player, a heckuva guy!

BW: Yeah, I did the "Hell to Pay" album with him. He explained his guitar playing to me: it's all a mathematical type of a deal for him. He can play straight-up; he can play with it hangin' on his shoulder, but he said, mathematically, it worked better for him with it on his lap. He's an incredible player. I took him around - I picked him up at his hotel room, in Memphis, and got up on the elevator, and he was comin' out his door, and I said, "You don't have a mind (someone to help him around) or you don't have someone! He said, "Nah, they just put me in here, and I found my way."

He got in my car and he said, "This is a '73 Mercedes." I said, "What? How do you know that?!" (laughing). He said, "I can tell by the smell. This is an old 72-73 Mercedes." I said, "You're absolutely correct!" (chuckles happily).

I took him to a record store - I called in advance and told them I was bringing Jeff Healy - he was opening up for B.B. King, down on the river. Jeff is the sweetest guy in the world. I called this record store down in Memphis and told them he's a 78 (record) buff - he's big on the old 78's. We went in - he could take a record - they had all of 'em down for him, so he could get to ('em) - pull it out, run his hand around the outside, his thumb across it, and touch the center of it, and tell you how many times it's been played, who it is, and what record company it is.

This is true! I've seen it. When it came time to pay for the records that he got, he took it out, took his money out of his pocket - say it was $25-26 - he felt the $10, put that down, felt another $5, and a $5, and a $1 - I mean, he could feel it! And he was exactly right. When I walked him out on stage - B.B. King was down on MudIsland - he said, "What are we looking at?" and I said, "You got the Mississippi River on your back, and you got a sea of Afro's in front of you. Sixty thousand Afros, and you could walk across, and you'd be right straight in downtown Memphis with a beautiful skyline." He said, "Thank you. Nobody ever tells me anything!" I took him out to eat - no one ever tells him anything or what it looks like - I find that amazing.

Me, too. Speaking of 'Kings,' I understand you played with Albert King.

BW: Albert--two weeks before he died--I was all bent out of shape about them rerouting my flight from New York down to Atlanta and back to Memphis, and I flew over, and I could see my house. I had to go to Atlanta, then come back to Memphis, and I was all bent out of shape--I told (ex-wife) Vivian, "I can't stand this, why did Delta change (my flight)?" Nonetheless, I got on the plane, and there was Albert! I walked in, and he was right there. I sat down and we talked the whole way.

He was goin' on, this was his last record that he'd done, at Gary Bell's place - it's now called "The House of Blues" - but it was the last record that he had done, and I always told Vivian, "You gotta meet Albert King one of these days!" and I said, "I guarantee you, the first thing he's gonna say, (drawls in a deep voice) "Ah known little Bobby since he coulda barely looked over the console!" (laughs with glee). And sure enough, I got on the airplane, and there was Albert, sittin' there in his bowler hat and everything, and all stretched out, and we sat there and talked, and he was all upset about what they had done to his last record - it turns out to be his last record.

He was all upset about it--he said, "It don't even sound like me!" I wrote a song with a boy named Danny Green, called "Blues Man," and that was on the record, and that was one of the last songs he ever recorded. Albert – he was a big, tall guy - he couldn't read nor write, but he could count that money! We walked off the plane and Vivian was there, and I said, "Vivian, this is Albert King!" and he said, (drawls in a deep voice) "Ah known little Bobby since he was barely" - just like I said! (laughs).

Would you believe that he has a new release that's just come out with Stevie Ray Vaughan?

BW: I wouldn't doubt that; it's probably the last session that Stevie Ray did (author's note: the session was in 1983), and that was done at Gary's studio as well. He had just come out of rehab, and he was havin' a difficult time, Stevie Ray was. He couldn't get the sound out of 13 amplifiers that he could get out of one. I mean, he literally had 13 amplifiers stacked up.

He was havin' a real difficult time with everything - I talked with him about it and everything, down at the Peabody. He said, "Goddamn, Bobby, when I was druggin' and drinkin', it wasn't a problem: I just used one amplifier. Now, we're up to thirteen!" (laughs). Tryin' to look for that sound!

A little more name-dropping, then I'm gonna jump back to your releases: Bill Graham?

BW: Bill Graham was cool. He was a cool guy - you could walk into his office - he had a real small office - you could walk in, and up on the right was a Derek and the Dominos poster.

His autobiography, <u>Bill Graham Presents!</u> (Doubleday, 1992) is really funny. I'm looking through (it) and don't see any mention of the Dominos; of course, they mention the Fillmore West, where you guys played - actually, you played at both Fillmores, East and West.

BW: Yeah, at the East, we did two nights in a row.

We were talking earlier, that there are two live Derek and the Dominos releases. One has the four of you guys leaning on the fence; that's the earlier one, and they (Polydor) just put one out about three years ago, called Live at the Fillmore, which has some alternate mixes that were not released. They were talking about how you guys went on and on - your piano was just rolling.

BW: I'm real basic when it comes to piano - I'm real basic when it comes to anything. Singin', I'm basic - I sing the song. I don't do no hot licks or aerobatics, or acrobatics or anything with my voice. That (imitates vocal squeals) makes me all nervous. I just sing the song. No, it's all real simple. The first song I ever did on piano in a recording situation, the very first song I ever played piano, was on George Harrison's <u>All Things Must Pass</u> album called "Beware of Darkness."

And it was just like, too cool: all of a sudden, a window - a door opened in my mind. It just happened. I listened to some of my early stuff with the Dominos, you know, like dink-dink-dink-dink; real sloppy but real basic, but real good and simple, no over-done things. I lost one of the tendons in my right hand and I told 'em, "Hook it up to the other tendon on my middle finger because I know me - I'll try to be playin' like Chuck Leavell, or something," 'cause I'll be trying to get fancy.

Chuck's one of my favorite players, and he's one of my best friends. He's my tree-huggin' buddy. He's got a big thousand-acre tree farm down there!yes, he's a sweet guy, I love him to death.

Back to your work: you've got <u>Bobby Whitlock</u> (1972), which is hard to find - it's out of print, but you've got a couple of things there: "A Day without Jesus"; "Dreams of a Hobo." George Harrison played on this album, too.

BW: "Dreams of a Hobo" is the very first song I ever wrote in my life.

How are we gonna find these things?

BW: I think MCA bought it.

Interesting songs you've got here: "Back Home in England." You've got a real thing for England, don't you?

BW: Yeah, but that was a song that I wrote in a dream. It came in a dream - I used to keep a tape recorder and a pencil and pad by my bed, and I was in California, and I dreamt that whole song, and I wrote it down and sang it - I woke up in the middle of the night and sang everything, right then.

Would you rather be living in England?

BW: No, I have an affinity for that place, that's why I think I'm so comfortable down here in these hills in Mississippi. Everybody thinks of Mississippi as the delta land - it's not. It's all hills and hollows and rivers and creeks and streams and stuff around here. There is the delta, but I don't live in the delta. This looks more like England or Wales or something with trees. I'm surrounded by a national forest, and I'm out here by myself.

You also did "Where There's A Will, There's a Way." That's the best song on that live album (with Clapton), as far as I'm concerned.

BW: (proudly) Thank you very much! I appreciate it. Delaney helped me with the very end of it. That song just came out of me - just fell out of me, as do most songs, just fall out of me. You know how baseball players get in a batter's slump, or a pitching slump - I get in a songwriter's slump sometimes. I always do, and it's a change - it's a growing period, it's a growth process. But "Where There's a Will, There's a Way" is just one of those things that came out.

On the live album, it's totally cool, the live Delaney album. I've got a new version of it that I'm doin' now, that's (growls) real funky and snaky. It's totally cool. I'm gonna put it on my next record that's comin' out.

Delaney did that on his last solo album: he changed "Let it Rain"; he did it as the original calypso idea.

BW: Delaney cut it the way he originally wanted it to be, with that calypso steel drum sound. I asked him about that, and he said Eric wasn't ready for the vocals and so he did it in that kind of rocker style. The original song was Eric's song, and it was called "She Rides." (sings) "And she rides, chocka-chocka-chocka, and she rides, do-do-do, and she rides like a new beginner." Then Delaney came in, and they changed it to "Let it Rain." It was called "She Rides." I'm not talking bad about Delaney or anything, I'm just sayin', this is the truth! If you want to do the in-depth interview, this is it!

Okay, I know you guys are close. You also have some other things out: <u>Raw Velvet</u> came out in 1972, <u>One of a Kind</u>, when your daughter was born; <u>Rock Your Sox Off!</u> (1976).

BW: They re-released it on CD, and it sold out the day it came out. I hope that this new thing that I've got coming out - it's taken me a long time to get emotionally, psychologically, and physically prepared for doin' what I'm doin' now, and all these songs that are on this album, all of 'em are sincere, they're the truth, they come from the heart, and hopefully, they'll make a difference, somehow, some way.

I'm 125-150 percent in my head and in my heart, I'm there, and I'll be there, and I'm gonna play the songs that no one's ever got to hear, like "I Looked Away" and "Anyday" and things like that. All those people bought all those records and everything - if I went out and bought a record, I would want the artist to play me the song, and Eric hasn't been playing any of those songs.

I'm gonna make sure that I do those kind of songs from the Dominos thing, because people paid a lot of money for those records and they're still paying money for those records! I would like to hear the people that created them - I would just like for the people to say thank you. So, I'm gonna be doing old Dominos stuff; I'm gonna be doing my new stuff. I'm gonna be doing some of my other things.

I know through my recording statements and stuff throughout the world, what's being played where, and it's very strange - like "Thorn Tree in the Garden" - people in Germany and France and Australia, they love that song. "I Looked Away," and "Anyday," there are all these great songs that Eric doesn't play at all, and that's okay, he's Eric Clapton, he can do what he wants to do, or he can not do what he doesn't want to do.

But, I believe it's my obligation because if I were on the other end of the role, I would want you to play me the song that I bought - the song that I love, the song that I listen to - if I went to your concert, I would really appreciate you playing me that song. Not something that Elmore James wrote - nothing bad on Elmore James, okay, or Robert Johnson, but, hey: can you play me "Why Does Love Got to be So Sad?" or "Tell the Truth" (laughs) - something like that? That's where I'm at, and that's what I'm gonna do.

Give the people what they want.

BW: Yeah! They deserve it - they paid a lot of money for those records! Those things - they weren't cheap! A double-album was not cheap! Now, a triple or quadruple CD is not cheap.

That's for sure. Last person in mind - I wanted to ask about how he influenced you: Ray Charles?

BW: Yeah! Totally cool. I got a good story: I wrote this song, and I couldn't get arrested in Nashville, because I was too soulful. I wasn't 'country' enough. And I wrote the song, called "Someone You Should Know," and I sang a lick in there, and it goes (rising vocal wail), "Hey-y-y, hey-y-y-y-hey-y-y, now that it's o-o-over, there's nothin' more I can say-y-y, 'cept that I'm too sorry for sayin' just a little too-o-o late!" It's called "Slip Away." But the lick, "Hey-y-y, hey-y-y-y-hey-y-y", that was me singin' Ray Charles.

Well, when he did the song, he did it exactly like I sang it, except he put a Ray Charles lick in at the end of it; you know, "Where you goin', woman, get back in here!" kind of a thing. He just really earmarked it, just totally cool. But "Slip Away," I wrote one night, just me and the piano, and I took it in to this lady at CBS, Bonnie Garner, and it was just a cassette, and I said, "This song is for Ray Charles!" and I left and went to California.

Six months later, I got a telephone call, and a tape in the mail, and a letter, in one day, the same day, and it said that Ray Charles told me that he was gonna - when he did his definitive country album - he was gonna do everything and mix it, and wait, and then do the world a favor, and go back in and cut "Slip Away." And that's what he did, and they sent it to me. And he sang it exactly, him goin' "Hey-y-y, hey-y-y-y-hey-y-y, now-w-w-w that it's o-o-over" - that's me singing Ray Charles singing me!

That's great!

BW: Yeah, I think that's the ultimate compliment. It sold, but I don't care if it sold one record - just the fact that he did that is like the ultimate professional, talented musical kind of compliment that anyone could ever pay - I mean, money would not compensate that. It's the best thing in the world for me, that suddenly, I realized, that (gesture) was too cool - there is relevance to all this.

Okay, Bobby, this has been an absolute treat and a treasure. Thank you so much for being a musician, songwriter, and an inspiration for so many of us.

BW: Thank you very much. Between yourself and this guy down in Nashville; he sent me some stuff and it's just him and his wife; it's not just, it is his wife and him, and it's just totally cool. He plays the slide, and bottleneck, and they're playin' the stuff, and he sent me a letter that just really inspired me, and at this point in my life, some people like yourself, and like this boy named Ricky Davis and his wife, that means a whole lot to me. You don't know how big this is in my world, that someone really does care, and that I've made a difference, and that's real important to me.

Well, we're gonna tell the story of those two red-headed curly-haired boys!

BW: I think that's perfect, and I wish that they'd get in touch with me. I would like to see them, because, you know, I'm partially responsible for that. That's why - Eric was playin', he had that song by J.J. Cale wrote called "Cocaine," and I took my kids to see it, to see him in Memphis. In the middle of the thing, he did that (sings notes) "duh-duh-duh-duh-cocaine!" It turned all of the lights on in the Coliseum. I told Eric, "Hey! You got a responsibility here. Anybody that doesn't have any on them is gonna go get it - because they believe in that."

I realize my responsibility and what you say and everything, what we have to say (as role models). It has an impact on people, and you've got to be cautious about what you have to say. It's all about love and peace and togetherness, being able to listen. I think that's where it's all at.

Thanks again, Bobby, for letting me listen to you, and much obliged for everything.

BW: Cool. Good interview - I appreciate your candor and frankness.

Lady sings (and honors) the blues and growing ripe with wisdom: Bonnie Bramlett

(It took a trip via Nashville to Muscle Shoals, Alabama, to coordinate this. From this trip came a wonderful friendship with Ann Sandlin, wife of Johnny Sandlin. I owe her many thanks for inside stories like this. Bonnie's latest movie work was a bar owner/singer who consoles Coast Guard rescue swimmer Kevin Costner in <u>The Guardian</u>.)

The resume's credentials are impressive, but you have to read between the lines to understand the classroom that helped shape her character: singer-songwriter; wife of a famous musician; actress; fiercely loyal and dedicated mother to many, hers and others; and last, a new role: Mentor-Spokeswoman for an awareness of women's lifestyles and transitional phases.

Bonnie Bramlett, featured again in <u>Gritz</u> with her second interview, welcomes us now to share her memories and reflections as she approaches six decades of intensity, determination, and strength to do what she loves: meeting a challenge head-on and giving to it all the energy she has within her very existence, and taking from it, the wisdom and understanding that comes with time, The Great Teacher.

I had the wonderful opportunity to meet with Bonnie in the Muscle Shoals Studio in June, watching her cut back-up vocal tracks with Scott Boyer, as Johnny Sandlin handled the mixing chores.

During a break in the session, we sat in the kitchen and talked about her life while enjoying a delicious meal of Ann Sandlin's chicken and mushroom sauce. There isn't anything that adds more flavor to good food than great company, and having both Scott and Bonnie there was a magic ingredient. Bonnie's warm hug upon meeting me was a door-opening experience; we had been chasing each other via phone and email for months.

We finished this via phone the following month. This is a story of reflection, contemplation, and thankfulness, for which I offer my gratitude to the people whom I meet. There's a picture of Bonnie on one of the walls in the studio; looking sultry and cool, she catches your eye. It's time now for her to capture your heart and attention.

Hello, Bonnie, what's on the menu for you tonight? I understand you're working with some old friends?

I'm doing some vocal work for Jamie Oldaker. (Eric) Clapton is on this project, too. I won't know a lot about it until I get there tomorrow, so I'm sorry I can't share more information at this time. I know it's some Okie tunes, and Vince Gill's doing "Magnolia; Brooks and Dunn will be there, too. They're all doing Tulsa and Oklahoma stuff. It should be fun. Jamie played on Eric's LP, <u>461 Ocean Blvd</u>, and as I recall, Jamie is from Oklahoma.

Sounds very nice. Tell me: how does it feel to be one of the most well-known and on-demand backup vocalists in the industry?

(laughs softly) I don't feel like I'm that—isn't that weird? It doesn't feel that way—but thank you! (Modestly) I do a lot of work, yes, but I can't say that I'm the most demanded singer. Yes, I do appear on a lot of people's stuff—if you really look at my resume, I'm everywhere. There's a whole big long list on my website of everybody.

I think of you most often in that capacity when I listen to Little Feat. Two songs that are truly classic examples of your work are

"Dixie Chicken" and "Fat Man in the Bathtub." Do you remember recording those two?

(enthusiastically) Yeah, sure! Lowell (George) was a friend of mine—they were doing their Little Feat thing at that time, and they came to play with me after that. Bonnie Raitt sang on that too, I think. It was the first time we did anything together, her and I. It was cut in L.A. at A&M studios, but I'm not sure about that. But it was a wonderful time: I just love Lowell—just so cool. I really miss him. He was one of the greatest guitar players that ever lived. As a man, he reminded me of Henry VIII.

He was intellectual—do you know what I mean? He was from (Frank Zappa's) Mothers of Invention. A phenomenal guitar player. The whole Little Feat group is incredible. That group consists of former members of The Mothers of Invention and Delaney and Bonnie & Friends.

How about some of those people: (bass player) Kenny Gradney, for example? Marvelous syncopation on tunes like "All That You Dream."

We had custody of him since he was about 18 years old. We had custody of Bobby Whitlock as well—we were taking minors over the state line, and Bobby was only 17 when he joined us, and so was Kenny. We were taking those kids to different states and out of the country, and needed legal papers for them. Sam Clayton was another great person—don't you just love him?

Well, <u>all</u> of them were great men. (wistfully) Kenny…I watched that young man grow up, and Sam…he and I were such good buddies, whether he was with Little Feat or Delaney and Bonnie & Friends. We still are—still great friends! He's a <u>warm</u> man. (imitates his deep husky voice) Yeah!

Speaking of Dixie Chicken, you just growled on that cut.

(Proudly) *Yeah, that's me, honey, I'm the Dixie Chicken! (laughs) I'm a Dixie Hen. (growls softly) Yeah! That group, the Dixie Chicks—it <u>thrilled</u>me when they said something in an interview that they named themselves after that song. Those are my little chicks, 'cause I'm the Dixie Hen! (cackles)*

I understand you're doing some new material for yourself. I heard they're 'torch' songs.

Yeah, I'm constantly doing that because I'm writing all the time. Some of them are very romantic—they're very deep. It's a very self-absorbed album. I took a risk to make it because I got the opportunity because David Corlews asked me. He said, "Bonnie, if you could make any album you wanted, what would you do?"

I wanted to do one that I would call a "pretty dress" album. I wanted to do one where you could hear <u>me</u> sing—where <u>I'm</u> the lead instrument. I wanted to do a "Bonnie-singing" album. It doesn't have monster-killer tracks; instead, it has monster-killer pickers. You're not going to be looking at the great producer of this album; hopefully you'll be hearing the great singer on it.

You wanted more of your 'smooth' side to come out, is that right?

Exactly! I want everyone to see my soul, and to hear my voice project that. I'll explain it this way: if you ever go to an acting class, the very first emotion you're going to get in touch with will be rage. It's the easiest thing to do. Everybody has an abundance of it, and if somebody gives you the green light and you can blame this character for being that mad. Being silly is not easy because you don't want to look stupid. Crying and being that vulnerable is not the easy thing to do as a beginning actor or actress.

But rage—everybody can get mad and loud really easy. I can scream and yell—I can kick butt!—everybody knows I can do that who remembers me by now. But now I'm a 58-year-old woman and I <u>really</u> want somebody to hear me sing (earnestly). <u>Then</u> I want to rock some more. No one *ever gave me the opportunity until David Corlew. He gave me the opportunity to put my songs on it: "NoMan's Land" is absolutely self-absorbed! That's my innermost, improvisational feeling, and that was totally about entering and going through menopause, and the fear that you feel. It's like, Omigod, where am I?—everything is so strange and different; and leaving a divorce and being fearful. Remember, I come from a home where my dad was the <u>boss</u> in my household, and we liked it that way.*

Believe it or not, I'm a submissive woman. I don't submit to a man because he has a penis—they have to <u>deserve</u> my submission, and I prefer it that way. I was so lost—I was betrayed and divorced, and going through menopause here (laughs), saying "What's going on?" I'm an older woman, coming to face up to important life issues. I really got into all that artistic freedom to write—I mean, I wrote exactly what I was feeling. "Give it Time"—my friend and I are standing there, and he's been through a horrible divorce, and me—I could tell you what every one of those songs are about because they're so fresh in my mind.

I never would have been able to do that without the support of David (Corlew) and him saying, "Bonnie, what do you want to do?" And I said, "I want to make a pretty-dress album where everybody can hear me sing." And I don't want to sing no lies—I don't want to sing any song that someone wrote for me because I'm gonna have some big comeback or whatever. These are <u>my</u> songs! I want to sing songs that I mean, that have meaning and a special place for me to show to the world.

They say women who are entering that phase are given an awareness of knowledge…

It's wisdom—a connection to the meaning of life! It's in the Book of Proverbs. They call wisdom "She" in a feminine sense of respect. I think I'm being blessed with knowledge because I don't do the medication and the hormones and all that—I do a very natural process.

I'm not on Prozac; I don't have hormones as I once did, but I'm not turning into some little old man! (laughs)

I'm not any more insane than I've always been—and I say that with self-assurance—all those female myths and everything about this time of passage. I've got hot sweats, but I call them 'power surges.' I've done <u>deep</u> contact with my inner self, and I look at the patience I now have. You grow into this ability to forgive, and it's one of the most powerful times I've ever had in my whole life. I'm embracing it with everything I've got—(confidently) <u>and sharing it</u> with other men and women to help them share this time with each other and not be afraid of it.

Your words and thoughts gave me the mental picture of another actress-singer who I feel you identify with: Cher.

Yeah! I totally do, and I have a lot of respect for her. I heard her sing—I don't mean make hit records—she can do that great a job, too, let's don't doubt that—she can <u>really</u> sing, that girl! I think Cher was always willing to go further than I would, and she was willing <u>not</u> to be herself. For that, she gets to be a star. I've always said to myself, "Bonnie, you're not a star," and I'm not. I won't let you (the industry) dress me up weird, and there's lines that I won't do for money.

Artistically, I don't know if that was the smartest move in my life. I compromise a lot, but now I don't feel like I'm compromising my art at all. In my youth, I took the stand that I'm not gonna be dressed up and I'm not going to do this or that—I was very intent on just singing. I don't know if that was the right thing—but it was how it was back then for us real purist blues men and women (laughs).

On the (now available only as an import) Delaney & Bonnie CD, <u>Motel Shot</u>, one song that stands out for me is your singing on "Don't Deceive Me."

Oh, yeah. Is that killer or what? Thank you—I loved that song; for many years, I used to sing that song for my daddy. (thoughtfully) Oh, yeah, that goes back…I was <u>so</u> drunk. And I listen to those performances, and I think, "That was really mediocrity." <u>Imagine</u> if we were sober and in control and healthy—what great abilities we had. You know, you go *through what you've gotta go through. I'd love to sing that song again, though, I'll tell you that. If I could sing that song today, you'd hear it sung!*

Would you consider re-recording it? It seemed you could make water boil by just singing that song—or playing it.

I'd consider re-recording everything I've ever done. I'm telling you, that was a killer song. I was drunk, coked out of my brain, hoarse, up for three days, hardly no chops—and everybody looks at that point in time and says, "Listen to her voice crack—how soulful!" (laughs). That wasn't soulful, it was just getting the note out, man! That was a great album, I'll tell you—it was <u>honest</u>. They were playing <u>briefcases</u> on that thing--Buddy Miles—we had Joe Cocker on "Talkin' about Jesus." We had Joe Cocker, talking about Jesus, honey! That was me, Leon Russell, and Delaney's mother, Mamo, singing "Rock of Ages." That was little ol' Mamo. It's so real, <u>Motel Shot</u>. A great piece of work.

It was worth every second to track it down—and I'm glad it's available through Amazon.com and other distributors. <u>Accept No Substitute</u> and <u>Home</u> are a little harder to find, but I've been lucky. So what do you think about Delaney and Bonnie putting it back together for this blues event? I think it's wonderful—so many of your fans (myself included) have been hoping for this. In the rock 'n roll history books and the legacies of the bands that had real impact, you two are considered one of the purest rhythm and blues couple. I think it will be great to hear what you both have learned over time…

I think it's going to be interesting—very, very interesting. I've been getting all kinds of phone calls from the guys, and they all sound <u>so</u> excited!

Would you tell me the rest of the story about a train ride? We talked about this at the studio in Muscle Shoals, about the Canadian tour via train in 1970 that had the Grateful Dead, Mountain, The Band, Janis Joplin, The New Riders of the Purple Sage, Buddy Guy and his band, Tom Rush, Ian and Sylvia, and of

course, Delaney and Bonnie & Friends. (author's note: This was detailed in an out-of-print book, <u>The Rolling Stone Rock 'n' Roll Reader</u>, edited by Ben Fong-Torres, available through Amazon.com).

(Laughs gleefully) You mean when we dosed that poor girl? With the Murine bottle? We dosed her with the Notorious, Infamous Murine Bottle—(mischievously) that carried the incredible, liquid, clear Owsley acid. You've gotta get the names right: she gave me the drink, and she gave it to Sylvia (Tyson), from Ian and Sylvia—but the other girl who was there with us was 'Frankie' Weir, who was Bobby Weir's wife (of the Grateful Dead), who used to be George Harrison's secretary before that. That's how I met her, when she was working for George Harrison.

So she and I were girl friends, (carefully) but because she wasn't a singer, this girl didn't want to give her (Frankie) that bottle. That was so rude, wasn't it?

Would you tell it from the beginning?

Well, it started with Janis, and now she's drinking vodka, 'cause she's mad at Southern Comfort because they gave her this hair coat. They gave her a full-length mink coat, but she hated that—she said, (angrily) "All the fuckin' money I've for them, what do they give me? A fuckin' hair coat! I'll never drink it again!" So she was drinking vodka. And she always had her own bottle because she didn't share it with anyone—she was afraid she'd get dosed! And she was a juicer—she didn't do drugs—although she did die of heroin, she didn't do acid, or speed, smoke pot—she didn't do none of that.

Then all of a sudden there was this little follow-cat girl—I used to call them band-aids, I don't care what they say in this new movie; I call them these little chicks who were there for the aid of the band! They don't care who the band is—so this is a little band-aid who was following—as opposed to groupies, who love you and know every song you wrote, and know where you wrote it, when you cut it—those are groupies. They have certain groups that they follow around, not just any band. That's what a band-aid does.

So this girl latched onto Janis, and she had <u>her</u> little bottle of vodka, too, so she came over to give us a drink out of her bottle. So she gave me a drink: "Oh, Bonnie Bramlett!" and she gave some to Sylvia, and she looked at Frankie and she said, "Are you a singer?" Frankie goes, "No." The girl says, "Well, then you don't get a drink." And Frankie just looked at her—is that rude or what?

So Frankie says, "Oh, Bonnie, let me give her a drink out of your bottle," and goes wink-wink with her eye at me. Now, I <u>know</u> what she's doing because she's the holder of the Murine Bottle (chuckles). So I said, "Can I have me another drink out of that bottle," and she said, (sweetly, drawing out the word) "S-u-u-r-r-e!" So I turned around, had me another big ol' drink, and then passed the bottle to Frankie—and she just (deep voice) <u>squirted</u> it. Usually, you just put a drop on your hand and licked it, and you've taken a full dose, but she squirted it (blurts): 'Squirt!' Boy, I'll tell you, we saw that girl about three hours later and she was like, <u>electric</u>!

So Frankie dosed this gal for insulting her. I remember you gave me a look when you told me this: both eyes crossed and your tongue lolling out of your mouth—a truly funny sight, I have to admit.

(laughs) She would have dosed her that night for being cute, too! It was a killer event, having all that talent there on a train. And quite an adventure!

Would you share with me the story you told about Bekka falling asleep in your arms onstage as you sang?

Well, she must have been all of about three, and Dad was taking a solo, and she walked out there and held out her arms to him and said, "I want to go to sleep." So he motioned for her to go to me. I was singing, and it's a beautiful picture, it is…John Hartford was playing with us that night.

She was originally off-stage in Mamo's arms, but Suzanne would sit next to Bobby Whitlock on the organ and play tambourine when they came. I have to tell you that we didn't bring our kids around a lot.

First of all, there was pot smoking, and we didn't want any of that around our children—none of that ever happened around our children. We lived with Mamo, and we had no drugs in our home—ever—if we wanted to go smoke a joint, we had to go for a ride and then squirt our mouths with mouthwash and put Murine in our eyes and everything else (giggles). We didn't feel comfortable smoking when we were home because our kids were there, and you know what? You don't feel comfortable being high around your babies. So we didn't get high while we were home at all. Our home was not a rock 'n' roll home. It was always a Christian home. Whatever bad behavior we had was not at our house.

You told me that when you first went out with Ike and Tina Turner, that Ike promised your mom that he would keep you out of danger.

(Matter-of-factly) Absolutely gave his word, and he did—absolutely. He was a gentleman in every shape of the word, and he always was—and still is. And Tina. When Delaney and I broke up, I went right to Ike and Tina, and they're the ones who gave me some money. You know how it is: when you first break up, you don't know where to go—where do I go, what do I do, how do I leave? Tina took me upstairs—this was before she started doing Buddhist chanting, and she prayed with me. She gave me some cash, and it was ironic that about four years after that, it was when she got up enough to leave Ike. And nobody was there to give her any money. It always killed me that nobody was there for her.

Have you watched the movie about them with Laurence Fishburne and Angela Bassett?

I can't watch the movie—it's too close to home. I've attempted to watch it twice while my mind's not closed, but I couldn't get through it.

I understand from a personal viewpoint. Divorce is hard to face, especially when you still love the other person.

It hurts. It's the theme of star-crossed lovers. You don't get the closure you need. That's what 'torch' singing is—'torch' as in 'tortured'—as opposed to blues, as in down-funky. Torch singing is a whole other thing; it's about pain, and expressing that.

Speaking of singing, I wanted to ask you in behalf of a friend, Sunny Stephens in Nashville, about a lady named Gus Hardin. She said Gus sang a lot like you.

Uh-huh, she used to be Delaney's girlfriend. Gus was a very talented girl; she had that Janis Joplin sound. I couldn't do someone else's style. I couldn't go to George Jones and do "D.i.v.o.r.c.e." with him.

Yes, you surely do sing with a sense of independent determination.

Thank you. I do love working with other people, but my best performances, no one could see or hear. They're the ones I do in my car!—the ones I do in front of only me. Some of the stuff that comes out—I go, "Wow!" I can recreate it, but it's a surrender process—when you surrender to your performance, then <u>you</u> don't know what's going to happen.

When did you first know that you were going to be a singer?

I always knew it—it was an innate knowledge—there never was anything else. I sang in front of people when I was about four years old in church, and I <u>never</u> wanted to be a nurse, or any of the other 'traditional' women's roles of that time. So was Bekka—she always knew she was going to be a singer—it's something you always know.

May I quote you here on that: You've said that she's a queen? As in a royal persona.

Oh, yeah, like "I give birth to queens"? (Directly) I don't give birth to princesses, honey! (laughs).

I see it as self-assurance. For example, Queen Elizabeth I—she took care of her country. You seem to be taking care of yourself and your career.

Thank you. I don't know if it's self-assurance, but once you face the facts, you have to manage your own affairs now. I've already let it go into two other people's hands—and mucked it up (laughs). It's my fault because I didn't pay attention. I do manage mine now, especially artistically, because I'm allowed to do so. My history has allowed me the respect that when I go into a performance, I'm allowed <u>a lot</u> of space.

Is that the difference for you as an actress and a singer? Is acting less demanding than singing?

More demanding. Much harder for me to speak words than to sing 'em. Acting gave me words and definitions for what I was already doing naturally on-stage. For instance, Stanislovski called it "The Circle of Light." If I'm in performance and I don't want to be there—I don't like where I am—I can just be somewhere else within myself. If I don't like who's in the audience, I make in my mind whomever I want to be appear right there to support me. I can do that. I've always been able to do that. It's something I've always been able to do and they have a name for it.

Any chance of returning back to the screen? Any particular role or situation that's playing now that you'd like to do?

Oh, yeah, first chance I get! I love acting now—I just love it. I want to do television very much. I love the theater—so yeah, any of that! I'm up for that expression, anytime. There's nothing special playing now that I'd like to do, but I'm always looking for new material. I want a sitcom that's a variety show as well, and I think we need that, where it's not just bashing music. It'll be fun. I just like the work!

I have to mention another actor-singer-musician whom I had the pleasure to meet: Mr. Levon Helm, who sends you lots of love and good thoughts.

Isn't he a prince? I just love him—he's an incredible person and I'm lucky to know him. I met him and the others just after Woodstock, I think. But I met them in the town itself—that's where they were living.

I think the world of him, too. A great man, and a great story-teller in his own right. Thank you, Bonnie; your thoughts are going to stay in my mind for a long time to come. I thank you for sharing so much and with such passion.

You're welcome, dear, it's always a pleasure. God bless you.

Sights and sounds from the drum kit: Levon Helm

(A percussive master of rhythm and blues and a terrific vocalist, Levon Helm has been one of my heroes since I first heard the double-disc Rock of Ages. *Thankfully, I am able to say now some years later that Levon has regained his health and can sing like old times. There's nothing better!)*

Yes, he's a legend in his own time as a musician, a singer, a leader, and as a living representative of the solid bedrock foundation of Southern charm and warmth. As the drummer/vocalist for The Band, Levon Helm's contributions have been touchstones of good music since the end of the '60s through today's times. The voice and persona captured a heritage of nostalgia that evokes images of the late 1800s county carnivals, of farmers hard at work in the fields with a mule and an old reaper, and a back-woods flavor that can't be bought from a trading post.

To watch Levon onstage is an extra bonus, because his shows with his group, The Barnburners, allows the audience to get up close and see the look of joy and happiness that radiates on his face as he plays. I had the pure pleasure of kidnapping my best friend and fellow music master, Mike Michel, from his seven-day-a-week landscape architecture schedule to drive up with me to Montgomery, NY and see a terrific show at the fairgrounds.

Even better, I had the chance to do some roadie work—and hauling gear for Levon Helm is a small token of appreciation for the endless hours I've spent listening to his workmanship.

As a means of thanks for agreeing to speak with me, I had found three books of recipes that a real farm boy like Levon would know, and mailed them. Two were from a noted food author/recipe collector and editor/writer from upstate New York, Mrs. Bunny Crumpacker: *The Old-Time Brand-Name Cookbook,* and *The Old-Time Brand-Name Desserts.* Illustrated with images and labels from scenes from the 1930s and '40s, it was perfect for someone like Levon and his wife, Sandy, who spent hours looking at the pictures and reliving thoughts and good feelings of their younger days—as well as some tasty opportunities. I also had to mail Lee two boxes of a Romanian pastry called *ruggalah* that my mother made—and he and his then-manager ate both at one sitting.

In a phone call, Sandy graciously gave me the acknowledgment that they helped bring memories to Levon about those hardscrabble days as a young boy on a farm, and shared with me the history of the Helm family. It's really "Helms," she said, and they dropped the 's' a while back. It seems that one of Levon's nephews had to go out of his way to prove his uncle was indeed the same man that was up there onstage with Bob Dylan, all because of that missing letter.

When he looked back at me from his drum kit in the middle of a song and gave a huge grin, I saw "the luckiest man I ever did see, doing what he loves to do." Levon doesn't sing any more, due to throat surgery, but boy, can he whack those drums!

Howdy, Levon, where have you been since I last saw you?

We (the Barnburners) were in Sackett's Harbor, New York, doing a show. We were there along with the Honky-Tonk Gurus. We'll play anyplace, anywhere! We're often found in New York City on the pier boats, and we'll be down by Atlantic City in July (the 12th) at Bubba Mac's Shack in Somers Point. We've been down to Missouri and Arkansas, too.

I want to say how thankful I am that you're enjoying those recipe books. Sandy said that they brought back memories of your early years.

Oh, thank you, you bet. I'm always interested in the samples myself. She found a heckuva good rice pudding recipe, and I can't wait! It'll be a flight test for her to try 'em and see how they taste.

I understand a website dedicated to the Band has information on a drummer's video of your technique, as well as links to the Barnburners music. I'm going to look it up for a copy.

That's kind of an old one; it's a few things that I did that I don't even remember, but I thank you for asking about it.

I watched you from behind the drum set at the outdoor show in Middletown, NY. You seemed to be having the time of your life—just happy as you could be.

Oh, yes. Nothing's better than that. Drumming is the best—there's nothing more fun than making music. When you get players like that (the Barnburners), you can get everyone playing above their head—it's just great. They're all good guys, too. They love the blues! It was just in the cards to meet them, I guess. It's a small world, and the music world is even smaller, so these are the kinds of guys you're gonna run across. They're all local musicians from the Henry Hudson River valley, right here in the old Woodstock area. There's guitarist Pat O'Shea, lead vocalist, harmonica player Chris O'Leary, and upright bassist Jeff Sarli.

There are a lot of good local musicians right here. I don't know what the per-capita population is, but for its size and number of residence, it seems like Woodstock probably has more studios than any town in the world—

maybe close to two dozen, or a dozen-and-a-half. So that kind of gives you an idea of how many musicians there are up here.

Like Muscle Shoals?

It reminds you of something like that. I can think of six or seven 24-48 track studios, and maybe a dozen-and-a-half homemade studios of different sizes and calibers. The Barnburners and I kind of hooked up because we're musically coming from the same place, and we were in the right location, too. It's our common denominator—they don't want to play anything but blues, and I don't want 'em too, so we get along great.

I see you and the Barnburners are playing a show in West Virginia in August. You like those small venues where you can get up close to the audience.

Yeah, they have a blues festival over there that we're gonna play (the Heritage Music Blues Festival in Wheeling, WV). (Matter-of-factly) We'll travel to the ends of the earth to make music! Those small shows, they're the best. It's like last weekend up at Sackett's Harbor, NY—that was one of those small town community festivals—same thing out in West Virginia. That's gonna be beautiful. That won't be quite as small town-like, but it's still got that good community thing like smaller venues: they really enjoy it and everybody comes out. We did one about three weeks ago, me and the Barnburners, in Williamsport, PA, at the county fairgrounds there.

I'll give you an example. The stage and everything and the music, that's all the same, but here's the difference (between the large shows and small ones): the people are friendly, nobody's got nothing to prove, nobody's trying to express their authority. Everybody you see has got a big smile and a thank you; if you ask somebody for something, they'll say, well, let me see if I can—they try and accommodate you.

And when it comes time to lean over there and get something to eat with that coca-cola, everything's home-made…all the cookies. One of the old boys made one of the best damn home—made bean soups you ever had. That's the difference—all the food was home-made, all the people were just bending over backwards to accommodate the situation—those things are always more fun. The food's better, the people are nicer, and it's more fun.

I heard you really enjoy Coca-Cola. Someone had told me to ask you about that.

Oh, sure. It's America's favorite—it's the real thing.

(Author's note: I wish Coca-Cola would jump on this as an advertising promotion!)

What's the difference between living in Arkansas where you grew up and living in New York? You go back home to visit when you can, right?

I go back to Arkansas two or three times a year. I just went there, and I'm due to go back again in a few weeks. I like to go down in the fall for the King Biscuit Blues Festival if I can, and I like to get home every spring to watch them cut the ground and get ready for planting season. I like to see that all go down if I can. If I get back there in the fall for the blues festival, I get to watch them cut the rice, and the beans, and pick cotton—I get to watch some of that harvest go down. That's fun to see.

That's what you personify to us as an audience when we hear your music with the Band. We see those images.

Oh, boy—I appreciate that! It's a beautiful place, it's so stark—it's got a beauty of its own. As ugly as it can be in places, it's still beautiful. It's flat as a pan, wet, swampy, mosquitoes, and so forth, but boy, there's nothing like a Delta sunset…or a Delta thunderstorm! You get close to the elements there. Growing up on a cotton farm, I got acquainted with 'em at an early age. I've spent my share of time in a stormhouse, listening to the wrath of God outside. You ever been in a stormhouse?

Not directly—but I once stepped outside in a lightning storm in New Hampshire that almost scared me back through the door without opening it.

(laughter) People have said that the buckle of the tornado belt is right there in the Delta, I've heard. We do get our share of 'em. They come rippin' through there—they can happen any time, and of course, they're most frequent in the springtime.

I understand you had the old milk-the-cows-and-feed-the-chickens type of childhood.

Growing up on a cotton farm, we pretty much had things on a regular basis. We didn't have electricity until I was in high school. If there was chicken for dinner or breakfast, we'd have to catch one and...well, you know the rest.

Would you tell me about your mandolin playing? One of my favorite songs where you play it is "When I Paint My Masterpiece."

A mandolin is one of instruments that's hard to get tired of—it's kind of like a harmonica in that way. There's something about it that you hardly ever get tired of hearing, and it seems to fit in some of the strangest places. Any kind of music can accommodate it—you don't think of mandolin in blues music, but it's a great instrument. You can put it up there in that tenor guitar spot, just to kind of spread out the rhythm guitar, the drums and the sock symbol and everything out together—just having that mandolin in there just makes that sock symbol and other parts of the drum sound like they're in tune.

If you've got that mandolin in there with the spread—in with the mix—we've always been on the lookout to use it when we could. Certain songs accommodate it better, but the mandolin, the accordion, and the harmonica, those kind of instruments make you want to sing along, too!

I like the Cajun-style accordion of folks like Buckwheat Zydeco and Clifton Chenier.

I do, too. I've always loved that stuff. Clifton Chenier was always one of my favorites—he reminded me of Little Walter. His melodies and stuff just cover the whole thing so well.

I have someone you'd know: the Allan Touissant Collection.

Mmmmm! Well, he's my favorite. He was the first man we went to when we had the opportunity to get some horns into the mix (for the Band). We didn't go anywhere else. Did you ever hear all those Lee Dorsey records he did in the Fifties? You ought to go and check out "Working in a Coal Mine," that was a big hit. That'll tell you how long he's been playing. His horn arrangements made our album <u>Rock of Ages</u> such a great success.

Tell me how I saw you use such minimal motion and yet get such a loud sound. What's your secret—wrist strength?

I'm trying to play pretty hard and keep my strength up, to save most of the motion for the lick itself—whatever you have to do to get there with as much correctness and touch and strength as you need—I try to play that way. I try to play hard—I don't want to hold back! I want to be free enough to hit it hard and not worry about it.

What about the 'muffled' sound you get—it's like the drumhead is made of a thick cardboard box.

I think it's the 'MemphisSchool of backbeat.' Drummers from Memphis have done odd things, like Jimmy Van Eaton—J.M. Van Eaton, who cut "Whole Lotta Shakin'. He taped a cigar box to the top of the snare drum and played on top of that, because the sound of the backbeat was better. It recorded better—the microphone heard it better, coming off that cigar box. It was too heavy coming off the snare drum—it was overbearing and overpowering. Coming off that cigar box, it was just right. Now that you know the story, you can hear that I'm right: it's a damn cigar box on top of that snare drum.

That's the way of Memphis drummers: they've always done special things to the snare drum to get that 'pop'. But at the same time, it lets them have that 'snap.' From what I heard, growing up and being conscious of the drums and hearing it that way, it sounded to me like every one of those backbeats was a rim shot, and the only way I could get it to sound that way was to hit a rim shot.

Consequently, that's what makes my drums sound the way they do—all the backbeats are rim shots, if I can manage it (laughs). You know, when you miss one, you can tell (laughs)—it sticks out like a sore thumb. Get every one of 'em right, and nothing sounds better.

We were talking at the show about live albums, and my friend Mike mentioned to you how much he had been enjoying <u>Rock of Ages</u>.

I appreciate you saying that. I feel that way about live albums—my favorite ones are live albums. <u>B.B. King Live at the Regal Theater</u> (note: Levon says it, "Thee-AY-ter" with the accent on the second syllable), <u>Ray Charles Live at Newport</u>, and so on. I feel the same way about us (The Band). And for me, I think the reason it's that way is that you get more than just the players, you get the audience, too.

You can <u>hear</u> that excitement—it comes out in the music—the excitement that the crowd brings to the equation. And if you're in the studio—a cold, hard, electric-lighted studio, you're not going to get the electricity that an audience can give to the situation.

On that theme--tell me about the feedback at the Fillmore East...

The Band always tried to bring the goods, that was our mission, to be one of the best bands, and when we played, we tried to make the music and the show as good as we could make it and do some of that fun stuff. The

Fillmore was one of the best—one of the most sophisticated musical audiences in the world. They treated us like gold—better than we deserved a couple of times (laughs).

How about with Bob Dylan on the <u>After the Flood</u> album?

That was real satisfying for me—that was the first time we had ever been able to play with Bob and get a round of applause. We had played with him and been booed all around the country, but all of a sudden, it was a new dawn—a new light—and I really enjoyed working with the Bill Graham outfit.

I thought Bill Graham and Barry Imhoff and the production crew did a great job, and it was fun to travel along with everybody and put that show on every night. All I had to do was play drums and do my part, so I was really enjoying it.

How about Watkins Glen? You have some great items from The Band's box set, <u>Across the Great Divide</u>, there, including some previously-unreleased material.

That was a good show—that was a good time! You know the difference in time in that a couple of years had gone by—that was only three years after the Woodstock Festival (where The Band played, but did not get featured on the soundtrack or the movie)—it made a difference—people were in a whole lot better shape. People weren't as zoned out. Traffic jams would happen on the way into the festival, and people would get out and throw Frisbees and play guitars, touch football and stuff, the traffic would move and they'd get back in their cars and go on up the road and get ready for the next game. It was just mellow and easy and healthy—it was over in one day; that might have had something to do with it. It didn't last for three days and nights. There wasn't time for a whole new nation to be born.

How do you feel about your acting career in the movies as a change from being a musician?

I've done a lot of acting—probably a dozen or so parts (laughs). <u>Coal Miner's Daughter</u> (with Sissy Spacek as Loretta Lynn) was the first. You ever see a movie called <u>The Right Stuff</u>? I was in that one—I was (Chuck) Yeager's buddy, Ridley. Yeager would ask Ridley for the Beamon's gum for luck before a test flight. That's two of my favorite things: I like to make records and I like to make movies. My favorite movie <u>is It's a Mad, Mad, Mad, Mad World</u>. (laughs).

For the cast or the action?

Both. The greatest cast in the world (including Spencer Tracy, Buddy Hackett, Terry Thomas, Ethel Merman, Jonathan Winters, Sid Caesar, and Mickey Rooney). I can't think of anything that would be more fun, unless you could be in a Mel Brooks and a Coen Brothers all at the same time. I'm also a big Strother Martin fan (laughs). Remember him in <u>The Wild Bunch</u>? (imitates him: "Awright, awright, help me get his boots!")

Levon, being mindful of the fact that you have recovered from throat cancer, is it easier for you to focus on playing drums and enjoy it more without having to sing?

Well, you know, I always enjoyed singing, when I do it, but I would rather play drums. I think most musicians I know would feel the same way. All of us will sing if we have to, but we'd rather be players. When I used to sing in The Band, that was just my turn. More than anything else, Richard (Manuel) was the lead singer in The Band. Rick (Danko) and I did enough so that they could call it The Band, with three lead singers—all that (sarcastically) 'record company jive,' But just between us boys, Richard was the lead singer and there wasn't no worry about it. But if no one else will do it (sing), I'll do it.

I'd like to think this is unanimous for many fans: <u>you</u> were the leader, as well as lead vocalist of The Band.

Well, I thank you a lot. I appreciate you saying that. That was really our mission—just to make some good music.

Speaking of Richard as a musician, I've read that you said he was melodic on the drums and rhythmic on the piano. From a drummer's perspective, I thought it was a great compliment.

(Proudly) Richard…oh, boy. Richard was just one of them self-taught people—it was almost like he was double left-handed. He wasn't, but he played like he was. Richard might carry the backbeat with his right hand, or he might carry it with his left. It just came off fantastic. Songs like "Rag Momma Rag," with me playing mandolin, Richard played the hell out of those drums.

What it did for The Band, it had the same sort of effect like me and Rick taking the lead on a song would have. All of a sudden, we'd have ourselves a whole new rhythm section, right? 'cause Richard's now playing drums, and I might be playing bass or mandolin or something else, and Rick's moving around to fiddle or something else—it's a whole other rhythm section. That's why The Band was able to sound different on different songs—'cause we wanted to!

It's like you all were musically ambidextrous.

We learned to be that way because of (keyboard/horn player) Garth (Hudson). Garth was the one of us who could really do that stuff. There's a few of us who could play a few percussion instruments, but Brother Garth can play percussion, woodwinds, and brass! (laughs heartily). Ain't that great?!

I've also enjoyed him on David Lindley's El Rayo-Ex album on the title track, listed as "The Horns." He really is a walking musical encyclopedia.

That's the truth. We look ambidextrous because Garth sure enough is! (laughs). It made us hustle our buns off, trying to make it appear so.

I love the variation he did on his solo (also known as "The Genetic Method) on the box set—here, he's called it "Too Wet to Work"

(recorded at Watkins Glen, previously unreleased). He sounds to me like Bach riding on a Harley-Davidson.

I'll let you in on this, because it probably went by without registering: when you watch <u>The Right Stuff</u>, when he (Yeager) breaks the sound barrier, forget about all the excitement and listen to the soundtrack. What you'll hear, down deep in there, is Garth Hudson. That's all him. I also love his saxophone playing as much as anything.

I want to take a moment and thank you for a song you did on the <u>Greatest Hits</u> CD: "Ain't Got No Home," from <u>Moondog Matinee</u>.

(Gleefully) Clarence "Frogman" Henry! Yeah, that's a good song. Well, you know that was the way it got---when The Band reached those days of collaboration being over, that was the best that we could come up with.

Wait! That song brought back some funny thoughts and memories—like old-time fairs and social events—scenes that have gone 100+ years past in the heartland of America, of good old-fashioned fun and dancing and eating—kind of like the smell that old leather does to you.

You know, nobody gave us credit for it—the critics certainly didn't, and the record company, they didn't know what was going on, anyway. That was all we could do at the time. We couldn't get along—we all knew that fairness was a bunch of shit. We all knew we were getting screwed, so we couldn't sit down and create no more music. "Up on Cripple Creek" and all that stuff was over—all that collaboration was over, and that type of song ("Ain't Got No Home") was all we could do.

I'll tell you something that they never gave us credit: you can't tell how good The Band is, or not, when they're doing their own stuff. Same with the Beatles, or anybody else. When they're doing their own stuff, you can't tell how good they are or how good they ain't. You let both of us do a

Chuck Berry tune—then you can tell how good the (two) bands are, can't you? So, that's what they never gave us credit for.

I think Eric Clapton said it best: when he heard the music from <u>Big Pink</u>, he said, 'That's what I want to do.' I also am certain that fans and new listeners are in your corner. Was Ray Charles an influence on you?

Oh, absolutely. Ray Charles is my hero. Ray Charles had the best band in town—whatever town you were in—since I've been around, anyway. I never got to hear Louis Jordan in a live performance.

Per your request, I gave Bonnie Bramlett a big hug for you when I saw her in the Shoals.

Ain't she the best?—ain't she somethin'? And her daughter, Bekka—looks and sounds just like her momma, just younger. I love her—she's just great!

Thank you, Levon, this has been a real treat. I am so glad we hooked up for this.

Thank you, too, Mitch, glad to do this, too. And thanks to your friend, Michael; it was a pleasure to meet him and talk with him.

Afterward, I just returned from a fabulous show at Bubba Mac's Shack in Somerset Point, just south of Atlantic City. Pat's '52-Cadillac-colored Les Paul was a scorching sensation, Chris was a titan of strength and power on harmonica and vocals, Jeff's vintage, upright, radiantly polished mahogany-cherry bass was a rippling wave of deep pulsation, and of course—the ground was shaking underneath our feet as Levon pummeled and thundered on the drums.

If you want to see the hottest, most dynamic R&B show on the circuit, break all the rules, take all the vacation time you've got, empty the bank account—or whatever is necessary to get there—

just go and see Levon Helm and the Barnburners before the clock turns another tick on the dial. It's worth every second of the effort, and the payoff is the best investment you can find.

2010 Update: Check out http://www.levonhelm.com for music, videos, and more. Levon's recovered his ability to sing, even though it clearly has impacted his range. But it's still the sound of one of America's greatest vocalists—and that's what counts.

Saving Our Planet

DANNY O'KEEFE SPEAKS UP FOR CONSERVATION AND LAND STEWARDSHIP, FEATHERED FRIENDS & TUNEFUL BUDDIES, AND MAKING MUSIC THAT HAS A PURPOSE.

(I have so much to be thankful for regarding my music: it has given me gifts beyond measure. I personally want to thank Danny "Good Time Charlie's Got the Blues" O'Keefe for his work: on the first anniversary of September 11th, as his tunes "Can't Outrun The Years" and "Never Got Off the Ground" (from <u>Runnin' from the Devil</u>) played in my office while we corresponded via email about upcoming plans, a call came from my mother. My father, at the moment of his death, had somehow found a way to tell my family and me goodbye and say what he never could do for us as his children: to learn and remember his life's lessons, accomplishments, and failures through the lyrics of Danny's songs.)

Danny O'Keefe's singing and playing bring immediate recognition as a long-time friend and ally. His warmth and reflective personal lyrics burrow deep into your heart and soul, and his guitar picking has found a place with anyone who has found the magic hidden in an acoustic. Danny's 1972 hit, "Good Time Charlie's Got the Blues" is a classic that evokes thoughts from audiences of long summer nights, wondering where time has gone.

Another tune, "The Road," became a huge success for Jackson Browne, and remains in my memory as a staple for an old navy buddy of mine from Michigan, the late Scott Harley Powell. Danny's versatility as a songwriter has made him a valuable asset on the West Coast, where he has found comfort and security on a small island near Seattle.

Danny has taken up a noble crusade that deserves national recognition: the preservation of habitat that is home to the multitudes of songbirds that populate our country. By tying this together with agricultural practices and resourceful preservation of land that has been devoted to a major product--coffee--he has dared us to be consumer-conscious and ecologically practical and responsible.

He has also been active again in the studio, and his latest CD is coming on strong and should be an immediate "must-have" for listeners who want the best. Danny is also a very articulate journalist-writer, and his website should be bookmarked for reading and composition samples for advanced classes. He also has a remarkable melancholy download available, "Ghosts of the Ascent," about those who have lost their lives on Mt. Everest, and a tune for whom I personally honor the memory: an American climber, Ms Marty Hoey, whose story I read about in Peter Jenkins' book about his travels, Across China.

Your voice--who influenced your style of singing? I've heard you do jazz (as mentioned, with John Klemmer on Magnificent Madness (and I truly dig "Lifesong"), you're known as a balladeer, and I know you did the Hank Williams-style "Honky Tonkin'." You were also very much at home on a Clarence (Pinetop) Smith-inspired song, "I'm Sober Now." May I mention that your timbre (to my ears) has the resonance of a cello being bowed--it has this phrasing that is like a spider's web: light but amazingly strong.

D'O: There are many influences that go into one's voice. My chief inspirations are Miles Davis, Billy Holliday, Mississippi John Hurt, Nino Rota, Stan Getz, Jimmy Rodgers and many of the country singers, but I couldn't say any one of these could be heard in my voice. They are, however, what and whom I listen to for creative ideas. These ideas go deep into the sub-

liminal conscious where they are called on by musical and lyrical ideas and feelings. Feeling is what you initially go for in your attraction to anything creative.

As long as I mentioned those songs, that bit with Klemmer--how did you meet? I just thought it was a surprise to find you alongside a jazz saxophone--but his playing is similar to your singing.

Our two managers thought it would be an interesting pairing. I wanted to write with a jazz player in order to explore many of the jazz leanings that I had. John wanted to write pop songs. The songs on that record (there were several others unrecorded) are the result. I would still like to write with someone more committed to exploring the possibilities of lyrics in jazz contexts. Bill Conners would have been someone whom I think would have been interesting to work with but I haven't heard of him for a while. I loved the work he did with Jan Garbarek on ECM in the '80's.

Obviously, your songs are autobiographical, and are just marvelous snapshots of life. Who was/is "Good Time Charlie"? and how did that come about as a song? Jackson Browne also made "The Road" a popular FM hit; can you fill in the legacy of that one?

I'm woven into "Goodtime Charlie's Got the Blues," but it is also about a good friend and mentor who is no longer with us. Friends in a band were headed for L.A. to build the next steps in their musical careers and I wanted desperately to go with them, and I did. The rest is the mystery of history. "The Road" is one of the truest songs I have ever written.

It's clubs instead of dance halls now, and the girls in daddy's cars are long gone (as are the drugs), but much remains the same about the road: You spend your days working towards that moment of performance where, ideally, you may be able to transcend yourself, if only for a moment.

Jackson originally wanted to call the album that became "Running On Empty," "The Road and The Sky." He had a wonderful song in "Late for the Sky" and thought "The Road" would work to complete the idea.

I showed him the chords and how I played the song and the rest is the history of mystery.

Speaking of autobiographical, you've released a new CD on Miramar Recordings as of this spring, <u>Runnin' from the Devil</u>. You have been quoted as saying this is an extremely personal album, one you have wanted to make for years. It seems that some of the songs ("Can't Outrun the Years," "Sheila," and the title) are what you do best: painting musical portraits of your experiences. What has made the biggest difference to you as a survivor of a very intense occupation: musician. How about your way of reflecting on life--you penned in "Good Time Charlie," 'You know my heart keeps tellin' me, you're not a kid at thirty-three.' Does it get better as you grow older and start confronting things with a greater sense of maturity?

What always makes the difference, then and now, is the song. It is the funnel through which you concentrate knowledge and experience of feeling and idea to create something in which you invest with your hope. My songs have saved my life many times.

The music business is a killing business and you must live for the creative moment that lifts you beyond and above the machine that is designed to grind you up and leave you behind. If what you do continues to open up your heart to greater life experiences, you are doing something right. If what you do makes you angry, depressed and bitter, you must change.

Someone brighter than myself said, "The only constant is change." The truth of that is the closest we ever get to experiencing the Creative Force of the Universe. If you can accept and love the changes you go through in your life, you will be ever closer to freedom and the responsibility it entails.

And-- a few titles for which you're well-known: "Magdalena" (a marvelous vocal--that excellent "yearning" touch that you have); "If Ya Can't Boogie Woogie (You Sure Can't Rock and Roll"; "Just

Jones," "Farewell to Storyville (Good Time Flat Blues)"; "So Long Harry Truman." You're pretty much a "west coast" wayfarer; home-based near Seattle. Is it the appeal of the city, the people, or just being able to live a quiet lifestyle on an island?

I have to live in a place that feeds my soul and my creative needs. It can't be a place that is only concerned with "the bizness." I have many friends in Nashville and L.A., but I can't live there. I don't want my songs based on the latest trend or to whom I can pitch a song.

I hope my songs find themselves in the voices of artists who truly appreciate them and can make them their own. That's the greatest compliment a writer receives. Alison Krauss recently cut a song of David Mallett's and mine called "Never Got Off the Ground," and it was a thrill to hear her sing it. She has one of my favorite instruments in the world: her voice; very "birdlike" and self-possessed.

The other reason I live in the Northwest is because I am a native Northwesterner. This is where everything feels best. I'm close to reasonably good fishing water, to good art and cultural interests, as well as many friends involved with creative living themselves.

Your friends are some of the most recognized names in the music industry regarding social responsibility and environmental concern: Bonnie Raitt, Jackson, Browne, Bob Dylan, Mary Chapin Carpenter. How did you first meet up with them (individually)--was it for the music or the environmental considerations?

I met Jackson through David Geffen in the early '70's. I have a great appreciation for his music, his character and commitment to ideas and ideals he believes in, and for the person he has always been and continues to become. I worked with Bonnie at the Troubadour in the '70's and we appreciated each other's humor and music as we continue to do. Watching her career is like being able to appreciate one of the great wines, the grapes of which you once saw growing on the vine, its heritage filled with promise and expectation.

What a great artist she is. I can't say that I know Bob Dylan in any personal sense, even though I have appreciated his work from the beginning, have met him a couple of times, worked for his company and written a song with him. Bob is the ultimate enigma and will remain so. Mary Chapin Carpenter came to a show I was on with John Stewart at the Birchmere in the D.C. area many years ago. Her musical partner, John Jennings, was with her. I remember her commenting that she'd like to sing "Pieces of the Rain." My mistake was never getting the song to her.

She is a great talent and very committed to social justice and environmental issues and has been a great support to my work with The Songbird Foundation (www.songbird.org).

With the exception of Bob Dylan, I am still involved with musical projects connected to environmental and social justice issues -the two are almost always intertwined- with these artists and many others to see if we can somehow make a difference while we are on the Earth.

You're the director of the Songbird Foundation, which is helping protect the forests and habitation of wildlife, especially birds. In response to this, you've emphasized the influence of the coffee industry and their bean-growing practices. Obviously, since coffee is such a largely- consumed commodity (and heavily impacts farming techniques), the public needs to be more aware of how our consumables affect our environment. What can we do to help?

The first thing we can do is to examine how we live on a day-to-day basis and what the impact of our consumption patterns has on the environment and others lives -not just humans but all others. We are in one of the largest extinction periods ever experienced on Earth and we're barely aware of it.

Coffee makes a good starting place in the understanding of sustainable strategies because it's the traditional "commodity of dialogue" We discuss things over coffee. It wakes us up, and it is indeed time to wake up to the urgent call being made by the Earth and the many species that are being pressured out of existence by Man.

Coffee traditionally was grown under a forest canopy, but increasingly over the last twenty years the trees are being cut down in "coffee country" and replaced by sun-tolerant hybrids, which require increasing amounts of chemicals. These shade trees are the wintering grounds for all those pretty migratory songbirds that come back to us each spring. We hope they continue to come back.

One way of helping them is to drink shade-grown coffee. Most organic coffees (although not all) are grown under shade trees, so you can be fairly sure when you buy organic coffee. By purchasing fair-trade certified coffee, you are helping guarantee that the farmers who grow the coffee are being paid an equitable price for their coffee and that the money is actually getting to them.

The farmers are the true stewards of the environment, and we need to make an investment in them if we are to be assured that those environments and habitats in which coffee is grown will remain for the birds and other creatures that depend upon them. You can find out much more about this issue on the Songbird Foundation website (www.songbird. org). Start by asking the people where you buy your coffee to please supply you with shade-grown coffee. Most retailers are very sensitive to their customers wishes.

You're a songwriter's magic lamp: Jackson Browne, Judy Collins, Elvis, Leon Russell, Charlie Rich, Waylon Jennings, Earl Klugh, just to name a few, have recorded your work. Is it more comfortable to let them carry on your legacy as a composer, rather than being up-front in the public?

I am very proud that other artists have found something of interest in my work, but I would love to be able to perform my songs more for audiences around the country.

My health precludes it a bit, and I'm afraid I've never had much of a musical business sense. I don't, at the moment, have an agent or manager to help put performance situations together for me, although I am a strong believer in synchronicity and the idea that when the time is right, the proper forces come together. Like the perfect wave, however, you must be ready to surf when it comes along.

Last question. What's it like being a bird-watcher? Anything memorable or special about a sighting? What's your favorite bird (mine, for the record, is the cardinal--I love hearing them call early in the spring here in New Jersey--I like to answer back to them, and their color just makes me glad to see them in the bare trees).

To me, birds have the ability to inspire and lighten the soul. Seeing different birds arriving at my feeders each spring is always a source of delight and anticipation. Seeing a bird I've never seen before, perhaps in a place I've never been before, always increases my perceptive ability.

As I watch the birds, I become more aware of the environment they, and I, am in. The flowers, the trees, the insects, other animals all begin to speak to me of place. We tend to become so detached from where we are because of electronics, houses, cars, etc., but to stop and not only smell the roses, but see how they grow in the garden they are in, and listen to the voices of the birds and others who share the garden with us, always serves to remind us that we are not really alone.

For more info on Danny's music and writing, as well as more information about the preservation of songbird habitat, please log into the following sites:

http://www.songbird.org/http://www.soundsofseattle.com/archive/artists/okeefe.htmhttp://www.dannyokeefe.com/

From the Delta to the Royal Albert Hall, Eric, Duane, and Albert, too: Glory be, it's Delaney Bramlett

(Delaney died just before Christmas 2009...and I got the news in New Mexico late that night while driving across I-40 to California from Alabama. Farewell to a man to whom I owe so many thanks and so much appreciation for the music he loved to share. This edited interview was the first I ever did—and I am so grateful that he gave me so much time.)

One can't say the name "Delaney Bramlett" without thinking of an ever-growing family of musicians and their music - hence the slogan, "Delaney and Bonnie and Friends." The term "Friends" was coined by Delaney to describe his band and soon the world became his friend.

There have been many beloved and famous people involved with Delaney over the years: Joe Cocker sang on the "Motel Shot" LP and Jimi Hendrix joined the "Friends" for a couple of weeks of touring. Eric Clapton, George Harrison, Duane Allman, Dave Mason, Leon Russell, and Billy Preston all have been by his side, too. John Lennon and Delaney collaborated together, and Delaney played the friend role as a guest member of Lennon's Plastic Ono Band. Jerry Lee Lewis requested Delaney's presence during the recording of his famous London Sessions album in England. Duane Allman and

Delaney became soul mates, sharing ideas, musical licks and a never-ending friendship, which to this day he fondly remembers.

Jerry Wexler, legendary producer and founder of Atlantic Records, said some of the best music he ever heard was played by Duane and Delaney on his back porch. They played many nights there, doing old Robert Johnson and Jimmy Rogers tunes.

A few of the artists who have recorded Delaney compositions are Luther Vandross, Ray Charles, Chrissie Hynde, Phoebe Snow, Staple Singers, Sonic Youth, The Osmonds, The Carpenters, The Everly Brothers, Crystal Gale, and even Lawrence Welk used "Never Ending Song of Love" as an opener for one of his shows. He has produced an assortment of artists such as Etta James, Dorothy Morrison (on "Happy Day") and wrote for and produced Elvin Bishop, John Hammond, and the Staple Singers.

Don't pass up the fact that Delaney wrote almost all the songs for Clapton's first solo album, laid down the basic vocal tracks as a pattern for Eric to follow, played guitar, and produced the results. He's been on stage with Rolling Stone cohorts Jim Price and Bobby Keys; alongside future Dominos Bobby Whitlock, Jim Gordon, and Carl Radle; Rita Coolidge, Booker T., "Duck" Dunn, Isaac Hayes, and Al Jackson. He did the late great King Curtis's last LP and taught Curtis to sing, out of which two hits came "Teasin'" and "Lonesome and a Long Way From Home." King Curtis kept a room at Delaney's ranch in California, and they spent hour after hour playing and recording together. The big man with the Flying V guitar, Albert King, was a personal friend and frequent guest at the ranch, and recorded there - and Albert was notoriously hard to please.

My search for Delaney began years ago, when I read in a *Rolling Stone* Music Review Guide that he had dropped out of sight. How could such a legendary musical icon be forgotten? After a little bit of research, in no time, I had seven discs of Delaney's material, including the soulful R&B sounds of <u>Home</u> and <u>Accept No Substitute</u> -

which I later provided to Delaney, as he had not heard them in years. For pure dynamite rock 'n roll, serve up <u>On Tour with Eric Clapton</u> - if it doesn't get you off the couch and into your dancing shoes, you need a doctor!

Hello, Delaney! How are you, and what have you been doing lately?

Well, I just came out of the studio; I've been sitting around and I want to go back to work, that's about what it amounts to. I've been writing for the last 25 years and I've got a lot of stuff here. I've been writing for a lot of other people, also, and writing for myself, and after this album, I'm doing myself a little blues album. I just got tired of not doing what I do best, you know? (laughs.)

I've been talking to people; everyone says just wonderful things about you, and they all know your work.

That's why I decided to do it again. I'm kinda like--oh, I guess (The Artist Formerly Known as) Prince, you know--I got tired of the way record companies treat people and I put it on a website.

I spoke to someone today who saw you playing in Staten Island, NY. She said, "Omigosh, I saw that man, and he was just a live wire!"

Well. I don't know about that; well, I always tried, when I was on the stage, or wherever, man, I tried to present my music and I tried to make people feel good - I always felt that anybody that paid a dollar to see me, I'm gonna give them their dollar's worth.

Bless you, Delaney, we certainly got more than our money's worth from you. Let me turn to one of the lyrics we talked about earlier, where you hit this beautiful high note. It was just like Roy Orbison: "She's been through enough"-- you just held that--it came from "It's Over."

You sure you don't want to hear it again? Well, let me get my guitar here (chuckles).

Delaney, you've got 13 great cuts here. First one up is Funky."

Well, that's one of my favorite things on there because it just kinda tells where I'm at right now. That song, actually, is kind of a preview of what my next album's gonna be. My next album's gonna be all little funky tunes, like a little shuffle. I just absolutely love "Funky" 'causeit''s funky, I like it, and I like it like that, you know? Lettin' mosquitoes bite you, you know, I've been out there, you see?--I like to write about the things I do.

Yes, you do. Ok, tell us about "Everyday's a Holiday" - is every day a holiday for you now, Delaney?

Well, it is, because I finally--I finally met a woman, this lady named Kim (Carmel), I produced an album of her now. And I've got it finished now. She's a really good singer. She brought me--she brought me back out of catastrophe. I was (hesitates)--tell ya the truth, I had kinda given up, not in myself or my music, or anything like that, but I'd gotten kind of gotten hooked on a down syndrome, you know?

I'd just have kinda given up, you know. I thought, well, at my age, I s'pose nobody wants to hear what I'll have to say. And this woman (Kim) came along 10 years ago. That whole thing, that's what that song's about. And she just kinda brought a little life back into me. I don't look any different than I did 20 years ago, I think I sing a lot better than I did 25 years ago, and I know I'm writtin' twice as good as I did 30 years ago, so I give her a lot of credit for that.

I think it covers a lot. Your (ex)-wife (Kim) played saxophone and flute for you, right?

I think it's one of the greatest albums I've heard in years - it's just absolutely a phenomenal album, but you know how things go these days---I don't know. I'm gonna be doin' my little blues like I was tellin' you about, and she's gonna be workin' on that, also. She's a great saxophone player, great flautist; she plays the flute like you won't believe it.

The next song we've got there, "How Do You Know": Delaney, that's a great spiritual album; I say "spiritual" because it sounds like you're talking about your early years learning about the Gospel.

To tell you the truth, I made up my mind up many years ago: I made a commitment to God, many years ago, and I let God down one time. I told Him that when me and Bonnie were together, I would never put out an album without a song that was praisin' Him, and the very last album I put out, it didn't have a song praisin' Him. It didn't sell diddly; it didn't sell nuthin'. And so I broke my word to God about that, and so I have since then been talkin' to the Lord and I said, "That won't ever happen again! That will not ever happen again!"

I'll call that "The Lost Years," when there had been some rough times. Later on, I heard that you had found things all over again, that you had found peace in your heart, peace in your soul.

Oh, yes—yeah, and, as a matter of fact, when I was producing Eric Clapton, I told Eric, I told him one thing. And he still remembers this, because I see it once in a while in a write-up when he talks about me. I taught him how to sing - I can't say I taught him how to sing, but I taught him how to phrase and do things, you know, the proper way?

I said, now listen!....but} he said, "I can't sing!" I said, "Yes, you can!" and if you don't, when God gives you a gift, He will take it away if you don't use it. I really believe that, because if you read the Bible, you'll find out that's exactly what the Bible tells you

ROCK 'N' BLUES STEW II

You're right, I think you did teach Eric phrasing. I happen to love his first solo album, the one on which you did so much work and songwriting. We have a reproduction of "Let it Rain." Delaney, how did you get the idea for a calypso sound on that?

Well, when I first wrote the song, that's the way I wanted to do it. And then, when Eric said, "I want to do that song," I thought, well, that won't work on this album. So, I decided to do it rock 'n roll (sings beginning guitar notes), and we did those, him and I played twin guitars, and we tripled 'em and tripled 'em, where it sounds like a wall of guitars. And we did it through little ol' Champ amps, you know, little bitty ol' Champ amps, and so that's how we got that sound. Matter of fact, that's in the Fender Hall of Fame because of the sound that we got (laughs).

Duane Allman had said that Eric could play a sound almost like a human voice crying or speaking.

Well, but he kept playing it through the Champ amp, but he just used the bottom pickup real basic, and I made him play just real soft, and we just got the sound on that, and that's what made that thing so effective. On mine, I played more growly (sings notes), if you remember how I played it. It's different; I didn't want to play it the same way, you know. Eric did a wonderful job and everything, so I didn't want to play it the same way.

So this was your original concept on that song?

My original concept was to do it with steel drums in the first place. But on that album, I just didn't think it would work on Eric's album.

I like the new version because it's yours; it was Eric's before, now I think you've reclaimed it.

Well, it's something like, when me and Duane played together, we'd never try to do anything that someone else did. We would try and capture the heart and the soul of somethin', but me and Duane, whenever we played twin guitar on stage and stuff like that, we'd do our thing and not try to copy, but we'd also give credit to where it belongs, you know what I mean?

That's why me and him got so close. When we got together, everybody used to ask me, and say, "Boy, you guys play twins on the stage and stuff, it's just off the top of your heads?" And I said, "No, me and Duane worked it out at the house!" Me and Duane worked out stuff, and he was a perfectionist!

Before we'd go on stage and stuff, me and him would sit down and work that stuff out, and of course, it'd sound like it was off the top of our head, and the artists would go crazy and stuff like that, but that was worked out! I mean, man, Duane, he was one of a kind. Now, he was a whole different kind of person than Eric Clapton and all those other people. He was a one-of-a-kind!

Let me ask you for a couple of Duane stories or Duane questions that I've had in my mind for years.

Well, that's where we stood out; see, Jerry Wexler said one time, me and Duane spent two weeks at Jerry Wexler's house over in Long Island (at Montauk Point), and we had a couple of weeks off, and we just sat on his porch over the water, and me and Duane would just sit out there and play all night long. Jerry Wexler said, "Man, the biggest mistake of my life was not having a crew out here to record that." He said that was the most beautiful thing he'd ever heard in his life. I think he even said that in his book, I believe.

I understand you met Duane because you were going to hook up with Ry Cooder, and someone said, I think, Jerry Wexler, "I've got somebody else as good as Ry, if not better - this is Duane Allman."

Well, it's kinda like that. We were gettin' ready to do a session in Florida. I said, "I want somebody to play slide better'n me, Jerry." Jerry liked my slide playin' and everything, but I said, "I want somebody that plays better'n me." So we sit there and worked this out and do this thing properly. He said, "Who're you thinking about?" and I said, "I dunno, maybe Ry Cooder or somebody, I dunno." He says, "How about Duane Allman?" I said, "Hell, that'd been my first choice if I'd have thought of that!" but I said, "Hell, he won't do that." He said, "I'll betcha a dollar he would." He said, "He loves your music," and I said, "You're kidding!" He said, "Let's call him!" So we called and he said, "I'll be there in a minute!" (laughs joyfully.) That's exactly what he said! "I'll be there in a minute!"

Let me ask you about Robert Johnson; I know he (Duane) loved him dearly, and I now understand why.

Well, when I learned to play what I called "southern blues"; I call it "country blues" myself, that's what my next album's gonna be. As a matter of fact, when Eric Clapton started livin' with me in Sherman Oaks, (California), when he first joined the band (Delaney & Bonnie & Friends), I said, "I want you to listen to somethin'." Well, Jerry Wexler said, and everybody else said, I had the biggest blues collection in the world. I mean, I had a room stacked full of albums, you couldn't even walk into it. Anyway, when Eric got there, I said, "I gotta turn you on to somebody." So I turned Eric on to Robert Johnson.

I was impressed with the soulful, emotional power of Robert Johnson's singing. No wonder you guys loved him so much.

Omigod, man; see, I grew up as a child on him. I had a guy named R.C. Weatherall, whom I wrote that song about, I put it on my live album with Eric, when we did it. (Singing and playing guitar) "Good morning, Robert Johnson's son--" Well, 'Poor Elijah' was---I couldn't say 'Poor R.C. Weatherall.' That's the guy who taught me how to play blues, man. His name was R.C. Weatherall. They called him

'Elijah.' (Sings) "Poor Elijah, livin' on the bayou way." He's the man who taught me the shit.

What was it like growing up in Mississippi?

Well, you gotta understand somethin' now, I was born in 1939. We lived in a log house and my daddy run off and left.it was just me and my brother (older brother Johnny) and my mom, and my mom---she worked for 30 cents a day, pickin' cotton, and me and my brother picked cotton right along with her and stuff. We didn't have no bathroom, no electric lights, we didn't have no nuthin'!

We lived in a log house - if you look back at that Home album, you see me and Bonnie and my grandpa sittin' there; that's the house I was raised in. There was no---we had to walk way-y-y down the hill, way down yonder 'bout a mile to get water to drink and to take a bath in our galvanized tub. We did that----pshaw, we didn't have electric lights! (snorts). We didn't have nuthin'!

My mom's the one who taught me how to play guitar! Santa Claus brought me a guitar, and my mom showed me---I'll tell you what, if there had been TV and radio in those days, my momma would have been a country star. She and her sister and her first cousin was the best singers I ever heard in my life. Did you ever hear of a group called The Chuckwagon Gang? Leon Russell wanted to cut an album with him and her, a long time ago, just him and her.

Your mom's living with you now, at the ranch in California. I have read that she was always sought after by the late, great Albert King, when he was in concert. He used to stand up and look for her.

Omigod, man, he rehearsed over here at my studio all the time. He fell in love with my mom, and she made him chicken stew---Mississippi chicken stew. Now, if you ain't never had no Mississippi chicken stew, you don't know what I'm talkin' about (laughs). It's different.

And so every time he'd come to town, he'd come here and she'd make him Mississippi stew. Every time he'd play, he'd insist that she'd be there.

Back to Duane--I understand that you found one of Duane's guitars in a pawnshop and wouldn't give it back to him - but that's okay.

I don't remember where we were, Texas or New Mexico or somewhere. Every town - I just love to go to pawnshops, I was a freak about that; I love to do that. In those days, you know, because people didn't know the values of 'em and of course, I didn't either. Well, I went down and there stood this little red - it's a Les Paul Jr., sittin' there. "What you want for that thing?" It's all scrubby-lookin', you know? And the guy says somethin', so I said, "I'll give you sixty bucks." So I took it back to the hotel (smirks).

So you gotta remember now, in those days, Duane would leave the Allman Brothers, and join my band at any time. And my mom can tell you, he called her at the airport any time we didn't know what was goin' on. 'Will you pick me up?' I'd said, "Where you at?" 'In the airport.' I said, "You're supposed to be on tour!" And he'd be kindacryin', because him and his brother was havin' a, you know, whatever; he'd be cryin' and sayin', 'Can I just go on tour with you?' and I'd say, "Yeah, man, of course you can, any damn well time you please! So, let's go!"

But anyway, I walked in with that little red guitar and he said, "Where'd you get that?" I said, "I found it in a hock shop." He said, "Well, boy, that really looks familiar to me! Damn." He said, "Would you look on the back of it? Is there a gouge there, looks like a big ol' thumb gouge?" And I raised it up and looked at it and said, "Yeah." "Hot damn, that's where I hocked that sunofabitch! That's where I hocked that bastard!" And I said, "What do you mean?" and he said, "Well, we were comin' through (laughs) here, and I was broke and I wanted to get high and I wanted to get drunk, but I didn't have no money, and so I hocked that sonofabitch!" And then he says, "That was the first guitar my momma gave me. (laughs).

That's great; I'm trying not to laugh at that story, that's wonderful. And you wouldn't give it back to him!

Ain't that awful? He said, "Would you give it back to me?" and right after that, he gave he his favorite guitar! He said to me, "Would you give it back to me?" and I said, "No." (laughs). And then - you know what's awful?

What's that?

Just before he died, we were playin' in New York, that Stratocaster that he loved so much, you know? - and I would always say, "You play my Gibson and I'll play your Strat." He knocked on my door one night; I guess I was too either drunk or passed out or whatever - and he knocked on my brother's door - Johnny, my brother - he said, "I've got to go, I've got to go down to Georgia." He said, "You guys are leavin' tomorrow." He wrote a little note, said, 'Wear it in good health.' And he said, "'Tell Delaney I said, 'Wear this thing in good health.' I know he's loved it, he wanted it, he's been wantin' this damn thing and I want him to have it!" Johnny says, "Okay."

The next morning, I got up and Johnny handed that thing, that damned thing to me, and I still got it. Well, it's got scrapes all over the back of it and everything, it's the greatest playin' Stratocaster in the world. I never felt so bad about not givin' him back.that guitar! (laughs).

I tell you what, I think you've been forgiven, Delaney, I think Duane would be happy to know you've been holding onto that guitar for all these years.

I'll tell you what: ain't nobody ever gonna get that unless they kill me! Ain't nobody gonna get that Stratocaster.

ROCK 'N' BLUES STEW II

You got a real special rosewood one from George Harrison. A picture of that on the website, a beautiful-looking instrument.

Sure did. Well, when I played---when we first went to - well, the whole deal was we were the openin' act for Blind Faith over here, for a tour. Everybody said, I was the reason I broke 'em up - I didn't break up Blind Faith, I really didn't. Eric just enjoyed the music that we were playin', so about half-way through the tour, he was just on the stage with us. And that group - they wouldn't even travel together, you know what I mean? So, he just started ridin' on the bus with us, and said, "Can I be your guitar player?" and I said, "Hell, yeah, you can be our---I love your guitar playin'."

And I wasn't even aware of Eric Clapton in those days, you know, I was a Duane Allman fan. So, it all came about that he ended up bein' the guitar player and all that stuff. We ended up goin' to England and doin' a big tour with Eric, you know, and I had started producing Eric's album, just, just started. It's an intertwined-type deal.

We did the Albert Hall concert, and Leo Fender had made a special guitar, a one-of-a-kind for George, a solid rosewood Telecaster. And so, after that show at Albert Hall, all the Beatles were out there, they were standing on their (chairs), just like the rest of the people, just goin' like - screamin' (laughs). We were havin' a good time. I looked out and saw the Beatles, standin' up on their chairs, and I went, "Jeez!" And here I am, I'm in awe, man, I can't believe it, the Beatles, for goodness sake, screamin' for me? (laughs).

You were a smokin, cookin' band!! I'd be on the roof, yelling!!

(laughs) Well, I couldn't believe I saw the Beatles out there, jumping up and down on chairs, you know? I went, "What in hell is going on?" And I was so in awe of the Beatles, you know, of course, everybody was in those days, especially me, as a songwriter and singer. But when I went back to the back - when I went to the dressing room - George Harrison presented me with this guitar. And he said, "This is to you for what you just did for me." And I went, "WHAT?!" And he said (again), "This is for you for what you just did for me."

I had a meeting with Leo Fender before he died, and I told him, "I got that George Harrison guitar." He said, "How'd you get that?" And I said, "He gave it to me." He said - Leo said, "Why would he do that? That's a one-of-a-kind." I said (laughs), "I dunno!" (laughs heartily). I said, "I just don't know, man!" I said, "I guess he liked me! you know." He says, "God, I guess he must have!"

Delaney, let me ask you about the New York City show of 7.26.71 you did with Duane, Sam Clayton and Kenny Gradney of Little Feat, and of course, a one-of-a-kind man was there: King Curtis. You did some slide; you said some really funny things, especially referring to Duane, you said, "Come on, hillbilly!"

I remember that! We were sittin' on stage, we were sittin' there, and I said, "Hey, hillbilly." What I wanted him to do was get up closer to me, 'cause he was sittin' too far away from me.

I recall a great song from that show; it's featured on a Duane double-CD bootleg (<u>Duane Allman-In Memorium</u>) called "Twelve-bar Blues," and you told Curtis to hold the solo, and he did a lovely job - that's where you said, "My fingers are so fast they hardly leave my hands."

(Laughing happily) Well, my hands were pretty fast!

Something else you did, you confused Bonnie, too, you said, "The next song is gonna be a 'ballard.' And she said (confused): "A 'wha'?" You said, "You heard of a mallard; this here's a ballard!"

(Snickering) Well, at that time, we were having a little trouble and stuff, and I really wanted to piss her off! That's the truth. You gotta understand somethin' - I had a room at Duane's house in Macon, and he had a room at my house in California. I had a room at King Curtis' house in New York. He had a room at my house in California.

So, we actually used to call ourselves 'The Three Mosquitoes,' because anytime you'd see one of us, you'd see us all. Whenever I'd perform, King Curtis would do the same thing with his band that Duane did with his band - he'd show up to my concerts. They'd both show up. We loved each other so damn much, man; I tell you what: if they had both lived, we'd have had a (musical) thing that people would be tryin' to copy to this day. To this very day!

For me, hearing your recollections of those two men is justification for my effort to find you and talk about them. Tell me about King Curtis: on that solo (on "Twelve-bar Blues"), it sounds like he was playing a saxophone of pure gold.

We used to sit and talk about it: he said he was 'me' and played sax like I sang, and I tried to sing like he played sax - me and him, we used to talk about that. Same thing with Duane: we used to play what we thought one of the three of us would do, and we'd do it, like what we thought the other one would have done, and that's what was golden about that whole thing. You have no idea - nobody will ever know---what the whole thing was about. Nobody will ever know.

See, me and Duane and Curtis would sit in one room, by ourself, and we'd play, and we'd sing. I'm the first one that ever taught King Curtis how to sing. And when he sang that song that I wrote for him - my God! - it was the most beautiful thing. He said, "I have a lisp, I can't sing," and I said, "Yes, you can; oh, yeah, you can." (Sings) "Out on the lonesome highway." Did you ever hear that song? You'd better find it! "Lonesome and a Long Way from Home."

I've heard you did that; I heard that (on Clapton's first album) and on <u>Motel Shot</u>.

Forget that---King Curtis! Hear King Curtis sing it. We all made a pact - I'm tellin' ya, we were 'The Three M'skeeters,' man: you get us three together, you're gonna need nobody else. I'll tell you right now: we'd walk in and sit in a nightclub, and people didn't know what to think. We didn't need no drums, we didn't need no bass, we didn't need no nuthin'! Just us three, just sittin' there. Bonnie didn't fit in that group; she's a good singer; no animosity, but she didn't fit in there. Like this here (picks and strums a blues tune): that was the three of us, that wasn't Bonnie.

Your singing reminds me a lot of the gospel sound of Edgar Winter in his early days.

Well, in another way, yes. I love his brother, Johnny, but I do it a lot differently. My phrasing is different than Johnny, but Johnny's wonderful! I do (sings and picks out tune). I'm a fan of Johnny and Edgar, both, but I don't do what they do, and they don't do what I do. But I'll tell you what: it's all in conjunction.

Let me ask you about something you did a while back - you did something for kids, about two years ago.

Are you talking about the kids in Indiana? I've done kids' things for years, yes, it's called "Kids First", I've been involved with that for like four years now. I only flew back there once to perform, and what this is about, is children - I can't believe that we're giving billions of dollars that's against us, (that's our enemies), to fight against us, and we've got all these children, that are walkin' around in their dad's poor, two-year old shoes. Kids First, whether or not I do a concert, I'm involved with them.

These little children have nuthin', and this is the poorest county in Indiana. To see those little kids, they have no coats, they got no shoes, they got their daddy's worn-out hand-me-downs to wear around in the snow and stuff. So, yeah, I'm involved in the kids - it's called 'Kids First'.

I wish more people would get more involved in those kind of things. I can't hardly pay the rent; I'm supposed to be a rock 'n roll star? I can't stand to see little kids walkin' around like that. Not just in Indiana, it's all over the world. So, yeah, I'm involved. I just think it's a horrible thing that in our country, as rich as we are, to give away billions of dollars all over the world, and see these kids, runnin' around and sleepin' on the streets. And I'll be involved this year, too.

You mentioned the Concert for Bangladesh at your 1971 show in New York; you always seem to have an awareness of people who are in need, people who have been suffering.

Yes, anybody in this country who don't get involved with little children, we got a problem, we have a problem. You look at the Bible, and (it says), "For God so loved the world," and it comes back to the little children. Can't we take care of (them)? First of all, our country - before takin' care of anybody else in the whole world, take care of our own children first - then let's go take care of somebody else. That's the way I feel about it.

Delaney, I want to leave you with a thought: I'd like to give you a very warm, open embrace on behalf of 'The Allman Family', all the folks amongst us who love the band.

Would you do me a favor: would you tell the boys---all the boys still with the Brothers---that Delaney says 'Hi' and that I love them very dearly. Ask them if they'd like to call me, to please feel free, and also say to Red Dog, I would really appreciate him callin' me. He's a special friend of mine. Do me another favor - do you know the boy - I say 'boy' because I'm an old man---that plays slide with them, now---I'd like the number of the guy that did the last show they did---what was his name? I'm talkin' about the slide player.

Ok, Jack Pearson was playing guitar with Dickey, he wore a hat onstage. Do you mean Warren Haynes? Warren's gone on with Gov't Mule. Derek Trucks, Butch's nephew, just joined them.

I'm just wonderin', is he ever out here, I'd like to hear him play with me. You think he'd be good playin' with me? Does he play anything like Duane?

Ok, I'll tell them, we'll find the right man for you, we'll tell all three of them.

Just tell 'em to give me a call. What about Dickey? Dickey must be 'the force,' now - I mean (the force behind) the guitar. Could you do me one more favor: just tell Gregg to call me, will ya? Tell him Delaney needs to talk to him.

Incense, Peppermints, the early Lynyrd Skynryd, Bright Lights, Country Music, and straight talk: Paul Marshall

(I saw an email address for a guy who signed himself as "Strawberry Alarm Clock" or something like that—and I remembered the song that made the group a hit: "Incense and Peppermints." Just follow the trail, I thought, and lo and behold, this interview followed. Paul gives his insights from the country scene as well as some well-placed comments about the nation.)

Paul Marshall is one of the best country singer/songwriter/bass players working today: a pretty cool achievement for someone who was once a member of one of the 1960's most psychedelic ensembles: the Strawberry Alarm Clock. I spoke with Marshall about the Clock, his country career, the state of country music in the 21st century, the Libertarian party and more.

A big question: how did some San Francisco psychedelics get hooked up with the Southern music scene?--especially considering Ed King (with LynryrdSkynryd)?

This is a question I can answer authoritatively, because I was there at the time. However, I must first correct you in your geographic characterization of the S.A.C. We were not a San Francisco band, we were an L.A. band.

We had done two tours of the South since my joining the band in '69. Each tour lasted about two or three months. Or maybe it was six weeks that felt like three months. Gene Gunnels (original drummer) was born and raised in the South, and his dad and step mom, and some family still lived in the Carolinas. They put us up when we came through Anderson, S.C. and Greensboro, N.C.

On the first tour, Lynyrd Skynyrd was booked to open for us on a lot of our shows in Florida and beyond. They were just out of high school, two or three years younger than we were. We liked them, we liked their music, and we liked hanging out with them. When promoters were setting up the second tour, we asked them to book Skynyrd to open for us again, and again we really got along great.

When we were deciding where to take the band in '71, and without a recording deal, Gene and Ed wanted to move to the South to try our luck from a different base of operations. Lee and I wanted to stay in L.A. It was a difference of opinion that got pretty amicably and fairly simply resolved by deciding to dissolve the band.

Ed felt that between Lynyrd Skynyrd and the Gunnels family, he knew enough people to help him get himself set up back there. Ed moved back shortly thereafter, resumed his friendship with Skynyrd, and quickly became a band member, first on bass, and then on guitar. Gene delayed his Southern Trip when he got a gig out of L.A. playing drums for the Everly Brothers.

Paul, you told me how the (early) LynyrdSkynryd came out to California--and were astonished at the sight of the geography. You also spent some personal time with them--Ronnie, and the others. Would you relive those memories, please?

ROCK 'N' BLUES STEW II

When we were doing shows together, Ronnie was clean shaven. I had a big old hippie moustache. Ronnie once told me backstage that he couldn't wear a moustache, because one time he had gotten a hair really badly stuck in his throat, and the experience had been so upsetting that it led him to avoid facial hair. And he was absolutely not kidding. He didn't tell me whose hair or what kind had been caught in his throat, but I empathized. He must have gotten over the phobia soon after that, though, because the next time I saw him, he had grown his own.

One of my favorite stories from the days when the Alarm Clock and Skynyrd were doing shows in Florida concerns our style of travel. Unbefitting our rock star status, but befitting our shrinking budget, we SAC guys were traveling from gig to gig in a big American-made station wagon with three bench seats: The one in front, one behind that, and then one in back that faced the rear of the car. Anyone sitting back there would have a great view of the U-Haul trailer carrying all our equipment. It was no Silver Eagle, let me tell you.

And we bitched and moaned about it incessantly. We were often driving hundreds of miles a day, as the gig scheduling never took the routing into consideration. Right after we had arrived at one of our venues, and were grumbling as we piled out of our heap, up drives Lynyrd Skynyrd. They're going to open for us. They also have a vehicle that they come tumbling out of and a U-Haul in back. Then Ronnie says, "Hey, somebody open up the U-Haul and let Chuck out!" Chuck was their roadie that tour. They had been so cramped for space that they had been taking turns riding in the trailer. We didn't complain as much after that.

Ronnie and a couple of other Skynyrd guys, Allen, I'm prettysure and I think Gary too, came out toCalifornia to visitus in '70 or '71. Ed, Gene, and I lived in apart of Burbankright by the Cahuenga Pass and Cahuenga Peak, a big hill separating Hollywood from the San Fernando Valley. When they got to Ed'sapartment, they looked upawestruck. "My God, you guys live right next to a mountain!"

Of course, if you know anything about Florida geography, you know that the entire state is perfectly flat. The horizon is the first group of trees, and no landmark protrudes. That was about all the sights they'd seen up to that time, so our little outcropping was quite an impressive sight to them. We had toured the Rocky Mountain states, and I'd been a frequent visitor to the Sierra Nevada mountains of California, so their characterization of Cahuenga Peak as a mountain amused me.

Larry Junstrom (of .38 Special) was the bass player who was with the band when we toured together. Leon joined shortly thereafter, so I never really knew Leon. Larry was one funny dude. He looked like a gigantic version of Cousin It from the Addams Family. He had very long blonde hair.

One day, a couple of older women came up and reprimanded him, saying, "You look just like a girl!" (a comment we long-haired types heard pretty frequently back then). "Evidently," Larry replied, "Yuh ain't seen mah dick."

As I look over your excellent bio on your site, the thought occurred: how (and why) was there such a transition from rock and the early classical music of your younger days to the country scene? You certainly seem to have found your niche in the industry. What was the attraction?

Come back with me, back in time to when my musical taste was a blank slate. I was younger than I can remember, maybe three or four, but I almost do remember the alleged incident. Out somewhere with my family, I sang a beer commercial jingle to a stranger. Burgermeister was the beer. I didn't know what beer was. I was happy to be singing.

See, it was the music, and the melodies, and I could hear the other instruments and parts in my head. I played all these old 78's at my grandmother's house: Peer Gynt Suite (especially "In The Hall Of The Mountain King"), "Rum and Coca Cola" (Andrews Sisters), "Come On

ROCK 'N' BLUES STEW II

A My House" (Rosemary Clooney). Lots of pop music from the '40s and early '50s. I was now about six or seven years old.

Then I discovered radio. That's where the rock and roll was. Elvis, Jerry Lee, Sam Cooke, Jerry Butler. Really, I loved almost everything I heard on the radio from 1957 until 1962. They didn't play country per se. But early top 10-20-40 radio was a real mix of styles and artists.

It wasn't compartmentalized. You could hear something as scary as Little Richard and as safe as Perry Como on the same station. And country music and artists were always represented back then. Elvis's country influence is clear. Jerry Lee rocked, but his string of country hits continued into the 80's. Johnny Horton was on the charts. I bought one of his albums because I loved "The Battle Of New Orleans," and there on the album were these beautiful country songs. I didn't even know they were country, I just knew I really liked it. "All For The Love Of A Girl"; "Whispering Pines"... very great tunes.

All this time, I'm still into all the sounds on the radio. Oldies like East Coast doo-wop and early R&B, New Orleans rock that's kind of second line, Chicago and L.A. soul music, and straight ahead pop-rock. I never even listened to the L.A. country station. I listened to the two or three top 40 stations. Oh, we can't forget the Great Folk Scare of the early 60's. Dylan, and all the others. After all, that was what made me pick up the guitar. And my first recording deal, for Bob Keane's Mustang Records, was basically a folk-style quintet that Bob morphed into a sort of pop-folk thing.

Then one Sunday afternoon, I was watching something on TV, and suddenly, there was all this amazing music. Porter Wagoner, the Wilburn Brothers, some other old country guys. This used car dealer in L.A., Cal Worthington, sponsored all these country music shows. It was very compelling. I made a habit out of watching those programs every week.

But the real turning point came for me in 1968. I was going to school in Santa Barbara, and I discovered the local country radio station, KGUN.

I listened to everything they played, and I didn't change the dial. I heard all the old Hank Williams songs, and Hank Snow, all the Hanks, in fact: Thompson, Locklin. And one of my old rock and roll idols, Conway Twitty. I thought he had disappeared. He hadn't disappeared--he was a country star. And I realized and recognized the connection to the country songs I had heard in the late 50's on top 40 radio, and that I had liked all that stuff back then.

More importantly, by now I was old enough to have had real love affairs, real breakups, real adult experiences, and that was the subject matter of most of these country songs. The pain and anguish and heartache and suicidal thoughts that were expressed by George Jones and Wynn Stewart and Webb Pierce actually had meaning for me, and it spoke to me in a very, very deep way. It is, after all, the White Man's Blues. I mean, it was in those days. And more specifically, the music of the poor and rural whites. Now, I was not that. I was a just barely middle class urban white kid with Jewish roots. But, like I said, the music spoke to me in an elemental way, and I immersed myself in it.

I started learning country songs. Ironically, within a year, I was auditioning for the Alarm Clock gig. I had to be told that they had had a hit called "Incense And Peppermints." Maybe I had heard it, I really couldn't remember. I certainly didn't know how to sing or play it. Of course, I still had a solid rock background. All the '50s and early '60s stuff. Beatles, Byrds, Turtles, lots of English Invasion songs, the Doors and Hendrix, Traffic, etc. I had been playing in a band in college that was doing all kinds of rock and playing frat parties. Beatles, Cream, Wilson Pickett… but on my own time, I was learning more country songs. Then I worked with another rock band as I was leaving school, and the whole band moved to L.A. and then they fired me for being "too country."

It was just about that time that I met Gene Gunnels. He lived in the same apartment building as my girlfriend's brother, and at a party one night, Gene said his band had a tour coming up and had just lost their lead singer. Did I know anybody who could sing? The members of S.A.C. didn't seem to mind my country influence, although they might have thought that my tastes were a little weird. But we even worked some country tunes into our sets. We did a good version of Doug Kershaw's "Louisiana Man," and a goofy original of mine called "The Smell Of Sweet Cologne," which was actually written as a country music parody, but we played it with such intensity that it worked.

After the Alarm Clock, in '74, I decided to start playing bass, and I bought a bass, and because I owned a bass and could find a few notes on it, and could sing, I got a gig almost immediately (remind me to tell you the joke sometime about the kid who asks his father for bass lessons).

Actually, I had a rough idea of how to play bass, especially to a lot of the country tunes I'd been listening to. I went down to the Musicians Union, looked on the bulletin board, and saw a 3x5 card that said something like: Bass Player wanted for touring country band. I called the number, and next week I was on the road with Frank Fara and Pretty Patty Parker.

I worked with this fine outfit for almost two years, all over the U.S. We were on the road about 48 weeks out of the year, and that was my real education in being a country bass player, expanding my country repertoire, and gaining some confidence and credibility.

What career choice (music, journalism, or other) created parental problems for you? I ask that because I can assume your parents must have had the traditional expectations that you would become a professional"my-son-the-doctor/lawyer" thing.

I can tell you, my parents were not happy campers the day I dropped out of college. Up until then, they were okay with all of my musical endeavors, and even a little proud of my small accomplishments. They loved music, too, so they had some visceral understanding of my passion for it.

For many years after that, they (especially my mom) kept making references to my "going back to school"; "having something to fall back on," etc. To her disappointment, that never happened.

Eventually, after fifteen or twenty years, they adjusted to the fact that I was not going back to school, or getting a real job, and began again to take some pride in my accomplishments in music, and in life. They came to some of my gigs, and were genuinely pleased that I was a professional musician, making real music. They were impressed with my travels and associations, if not my bank account. And they were proud of me for creating and maintaining a successful marriage and family in these difficult times. Any regrets they may have had, they now kept to themselves, and we got along very well. My mother died unexpectedly two years ago at the age of 74. My father is doing well at 87, and was over to the house for dinner last night. But you hit the nail on the head with that question.

Just to add some more wood for the fire--any controversial issues or personal platforms: Danny O'Keefe mentioned the destruction of songbird habitat, the Mighty Field of Vision, dedicated to help gain financial and medical support for musicians on the down-and-out; Delaney Bramlett is pushing for more Robert Johnson airtime. Anything hot on your hibachi? I know that country musicians have been very big (Willie Nelson, for one) with Farm Aid.

I wasn't much of a joiner when I was young, but eventually I found several causes that I had to ally myself with as a matter of conscience.

About twenty years ago, the big push began in California to divest law-abiding citizens of their legally held weapons. I'm a big believer in the Constitution of the United States of America, and I think it means what it says. So, even though I had never owned a gun, I joined the NRA.

Eventually I acquired some firearms. Now I'm a responsible gun owner who enjoys shooting at ranges. But I also know that if I were to depend on the LAPD or the state for protection, to defend my home and my family, I would be at the mercy of the criminals and plain old luck.

I think the 2nd amendment is in danger. And if that's in danger, the rest of the Bill of Rights is in danger, too. (You can probably find many exam-

ples of threats to the 1st amendment, and the 9th and 10th are routinely ignored. The 4th has been in trouble for a while, too.) So I am a proud member of the NRA.

I think we should all be held responsible for our actions, specifically, actions that directly harm others. What we choose to do to ourselves should be our own business. Like the song says, "ain't nobody's business if I do." Well, the laws against drugs, and the War on Drugs, have caused more harm to our society than the drugs themselves ever could. I don't think I even need to elaborate on this, but just to single out one drug, let's talk about marijuana. It's much less harmful to the body than alcohol. It doesn't cause anti-social behavior. It has great medicinal value.

I could go on and on, but I'll just say that I support NORML, MPP (the Marijuana Policy Project), the DPF (Drug Policy Foundation), and other groups that want to end the Drug War, legalize or decriminalize drugs, make drugs available medicinally and recreationally, and hold people, not inanimate objects (guns, drugs) responsible for their actions. Remember, the Declaration of Independence, another document I'm very fond of, includes the right to "The Pursuit of Happiness" among the inalienable rights given to people by the Creator. We should not dismiss, abridge or revoke it.

Well, here were two seemingly diametrically opposed political viewpoints. When I was in college, the right wingers believed in guns, and the left wingers believed in drugs and the twain almost never met. Except in the real radical camp. For instance, the radical Black movement, Black Panthers et al., realized the importance of guns to a revolution. And so, obviously, did the police state, which tried to disarm them at every opportunity, often using illegal means to do it. Hmmm. The importance of weapons in a battle against an unjust power...that rings a bell...like a Liberty Bell.

Enter, not long after that, a new political party. A party dedicated to the Constitution. To the Bill of Rights. To individual liberty. To responsibility for one's own actions. As soon as I heard about it, I knew it was my political party. And for about twenty years, I have been a registered Libertarian, and a member of the Libertarian Party. They support the 2nd amendment without hesitation. They call for an end to the Drug War. They say what happens between consenting adults in the privacy of their room is nobody's business, least of all the State. You want to try an unproven new cancer drug? It's your right. You want to allow smoking in your establishment? It's your right. You want to have a no smoking policy in your establishment? It's your right. Want to drive without a helmet, or a seat belt? It should be up to you.

You want to kill somebody, and then blame it on the gun, the knife, the car, the bartender? Sorry, pal. You want to smoke for 50 years despite official warnings and common knowledge that it's bad for you, and then collect billions from the tobacco companies? I object. You want to drive balancing a cup of hot coffee in your lap, and then blame somebody else when you spill it and burn yourself? You give freedom a bad name!

The Democrats abandoned their support of individual rights and responsibility in favor of group rights and society's responsibility. The Republicans give lip service to small, less involved government, but continue to grow it, sometimes at a "slower rate". The differences between the two parties are minor. Their similarities are many. Prime among them is their lust for power and their collusion in excluding third party challenges.

America needs another point of view. Perhaps it could use many points of view. I'd be happy to see almost any party challenge the dominance of Republicrats. But my choice is Libertarian. Register Libertarian, vote Libertarian, and join the Libertarian Party. The best hope for the United States of America.

Let's call it a wrap with two ideas: (1) sing a song of praise for the city of Nashville--and include any special places that will bring in the tourists. I guess, since it seduced you from the California lifestyle (and career influences), she must have some special kind of charm.

ROCK 'N' BLUES STEW II

Well, yes, I've spent a little time in Nashville, but that's not really newsworthy. It's not my city, but I'll tell you what I can. I like that Nashville is a big little city, if you know what I mean. In some ways it reminds me of L.A. in the '50's. Entertainment oriented. Lots of things to do and places to go. But not yet overgrown.

I can tell you a few places I've enjoyed while I've been there. The Hermitage, Andrew Jackson's home, is worth visiting. It's an interesting slice of American History in a lovely setting. Another place I like to hang out is CentennialPark. It has a full size replica of the Parthenon, and a statue of Athena inside. It's something to see, and it is a lovely place to spend a sunny afternoon, with a friend, or a good book. They often have concerts and other events there.

I can also recommend that visitors go to one of Billy Block's Western Beat shows, every Tuesday night at the Exit-In, 2208 Elliston Place. Billy's shows are cutting edge, and you can see some amazing artists in an intimate setting. For singer/songwriter shows, there's also the world famous Bluebird Cafe. You should go just to say you've been. The Ryman Auditorium, of course, is country music history. I haven't been there since the renovations, but I hear they've really made it a great place.

Some of the most adventurous and retro country music (not necessarily represented by my CD), is coming out of L.A. Here, a visitor might want to check out Ronnie Mack's Barndance the first Tuesday of every month at Crazy Jack's on Magnolia Ave. in Burbank.

Another great attraction is the Autry Museum of the Southwest. Founded by Gene Autry, it contains history of real cowboys and Indians, beautiful art and exhibits, the story of Hollywood's movie cowboys, and temporary exhibits like the traveling Woody Guthrie exhibit, the story of Chinese immigration to California, famous guitars, etc. It's in GriffithPark, which also has the Los Angeles Zoo and the Observatory. The Autry often has music, too. And while he's still with us and playing every weekend, take a trip up to Bakersfield to Buck Owens's CrystalPalace and see the master.

I've calmed down now, Mitch, just thinking about the Parthenon and the Autry. Sorry I got so excited before. Your last question really got me started. Don't get me started!!

Can't stop now!!--all right, another one: the country scene has seen quite a rise (again) in popularity by crossing over to other audiences--in particular, Rickey Skaggs, Shania Twain, and Garth Brooks. Dolly Parton, of course, had a significant share of the attention, as did Reba, Loretta, Kris, Johnny Cash, and a Rolodex of others. Care to share a few comments on the impact that you have seen by mainstream America's enjoyment of their music? It seems like we need a gentle nudge every now and then to remember how natural and honest country music can be.

The currently popular or top 40 brand of country music is in sad shape. It's slight rise in popularity is proving brief, and at great cost to the form. The core elements of Country Music have steadily eroded under a flood of pop sensibilities that have watered down the 100 proof emotions and worn away the rough and ragged edges of the music I loved. I knew we were in trouble when I was pitching songs in Nashville and they turned down every tune that had a reference to alcohol consumption because "We don't want to record any more drinking songs." Blasphemy!

Now, as the current crop get younger and younger, and prettier and prettier, I long for the days when average-looking people were the meat and potatoes of Country Music. Ever take a good look at Porter Wagoner or Ernest Tubb? And as a recent editorial pointed out, you can't have teenagers and children singing country music.

Country is supposed to be adult's music (exceptions like the young Tanya Tucker are acknowledged. Leanne Rimes is in that mold.) And just watch the country videos. Holy cow, it's clearly not about the songs. It's just muzak for these juniors to pose, posture and writhe to. This is not sour grapes or "in my day..." You can hear real country music. You just have to tune in to AustinCity Limits more often. Or come to Ronnie Mack's

Barndance in L.A. It's here, it's just not as easily or readily available. You've got to want it.

The people you mentioned: Ricky Skaggs--his first big solo success was part of a roots revival movement that I thoroughly supported. His credentials are impeccable and he is a musician and singer of enormous talent. Did he cross over to other audiences?

Shania Twain--Well, I suspect she can really sing, although you never know how much is pitch correction these days. God knows she's a beautiful woman. Mutt sure knows how to make hit records. Is it country? Please!

Garth Brooks--A country singer who wanted to be The Who, and at his zenith, almost was. He outgrew his need for country material, but he may return to it again.

Dolly Parton--I bow down. I am not worthy. She is a talent, a genius, a goddess, a woman. She has been to the mountain. She took her music to a wider audience solely on the strength of her being Dolly. But despite her forays into acting, and despite experimenting with musical styles slightly beyond country, she never abandoned the real music, or the real deal. Do I kiss ass? I think not. But if there was a line for it, you could save me a place.

Reba--when she stopped singing real country music, it always sounded like the performances were more about her than about the songs.

Loretta--the real deal. Outside of Sissy Spacek'sCoal Miner's Daughter, do non-country audiences know who she is? They should, but I have my doubts.

Johnny Cash: Yes, his TV show probably spread some country music around. it may have been more effective at introducing Dylan and Kristofferson and people like that to a country audience.

Non-country audiences who have been exposed to people like the above mentioned stars seem to accept the people and their image, be drawn to them, and embrace them, and welcome them into the larger culture as people and personalities, but for the most part remain oblivious to the musical form and style from which they sprung.

Unfortunately, mainstream America's enjoyment of country music today is predicated on what the Big Record Companies and Big Radio Conglomerates want to sell. Many Americans still think of traditional country music as whiney, twangy, corny, and maudlin. At the same time, the current country music that is none of those things (well, okay, it is maudlin) still suffers from the same misconceptions, and fails to garner a significant marketplace chunk.

Fortunately, there are still independents. There are the Derailers. There are pockets of traditional music preservation, and new music written in the traditional form. And I still sing at least three Wynn Stewart songs every gig.

Visit Paul at www.paulmarshall.net

On and off road with Dick Cooper: managing LynrydSkynryd and their last days; Jerry Wexler and Otis Redding; and the late, great, Muscle Shoals Sound Studio

Dick Cooper wears many hats: music museum curator, band road manager, free-lance writer and photographer, motorcycle racer, traveler, martial arts disciple and all-around wellspring of rock-solid advice and counsel.

He's been there with LynrydSkynryd, especially at the time of the tragic crash and afterward for the regrouping and healing process of the surviving members, the legendary recording sessions with Jerry Wexler at Muscle Shoals and in FAME Studios with Rick Hall, the man who gave Duane Allman his first break, and Dick's a man who served as keeper of all things sacred for the Alabama Music Hall of Fame Museum. If you've ever read anything about music in popular magazines, then you've surely seen his by-line or noticed a Dick Cooper photo.

I had the great fortune to meet Dick during my Road Trip in May 2000 during the Memorial Day weekend, courtesy of Johnny Wyker, and we traveled together from Muscle Shoals to Bobby Whitlock's farm/studio. The opportunity to learn from such a well-rounded man was never better: *I plied Dick with questions and tried to soak up as much knowledge as possible. His storytelling is as clear and well-spoken as any I've ever hoped to collect.*

You had a very clear definition of the working differences between the Muscle Shoals and Fame studios: would you elaborate on them, please? You also specified some of the artists and their impact/contributions to the studios: would you outline their work, please, and how each studio brought out different material and styles?

DC: When I first began writing about music in the Shoals, I had a weekly column in the Florence Times-Tri-Cities Daily. At the time, I didn't know a great deal about the behind- the-scenes working of a recording studio, and concentrated on the people involved: both the artists and studio personnel like engineer Jerry Masters. To me, the "news" was the latest artist to hit town, and I would start each week's column with who was starting work that week.

While this seemed like the obvious way to handle the column, it didn't take into account the differences between the two principle studios, FAME and Muscle Shoals Sound. At that time, Muscle Shoals Sound was primarily a tracking facility that would see a different producer come in each week with a new artist. They would record the tracks, and then in some cases go to other studios to overdub and mix. FAME, on the other hand, was a workshop for record producer Rick Hall. Hall was one of the pioneers of Muscle Shoals music, and was so good at his job that he was named "Producer of the Year" the year before my arrival.

I was oblivious to the fact that when Rick recorded an act, he did it from start to finish. During pre-production, he would meet with the artist, review the material, and select the songs to be recorded. They would then go into the studio and record the tracks and pilot vocals; when they were finished, the tracks would be "sweetened," the vocals recorded and then the album would be mixed, mastered, and turned over to the record label to be pressed and distributed. The overall project would take four to six weeks.

Muscle Shoals Sound would have four or five producers with different acts through the studio in the same length of time. Brad Shapiro would bring in Millie Jackson; they would be followed by William Bell, who might be producing The Staple Singers, then Ron Hafkine would bring in Dr. Hook, and they would be followed by Jerry Wexler producing Willie Nelson. That time sequence isn't correct, but that is an example of how things were done.

There were also six or seven other studios in town, and so Rick felt he wasn't getting the respect he deserved when he would have Andy Williams here for five or six weeks, and get the top of the column only once during that time. After a few months, I expanded the column to Billboard magazine, and Rick really got pissed. He called the Billboard editor and told him to fire me, because I didn't know what I was doing. So I was fired. Fortunately, over the years, Rick got over being mad at me, and eventually was the person on the Alabama Music Hall of Fame board of directors who recommended that I be hired as the assistant to Executive Director David Johnson. I eventually became the curator at the Hall of Fame and created the bulk of the exhibits in the facility.

Muscle Shoals made a name for itself in the î60s, cutting R&B hits for Aretha Franklin ("Never Loved A Man (The Way That I Loved You"), ("Do Right Woman, Do Right Man"), Percy Sledge ("When A Man Loves A Woman"), Arthur Alexander ("You Better Move On", "Anna"), Wilson Pickett ("Mustang Sally", "Land of 1,000 Dances"), Etta James ("Tell Mama"), James and Bobby Purify ("I'm Your Puppet"), and many others. The music was being made with black vocalists, and white musicians, with a few exceptions.

When Martin Luther King was assassinated, much of that changed. By the time I arrived in the Shoals in the early î70s, FAME had begun focusing on pop acts like the Osmonds, and Andy Williams, while the newly-formed Muscle Shoals Sound worked with Cher, R.B. Greaves, and Boz Scaggs. There was a good bit of competition between the two studios. Muscle Shoals Sound had the most traffic, but Rick was producing the acts that came through FAME, and the guys at MSS aspired to produce as well. David Hood had some success in Europe with Smith, Perkins, Smith, a group consisting of Wayne Perkins and Tim and Steve Smith. The band moved to England where Perkins ended up playing on Bob Marley's first album. Jimmy Johnson produced an overlooked gem by Roy Lee Johnson and the Villagers, and Roger Hawkins and Barry Beckett teamed up to produce "One More River To Cross" on Canned Heat.

The diversity of the artists coming through Muscle Shoals was astounding. The same 25 or 30 musicians were playing for Herbie Mann, Aretha Franklin, The Osmonds, Joe Cocker, Mac Davis, Ronnie Hawkins, Paul Simon, Rod Stewart, Paul Anka, Leon Russell, Andy Williams, Bobby Womack, The Staple Singers and Linda Ronstadt. Despite all the changes in personnel over the years the number of studio musicians that have made their living in Muscle Shoals is probably still under 100. And there was an effort not to develop a distinctive style. The effort was to become the band of the artist on the studio floor at that time.

The strong points of Muscle Shoals were the willingness on the part of the musicians to work, their improvisational talents, and arrangers like Barry Beckett and Clayton Ivey. The musicians built their reputation on being willing to take whatever time was necessary to cut a hit, while in Nashville, the three-hour session was sacred. Muscle Shoals sessions would run late into the night if necessary. If Muscle Shoals had a style, it was minimalism. Less is always enough. Let the vocalist carry the song; after all, it's his/her album.

You were the road manager for LynrydSkynryd for a while--and were there when the news came about the plane crash that took the lives of three members, including Ronnie Van Zant. What do you remember about that day, the early days of the band, and

ROCK 'N' BLUES STEW II

Ronnie? What was it like to do what you did for them in your capacity as decision maker and planner? Where might they have gone as a band?

I was actually the road manager for the *opening act* both times I was on the road with Skynyrd. In 1977, a Muscle Shoals group, LeBlanc-Carr (led by Pete Carr and Lenny LeBlanc) was the opening act on the Skynyrd "Tour of the Survivors." This was at the time of the group's Street Survivors album.

We opened the warm-up date in Statesboro, GA., and the dates in Miami, St. Petersburg, and Lakeland. The night of Oct. 19th, we played a gig at the auditorium in Daytona Beach, FL, Pete and Lenny's hometown, while Skynyrd flew to South Carolina for a gig. On the 20th, we were driving to Baton Rogue, LA, to rejoin the tour when the Skynyrd plane crashed near McCombs, MS.

Pete and the Eddie Struzick, the sound engineer, were writing a song in the car during the trip. We had a tape recorder rolling, and were totally unaware of the plane crash until we arrived in Baton Rogue. I was checking into the hotel, and the band was asleep in the car when the clerk in the motel said, "Oh, I guess you know your show has been canceled." I said, "No. Why?" And the clerk said, "Why because of the plane crash, of course."

That was a horrible night; we couldn't find out anything about Skynyrd. Many of our friends were in a near state of panic, because they weren't sure if any of us were on the plane. We had the same management company as Skynyrd, and we were suddenly abandoned, because everyone was focused on them. It was chaos.

In 1988, things were a bit different. I was still the road manager for the opening act, Rossington, but since Gary was the lead guitarist in both Rossington and Skynyrd, and his wife Dale was the lead singer in Rossington and a Honkette, the background vocal group for Skynyrd. I doubled up and helped with some of the Skynyrd chores. I got the fun stuff, like herding the luggage through airports, helping with wardrobe, etc. You should have seen the look on the face of the skycap in Albuquerque, NM, when I asked for some help with some luggage, then led him to a carrousel overflowing with 155 bags for our group.

It was really great getting to work a show like that. We played all the major cities, and were in almost all the continental states. I don't think I hit Vermont that year, and some of the other states we just drove through, but it was really great to see how much this country had changed in 10 years.

After the Skynyrd crash, Leblanc-Carr had continued to work with groups like the J. Geils Band, Journey, England Dan and John Ford Coley, Robert Palmer, Sammy Hagar, NRBQ, and Taj Mahal. We did a nationwide tour in rental cars, and really got to see the country up close. When you were in Iowa, people had Iowa accents, and when you were in Cincinnati they had Ohio accents. When I went back in 1988, there weren't as many regional accents any longer. Everyone talked like Dan Rather.

I met the guys in Skynyrd on April 22, 1974. They played a concert at the Florence-Lauderdale coliseum, headlining a show that included the Outlaws and Jimmy Buffett. Buffett had been added to the show as an upcoming act. He and Roger Bartlett drove down from Nashville for $75 and played between the two bands during a set change. Buffett was playing a Martin guitar that he had glued a plastic hula dancer to the side. When he strummed the guitar, she would sway back and forth. I thought he was great, but he got booed off stage. Everyone was ready for Skynyrd. I had met the guys that afternoon behind the coliseum. Ronnie was standing at the door to the van, directing traffic, and I was invited to join in the fun and frolic inside, but declined.

I later interviewed Ronnie at Muscle Shoals Sound, when he was there working on material that went into <u>Street Survivors</u>. And although Ronnie was always gracious and polite, I can't say we were more than acquaintances. Gary and I got along better, and although Allen and I had our differences, he ordered me to catch a spider for him, and my refusal almost led to a fight, but we got along o.k. I got along well with Ed King on his good days, and would speak to him even at his worst, although there were times he wouldn't speak back. His brother Jim, on the other hand, was a great guy, and I have often wondered what has happened to him.

I was close to some of the Rossington people before we went on tour. I had known Jimmy and Ronnie Eades for years. Jimmy was the head for Muscle Shoals Sound when I went to work there as Barry Beckett's assistant, and I had worked for Ronnie Eades and the Muscle Shoals Horns as a publicists during the mid-î70s when they had out their first album, and later when they were touring with Elton John.

I had also known Jay Johnson since he was 10 years old, and had known drummer Mitch Rigel and Stage Manager Tim Facok for a couple of years. I still live in Facok's house, even though he has moved to Athens, GA to run sound at Tasty World. Tim Lindsey was also a member of Rossington, and he and I shared a room for a part of the tour.

You've written for many prestigious magazines, including *Rolling Stone* and *Billboard*. What stands out in your mind that you would want to tell a newcomer to the journalism industry, or as an instructor at the university, what did you say to students?

That's easy. Don't take no for an answer. I've been very fortunate when it comes to my writing and my photography. A lot of my early music writing was terrible. I really didn't know what was going on from an insider's perspective, and I wrote as a fan. That was one of the reasons Rick Hall told Billboard to fire me. He was right, I didn't understand what was going on, but I learned. The second thing I would tell a young writer is never be too proud to say, "I don't know what you mean, please explain it to me.

At the grand opening for the Alabama Music Hall of Fame, Russell Gulley, who had been with the group Jackson Highway, brought Charlie Louvin to meet me. Charlie, said, "You don't know nothing about country music." I told him, "You are right, but if you will sit down and tell me your story, I'll know a lot more. It took Charlie off guard, and we became friends. He did sit down and talk to me, then gave me Ira's mandolin and one of the most famous Louvin Brothers costumes for the Hall of Fame exhibit.

As my Louvin education proceeded, I became a hardcore fan. Although country isn't one of my favorite styles of music, you can't listen to songs like "Cash on the Barrel Head," "When I Stop Dreaming," and their live version of "Hole in the Bottom of the Sea" without becoming fans. A few years later, the Louvin Brothers were inducted into the Hall of Fame.

You were mentioned in Jerry Wexler's autobiography - you obviously were very important to this man. What did you learn from him?

Jerry Wexler has had the greatest influence on my life, despite all the things that Jimmy Johnson, Barry Beckett, Pete Carr, Lenny LeBlanc, Johnny Wyker, David Hood and Roger Hawkins have done for me. Wexler is that beacon that you know is the way. He has been that to those I mentioned as well.

He is so much larger than life, that every day is a new lesson. I had the pleasure of working with him on two Dylan albums, a Dire Straits album, a Mavis Staples album, a McGuinn-Hillman album, a Carlos Santana album and an Etta James album. The first six were as an assistant to his co-producer Barry Beckett, and I was the project manager on the Grammy- nominated Etta James album, <u>The Right Time</u>.

Wex had a way of hitting that nerve. Whether it was just the right amount of track when you were mixing, or knowing when to stop messing with a song, he had the touch. Before I knew him well, I had asked if he could help get me tickets for a Clapton show in Birmingham. I was working with the *Times-Daily* at the time, and had interviewed him when he was in town producing a Barry Goldberg album, which he had co-produced with Bob Dylan.

He had pulled the strings, and I had ended up with great seats, free. The next time he was in town, I went by to see him, and took him a small gift to show my appreciation. I handed him the gift, and he asked, "What is this?" I explained it was a "token of my appreciation." He tossed it backed to me and asked, "What could you buy me that I would want?" He then softened the blow a bit by saying, "Go find somebody that needs your help and give it to them. You can never really help those that help you."

I've tried to live up to that. He also told me the secret to recording hit records. He said, "It's easy, put a hit act on the floor."

Photography versus journalism - is it more fun, or do you miss the writing?

I don't really miss either, because I do a lot of both. I began both at the age of eight. My father was a commercial photographer, and I started helping him when I was eight. I also started an elementary school newspaper that year.

I have been very fortunate with both. I'm not a good photographer, I'm an opportunistic photographer, and I've learned to take pictures through trial and error--and I have been heavy on the error part. However, the Smithsonian used one of my photos in its 150th Anniversary exhibit. The same photograph, of Wexler and Willie Nelson, is in and on the dust cover of Wexler's biography. It will also be in an academic book on Southern culture to be published next year by the University of Chicago Press.

Some of my other photographs have appeared in Rolling Stone, Mojo, Zoo World, and many other music publications, and on MTV news. I've had pictures in a Dylan CD booklet, on record covers for Delbert McClinton, Lenny LeBlanc, and in Etta James's biography. I still write some articles, and will have some work in *Gritz* in the near future.

You've had a passion for motorcycles; part of your connection to John D. Wyker is your days of riding up and down throughout Alabama. Any good stories you can share about those days - (we know there are plenty!)

Well there was the day I ran over Johnny about six times. He was learning to wheelie his 185 Suzuki dirt bike, and he kept twisting that throttle and jerking the front wheel off the ground. The only trouble was he didn't know when to stop--does this seem like a trend? Anyway, he would hit the pavement, and I would ride over him. He finally realized wheelies weren't for him.

I'm wondering why he needed five more times--but then, he chased after us with a pickup truck and a 35-foot camper-trailer. all the way from Decatur, AL, to Whitlock's house in Mississippi. Maybe he wanted to return the gesture?

Our friendship really developed around bikes. You can't rip and roar like we did without doing a little bonding at the same time. It all started one day when I went by to see Johnny about some information for a music column I was writing for the *Times-Daily*. While we were standing outside his apartment, Bill Tucker, who has since become a drummer, rode by throwing the afternoon paper. Tucker had a 185 Suzuki, and he could wheelie halfway down the block. It looked like great fun. So the next day, Wyker had a Suzuki, then I traded my Yamaha street bike in for a 350 Yamaha dirt bike, and the next thing you know, the whole neighborhood is ripping and roaring.

We started out at an abandoned industrial area between the river and Wyker's apartment. That was great for a while, but then we discovered Bruton Branch Recreation Area just north in Tennessee. I was there all but six weekends in 1976, and had been there most of the weekends in 1975. The area was great. There were all these power lines coming out of Pickwick Dam carrying power into Alabama and Tennessee. There were waterfalls, steep inclines, rock, dirt, and all that fun stuff. I kept breaking stuff off my bike until at the end, when it was stolen--it no longer had any lights, brakes, or anything else that wasn't absolutely necessary.

Most of our riding was "unstructured," but we did occasionally participate in organized events. At a Hare Scramble on LaGrangeMountain near Muscle Shoals, I took second place in my class, beating out sound engineer Jerry Masters by less than a minute. That was even though I had fallen 15 times during the race. It seems I was running faster than the bike could go.

We'll have to contact Jerry and ask about his style of riding.

I had a couple of spectacular crashes along the way. Once, attempting to climb "The Big Hill" at Bruton Branch, I had the motorcycle run out from under me. I slipped off the back of the bike as I got near the top. I was standing on a small ledge a hundred or so feet up the hill with the motorcycle stretched out overhead with the wheels pointed away from the hill. Just as I realized that I was in trouble, my toes slipped off the ledge, and the motorcycle and I locked in a wild tumble to the bottom. I'm not sure who rode whom on the way down. I just know there were no injuries that washing in beer and wrapping in a bandana couldn't cure. At that time I was married to a nurse, and her skills patched me up a couple of times.

Those were great times. We would go to Bruton, and camp out in a dirt field. We would bang around the woods, and with any luck come home with nothing broken. In general, we had more fun than the law allowed, but since we were in the middle of nowhere, it didn't matter. Once during the winter, it was snowing, and there were only about six of us there. The parking area at Bruton was a large flat muddy area on the power line between two hills. One was "The Big Hill" and the other a terraced affair that the average rider could negotiate. We circled up the vans and built a huge bonfire in the center. There was an area nearby of clear cut, and there was plenty of limbs and tree tops for wood.

The next morning, I got up and went for more wood. When I came back I saw one of the most beautiful sites I've ever seen: it was still snowing, and there was this incredible blue light illuminating the area. The muddy field was covered in about six inches of powder. At a distance, the circle of vans was silhouetted against the bonfire. The heat from the fire was rising, and the snow was being diverted to the outside of the circle. It looked as if there were a vale over the circle. It was beautiful.

We went riding later, and it was hilarious--it was so slippery, no one could ride more than a few hundred feet without falling down. It was so cold, B.J. Malone sat a beer down to adjust his chain, and when he picked it up there was a sheet of ice over the top. But in the circle it was warm enough to walk around in a tee-shirt.

Would you share your memories of a great musician and legacy of Muscle Shoals? I'm speaking of Eddie Hinton, and the efforts of those who are part of the Mighty Field of Vision and their charitable aspects.

I hadn't ever considered that there was a difference between the purpose of most records labels and MFV. The label, tribe, whatever it has become, was created to generate cash flow. That cash flow was necessary to keep Eddie Hinton alive and functioning.

My first reaction, when Johnny got me involved after finding Eddie homeless, was to form a publishing company to publish Eddie's songs. We couldn't get anyone to record the songs, but the people we played the songs to kept trying to buy the tape, so it finally dawned on us that we had a record.

It's a smoking machine--Eddie's voice just grabbed me when I slid the tape (Letters from Mississippi) into the car stereo, and the horns on "Everyone Meets Mr. Blue" are the best thing!!

We only had six songs, but Jimmy Johnson had produced six songs on Eddie a few years earlier. He had been unable to get them released, so he donated them to the cause, and we had enough material for an album.

No label in this country was interested. But in Europe, many of the facets of Eddie's personality that led to his downfall made him intriguing. That, coupled with the European propensity for minutia, created a viable market for Eddie's songs. Unlike most Americans, fans in Europe knew who Eddie was, and knew the songs he had written and on those he had played.

I had known KalleOldby for about seven or eight years. Kalle, a producer with Swedish National Radio had initially contacted Muscle Shoals Sound while a journalist with LARM, a Swedish music magazine, and since I handled matters of that sort, it landed on my desk. Kalle was unbelievably knowledgeable about Muscle Shoals music, and his questions caused me to look into areas I hadn't considered examining. We became close friends.

When we were ready to find a record deal for Eddie, I turned to him for a short list of potential European record companies. Kalle eventually wrote the liner notes for <u>Letters From Mississippi</u>. Kalle is still one of the biggest promoters of Muscle Shoals music in Europe. He comes to the Shoals every year, and even used MSS to record the music bed for one of his programs.

The Mighty Field of Vision is an ad-lib vocal from one of Eddie's songs, and I had nothing to do with its selection as the name of the company. On the other hand, it fits perfectly into my personal philosophy. I have studied Kung Fu for a number of years, and you are taught that your Chi, or life force, follows your vision or focus. I had no problem with following Eddie's vision. Here was a man who was relentless in the pursuit of happiness in the face of hopelessness. There were times when I didn't agree with what constituted happiness. I don't like 190-proof grain alcohol, but there was no denying that Eddie felt happiness was achievable under any circumstances.

That has been a wonderful lesson. I recently was hit head-on by a woman who had no license, no job, and no insurance, and now I have no car. But in retrospect, Eddie's most uplifting songs were done when he had much less. If you live your life right, you will go where your vision is focused. That is the lesson of Eddie Hinton. The focus of his Vision continues today, five years after his death.

As far as the charitable aspects are concerned, I refer back to Wexler's comments about never being able to pay back the people that have helped you. So I worked with Eddie, and I helped organize events like the Donnie Fritts concert we held in January.

That's a tremendous tribute - you certainly did him honors. One last question: what's the most unusual thing you remember about the studio days?

You know, there were always weird animals roaming the halls. What about the copperhead Wyker killed in the tape vault, or the baby rattler that was killed in the men's bathroom in the back of the building--and then there was the woman that showed up from Boston during the first Dylan session…?

Looking for Adventure in Whatever Comes Our Way: Larry Byrom of Steppenwolf

(Before becoming one of Nashville's finest session guitarists, Larry Byrom rocked it hard as the axe man for one of rock and roll's hardest working bands, Steppenwolf The late Ray Brand, lead guitarist and vocalist for the Crawlers, graciously made the introduction for me. I brought Ray a gallon of kosher dill pickles and a pound of corned beef from New Jersey in return. Getting that safely into a carry-on luggage rack was another story.)

From the beginning: how did you come to be a guitar player for a super group like Steppenwolf?

It came when I was a boy - there was a Dick Clark ("American Bandstand") Caravan of Stars tour that came through Huntsville, AL, and I was on a local warm-up band called 'The Precious Few.' I was kinda aced out by this guy, Rudy Romero, who was in a group called 'The Hard Times.' They were doing the "Where The Action Is" tour and television show. So, I went out to California and played bass with them on their first record (*Blue Mind*"). That lasted for a while until it broke up, and Billy Richardson, who was a member of the band, Nick St. Nicholas, Steve Rumph and I formed a group called 'T.I.M.E (Trust In Men Everywhere),' which was on Liberty Records. Nick St. Nicholas was the bass player for Sparrow, which later became Steppenwolf. At a certain point, Nick left the group to join Steppenwolf - I think it was around their third album, *At Your Birthday Party* (ABC Dunhill). Shortly after that, Michael Monarch decided to leave the group - he was having some personal relationship problems with John (Kay) and they called me. I auditioned for the group and they made me a member on the spot! That was around November 1968.

Let's look at your body of work - I'll start with *Monster*.

Monster was my first record with them. Michael Monarch had done some cuts and then he left, then I came in and wrote "Monster" (the title song) with John and (drummer) Jerry Edmonton. I wrote an instrumental on that record called "Fag," and co-wrote a couple of other things.

Why was *that* song written?

(Laughs) That was obvious (for the timeframe and location): it was Santa Monica Blvd. It was written in mind with the gay crowd and was sort of something that described the way they walked. It was a piano-bass thing.

Sort of like Lou Reed's "Walk on the Wild Side." But weren't the nights in LA more interesting than that?

Sure, part of *our* scene was cruising the streets to look for chicks and going down to the Troubador and hearing the new acts that were coming in - however, in time, Santa Monica Boulevard became a gay center. After getting hit on a couple of times because I was a good-looking young man, I just said, "This is bullshit!" and so I wrote a song about it (chuckles).

The current edition of the *Rolling Stone Record Review* guide's comments about *Monster* says, "Intended as a blow against the empire, *Monster* tried for a revisionist look at the entire history of America, from the slaughter of Indians to the Vietnam war."

It was basically a political look at the way we felt our generation viewed the hows and whys as to where we had gone as a country. We were totally rebels - we didn't believe in "The System," as they called it back then - the "Nixon World" - all that Vietnam bullshit - we didn't feel like we needed to be over there. We always thought marijuana should have been legalized, too - the album was basically an out-and-out protest album.

How about *Steppenwolf 7*?

Yeah, on that one, I had a lot to do with it - I wrote just about every song on that record (proudly): "Ball Crusher," "Fat Jack," "Renegade," "Foggy Mental Breakdown," "Who Needs Ya," a song called "Earschplittenloudenboomer," and "Hippo Stomp." "Who Needs Ya" did pretty well; however, just before *7*, there was *Steppenwolf Live*. That was recorded at shows like the Santa Monica Civic. On that record, we played a song that I wrote called "Hey Lawdy Mama."

Yes, it's one of the band's classic cuts.

Yes, that song did very well - it made it to the top 20 on the charts, and I was real proud of that one. At the time of *Steppenwolf 7*, I was writing a lot of grooves - what would happen is, I would write an instrumental groove, lay it down with Jerry, Goldy (GoldyMcJohn, organ/piano), and George Biondo, who took Nick's place - and we would send them over to John's house - he was living over in Nichols Canyon - and he would come up with a melody and a lyric for these tracks.

What about "Snow Blind Friend"?

That's a good look at someone who was literally, totally snowed under by cocaine. We were pro-pot/anti-coke. The consequences speak for itself. It's a Hoyt Axton song.

You mentioned GoldyMcJohn on the organ - what did he do to it to get that intense, behemoth sound?

A lot of people think it was a B-3, but it was a Lowery with a B-3 Leslie with a cracked speaker horn. It made for a crackling, break-up sound, and of course, we had it as loud as it could go. That was his signature sound.

You left the band in 1971, right?

I didn't leave until the latter part of '71, and formed a group called 'Ratchell' (pronounced "Rachel"), and had two albums released on MCA.

Take me on the road with Steppenwolf - what was it like?

(Enthusiastic) It was *incredible*. We approached it as a business - we never did long tours - we actually did it weekly. From Thursday through Sunday, we'd be hitting the cities, then from Monday to Wednesday, we were home - actually getting home Sunday night. We'd do three shows per weekend, along with 3 Dog Night and some other people that Bert Jacobs and Red Foster Associates were booking on the road - we had a little package deal at a certain point. The limo would come by on Thursday morning, pick us up, we'd fly to our date, do the show that night, fly to the Friday night gig, then do the Saturday night show, and be back traveling home by Sunday. It was great! I never got too tired of it - I did that for three years.

I guess with John Kay's German background being considered, you did some European tours.

Absolutely - we did a couple of European tours - a lot of things in Germany, and very well-received over there. We did the Lyceum and Albert Hall in London, we played near the Louvre Museum in France - we played in Amsterdam, Sweden, and Denmark. We were very successful - they loved us. They were really proud of John's heritage - he was one of the "Motherland" sons who had escaped communism. Actually, he and his family had left under the cover of the Second World War - he was a boy back then, and remembers going through places and barely being missed by bombs and things like that.

(The late) Ray Brand told me you knew some interesting folks back in the LA days: The Doors, Janis Joplin - can you tell me about working with them?

We all sort of lived together in a place called Laurel Canyon - now, it's been turned into a pretty trashy den - but back then, it was nice, clean, and there were a lot of us who were close friends. Mama Cass was there - Mickey Dolenz of the Monkees lived right down the street - Janis Joplin was someone we associated with on the road quite often. Jimi Hendrix was a good friend - we jammed together. The guys from The Doors - I knew (Jim) Morrison a little bit, but I knew (guitarist) Robbie Krieger even better. I just hung out with those guys - I met Neil Young, too. I went on the road with him in 1983 - we did the "Shocking Pink" tour. I'm real proud of the association I had with them. I was out on the road with Peter Frampton last year. I had a good time with him - it was a great tour, and it was a wonderful time. I was out with a few people in 1991, like Steve Winwood on a world tour. In 1992, I went out on a Canadian tour with Rodney Crowell.

And of course, the opportunities come up to go out with people like Neil or Peter - I really relish that - I like getting back out in front of people again. Most of my years - the last 25 or so years - I've spent in the studio. I've been a backup musician on these country records that have been coming out of Nashville, along with a few pop things.

What's your main instrument - that is, what model?

I have a Strat that I like a lot; I have a 335 that I love; I have a white custom Les Paul that I really love. Acoustically, I play a Gibson J-200 and a large Taylor.

As a guitarist, who were your early influences?

Eric Clapton, Jimi Hendrix, Chet Atkins - most notably, Chet, when I was younger. Also, Reggie Young, who is a great studio musician, whom I see all the time in Nashville - he has a track record that goes back to the '50s - he toured with the Beatles as a warm-up. He's one of my favorite guitar players and somebody that I modeled after - Reggie Young, he's great.

If I could do something with anybody today, it would be Paul McCartney. I would love that (sincerely). Right now, I'm working in Nashville with some other musicians on a project that is based around Beatles music - we're writing new songs in that style. Paul has done country material before; it would be wonderful to do something like that with him.

I was fascinated by Chet Atkins as a young boy because I heard him play "Yankee Doodle" and "Dixie" at the same time. I was originally a trumpet player and into Dixieland jazz - Pete Fountain, Al Hirt - that was my first love as a musician - Louis Armstrong, too. I started playing trumpet when I was about seven years old. Then I picked up guitar through records and friends, just after the Beatles came out, and I was digging into what they had appreciated - of course, I loved Elvis, too. However, Chet Atkins seemed to be the catalyst for a lot of these parts of me - Merle Travis and Chet. So I sat down when I was 14 and learned to play "Yankee Doodle" and "Dixie" at the same time! It was great - you can accompany yourself on an instrument. I thought this was great - you could have the bass part going at the same time - it was fascinating to me. And - you know - girls! There were always girls (laughter).

I worked with Carl Perkins, too, and Bob Dylan - oh, gosh, Glen Frey, Jimmy Buffett. I'm really proud of what I've done - I'm about three years from retirement - I can collect my pension in three years - but I'm still not slowing down - I can collect a pension and still work!

Tell me about John Kay.

John Kay is a wonderfully sophisticated, intelligent human being with a good sense of politics (he ran for a city council post). I think John is one of the most underrated poets of our time; he's a master of the English language. If you listen to the lyrics on *Monster*, there's a song called "Power Play": just incredible lyrics about the government and how out-of-hand they had become.

I guess at the time, we didn't understand what the hands of power were really trying to do and they were misleading us (as a country) in a lot of ways - they were doing the things that they felt they had to do. Even John looks back at those lyrics today and says the same thing: I don't feel the same any more as I felt back then. But, I feel for the time in mind, he was a helluva spokesman.

I see Jim Morrison as doing something similar, but I think that he was more charismatic than John as far as getting across a social message.

I disagree with you - I think that John was and is every bit as charismatic. I think John has stage moves that Morrison didn't - John has a presence that could be termed as "a menacing authority." He was really great - I learned a lot from John. There are some good videos available of the band!

Okay, last questions: Larry has gone fishing - what has he set out to catch?

I go for big bass - I'm down here on the Tennessee River in Scottsboro, AL. I love it down here! When I'm not fishing, I'm golfing, and when

I'm not catching bass, I'm looking for a good school of crappie to eat. My golf game is pretty decent - I'm shooting around 90, and every so often, I break the high 80s.

How is it that the game of golf is so popular with rough-and-tumble rock 'n roll musicians?

Well, as a rock 'n roller, you dive into dark hotel rooms with drugs and women and all that, and after a few years, you come out into the light and realize that there's a beautiful world out here. Golf is a great way to see it: some of the most beautiful places in the world are golf courses. That way, you can be outdoors doing something and casually enjoying yourself. We all grow up - I'm 51 years old now, I've been doing this business for about 35 years, and it was time to do something different. It's also about health.

Final question. In the liner photo from *Live*, what's the story with that headset? Did you go to a Native American gathering?

The hat was an accident that was on time. I was a little overweight at the time, so I thought, what the hell - I need a prop! I've had so many comments over the years - it's funny what a small move can do.

It sure competes with that scary-looking wolf on the cover! Larry, thanks again for everything - including your well-merited stand on John's showmanship. This should be a good reason for readers to explore the other material of the band that has been passed over by "Classic Rock" stations.

Check out *Jupiter's Child*. I didn't play on that one, but I particularly like it. Jerry Edmonton was the pulse of Steppenwolf; John Kay was the lyrics and the front man, but Jerry was the driving force of the band. We lost him about two years ago in a car accident. He was *the* guy.

Peaceful Easy Feeling: A Conversation with songwriter Jack Tempchin

(Jack Tempchin is the writer of such legendary hits as "Peaceful Easy Feeling," "Already Gone," "Slow Dancing," and "Smugglers Blues." In 1995, he toured all of July and August as solo opening act for Ringo Starr & His All Star. Thanks go to Bobby Whitlock for this introduction.)

When did you know you wanted to become a musician?

Well, let's see: although my dad sang around the house, there weren't any musicians in the family. I bought a harmonica when I was 16 - I rode my bike to the store to buy it, and then I heard a Bob Dylan album at a party in high school. Nobody else liked it, but I thought it was really great. Everyone else was into playing guitar at that time, but I didn't take it up till I was 18.

My first gig was as a harmonica player - the other guy played guitar. I just got into the folk scene - I was really just a fan. I was into all the old blues players who would come to the coffeehouses and little bookstores in San Diego. There were folks whom I heard like Mance Lipscomb, Bukka White, Lightning Hopkins, Sonny (Terry) and Brownie (McGhee). I ran a folk club at the college, so I actually picked up Brownie and Sonny at the airport and booked 'em in there.

My friend reminded me a year later of that when we were playing up the coast in some little place and we were opening for them - Sonny Terry came over to me and said, "You play harmonica real good, you're gonna be all right!" (laughs). I had forgotten about that over the years - Sonny Terry told me that I was a good harmonica player!

That's a great compliment. When did you pick up the guitar as your main instrument?

My friend took me downtown to the pawnshop and we bought this Stella for $13. That was it - I just started carrying it around everywhere. I met this incredible guy, Joe Faulkner - he used to sit around and start strumming and make up songs for hours, and they were always incredible. He never wrote them down, nor did he see any reason why he should do so (chuckles). I did that with him for a year or two, and finally, I thought, well, I ought to get on a stage and try some of these.

There was a coffeehouse called "Occam's Razor," and later, there was a place called "The BiFrost Bridge." The BiFrostBridge was in LaMesa - it was kind of a suburb of San Diego - and I went there for years and hung around, and that's where I actually started playing. Hoyt Axton played there and all these other people. (Unbeknownst to me, I didn't realize that they were making LSD upstairs and selling it - they had a lab.) While I was there, some blues guy came down and broke off the neck of a wine bottle, sanded it down on the sidewalk, and used it for a bottleneck. After that, I got totally into the folk and blues thing.

What blues players influenced you, especially on bottleneck?

Well, of course, Robert Johnson, from 'way early on - I had a friend who was a blues fanatic who delighted in turning me on (to Johnson's songs). Of course, at that time, the name "Robert Johnson" was still generally unknown. I learned about Lightning Hopkins, too - to me, he's one of the most-underrated guys, just an incredible player and entertainer, and an old gentle finger-pickin' guy, Mance Lipscomb. Basically, if anybody was there (at a gig), I was into their music.

Let's jump ahead in time a bit. How did you meet Jackson Browne?

I was playing in a club called "The Candy Company" - that's where I really became a performer. Every club had a "hoot" (hootenanny) night. I heard this song, "Adam Was a Friend of Mine," and I thought, "Hmm, this guy's pretty good. These songs are great!" And then I thought, "This guy's almost as good as me!" (laughs). Then I heard a few more songs and I said, "This guy might even be better than me!" (laughs again). I guess he heard a song or two of mine or something. I went out right after that and went hitchhiking around the country. When I came back, I saw Glenn Frey and J.D. Souther - they had a band called "Long Branch Pennywhistle," and they were playing there.

They were going to stay at this house with the owner of the club. The owner of the club wrote a stock market tip sheet, and rode a motorcycle - he bought the club just for fun, but his wife was into what we were calling "encounter groups." You know, you sit in a circle and tell the truth in those therapy groups that were big at the time - they would get people to stay at the house and then they would bombard them with these therapy groups.

So I told J.D. and Glenn - whom I didn't know yet as personal friends - that I didn't think they'd want to stay out there. I had a big house at that time, with five guys living there, and so I invited them to come and stay there. And that's how I became friends with them - every time they'd come to San Diego, they'd stay at my house. Jackson came down a couple of times and stayed with us, and I visited those guys in SilverLake, near L.A. - Glenn and J.D. had a place, and Jackson had a home up on the side of the hills. Jackson would practice his piano all day - he was the only guy in our crowd who would practice his songs!

I was also there when the Troubador was really happening - it was before the (Glenn's) group, Long Branch Pennywhistle - I was playing harmonica with Glenn and J.D. - the whole folk scene was coming through there, like Joni Mitchell and others. Doug Weston, who owned the Troubador, offered me a contract, and drove me around in his limousine. I thought, "Hey, this is where it's at!" (laughs). Then it all dissolved!

Where would you have been if you hadn't discovered music? I'm just trying to see what we would have missed.

I started out at UCSD - the University of California at San Diego. Everyone assumed I was going to be a scientist. However, I quickly dropped out of that. I could have wound up as a teacher or an inventor - I always liked to think about inventing things. Of course, I never actually did anything about it - except write music!

I was always ahead of the Baby Boom Bowl, so it always seemed to me that whatever I was into at the moment, everyone else would find for themselves a couple of years later.

You put together some very famous Eagles tunes for us: "Peaceful Easy Feeling" and "Already Gone."

I was sitting in Jackson Browne's house in Hollywood in a room with a piano darkened by heavy curtains on the windows. Jackson liked to compose in private. I was playing my new song, "Peaceful Easy Feeling." I had been calling it "Standing on the Ground," but when I went to buy a car, the salesman asked me what I did. I said I was a songwriter, and he asked me to hum a song. I sang a few bars of the chorus, and he asked the title. When I told him, he said, "Well, you ought to call it "Peaceful Easy Feeling."

I wrote it in the desert and finished the last verse standing at the *Der Weinerschnitzal* parking lot (at the corner of Washington Blvd.), playing my $13 Stella guitar, which I always had with me. First, I wrote it as a strumming song, then I changed it to a more sensitive finger-picking song.

My buddy Glenn Frey was walking by the room and heard me and came in. He asked if he could tape the song, and I played it into a cassette recorder for him. He said his new band was eight days old and they were going to play a showcase in a few days for the labels. The band rearranged the song back to a strummer and he came back and told me the next day.

When Glenn returned from recording the first Eagles album in England, he came down to San Diego to see me. He played us a tape of the album. The first song was "Take It Easy," then "Witchy Woman," then "Peaceful Easy Feeling." After three songs, I thought, "This is the best album I've ever heard," and I said it to him right there. Well, time has proven me not too far wrong on that.

In the summer of '72 I was traveling with my girlfriend (now my wife) in a VW bus. I was in a kitchen of someone we had met on the road when I heard the song coming from a little radio on top the refrigerator. That was a thrill. I realized I might not have to get a "real" job but could perhaps have the life in music that I wanted. It has, of course, been fantastic.

The other song, "Already Gone," was because I wanted to write something about being from California. I had heard country music ever since I was young enough to listen to the transistor AM radio I hid under the covers in bed. I didn't know quite how to write country-style, so I asked a friend of mine, Rob Strandlin - he wore cowboy boots, drove a pickup truck, and had a bunch of dogs, and he listened only to country music. We sat around before a show with some hard cider and drank it - I got a little drunk, which I had never done in my life, and we wrote it backstage in 20 minutes. I did it onstage right after that.

The way the Eagles got it was really great - Glenn just heard me playing it. A few years down the line, I got a call from him and he asked, "Hey, remember that song, 'Already Gone'? I think that would make a big hit record - don't you?" I said "Sure!" The next time he called, he said, "Listen to this": he just held the phone up to the speakers in the studio and there it was.

How did you meet a mutual personal friend of ours, Bobby Whitlock?

I was sitting in my little house in Hollywood one day when I got a phone call from a stranger- a guy named Bobby Whitlock. At that time, Glenn Frey and I had a number two hit in the billboard charts, "You Belong To The City" (featured on the television series, Miami Vice). Whitlock had just arrived in Hollywood and was looking for co-writers. He later told me he just opened the Billboard and started calling the writers of the hits in order.

I was not looking for co-writers, and I had never heard of Bobby Whitlock. The really strange thing, though, is just something in his voice and his accent made me instantly decide to meet with him. I think he came right over, he was right down the street and we hit it off big-time. We started writing, got some pens, a few yellow pads, and guitars, and then he said, "What shall we write about?" I looked around the room and sang "Four Walls, Two Chairs and a Doorway," which was just what I was seeing and that was the first line.

We had a great time and when we finished the song "Someone That You Used To Know," we both agreed we were great and the song was great and that it was perfect for George Jones. A few years later--I never really found out how--George Jones did get a copy of the song and he did record it! Things like that just don't happen in real life.

Bobby and I wrote a bunch of songs and recorded them. He put together a session for the demos and it was guys I had never met. Guess what?--it was Jim Keltner, Tim Drummond on bass, and Steve

Cropper (one of my heroes) on guitar. Whitlock was amazing. The key thing was he told a lot of very interesting tales about all kinds of people...and eventually I found out that everything he said was true - and he never exaggerates.

Aside from the places he's been, everywhere he was, and the people he's been with--the Rolling Stones, Eric Clapton, the George Harrison thing (All Things Must Pass) - I mean, he's got great stories. It's just the fact that he's himself. He had been in town a few weeks when he said he was going to throw a benefit for the families of the Ricky Nelson band that died in the plane crash. He knew some guy whose father was a big Las Vegas Mafia entertainment guy and this guy helped him put it together. I had dinner with them in an Italian restaurant on Sunset. It looked like the Godfather and his cronies at the long table. The conversation was going along when finally the old guy spoke. He just said one line-"I never met a woman I could respect."

Well, a few weeks later the concert took place--I think it might have been the Wiltern Theatre. It was packed, and my band played and Whitlock played, and several other bands. I didn't see how a guy could come in from out of town and put that all together and have it work. We still write together and are great friends.

You're currently "moonlighting" on Monday nights with Waddy Watchtel.

I have a super band. I can say that because it's not just me. I've got Waddy, Rick is on bass, and he played for 15 years with Joe Walsh, Phil Jones, who played on Tom Petty's Full Moon Fever, and then I have two other singers: Terry Reid, who was discovered in London when he was 15 years old and opened for the Rolling Stones and Ike and Tina Turner; and Bernard Fowler, who sings backup with the Stones. Every Monday, I have people who sit in with us - Johnny Rivers comes sometimes, George Thorogood, Randy Meisner, Chris

Hillman from the Byrds. Anybody I've known, I just ask them to come on down and play. I'm just having so much fun with it!

Have you thought of recording some of it?

It would be hard to figure out right now - I do a bunch of my songs, and then we do just covers - Neil Young and stuff like that. Yeah, we're gonna do some recording at some point. I haven't really clarified where I'm going. I'm working more on creating a big scene - the place is packed every Monday - I'm trying to build a big happy musical family.

Do you mostly stay in California or do you visit other folks?

I come to Nashville - or as it's known, "Tin Pan South" - in April for a songwriting event, and I just get into the habit of going there for that. Mostly, I stay here (laughs). I was in a band in L.A. called "The Funky Kings, but when they broke up, I started going on tour as a solo act. I worked with Kenny Loggins for about a year; Christopher Cross, when that album came out - I worked with Chicago for a while, and I opened for Joe Walsh. I did about seven or eight years as a solo act. That was fantastic - I loved that.

The Funky Kings - tell me about that.

I really loved this band called Hawk. They had just one hit - they were in Hawaii and they wrote a song for a surfer. They broke up when I went to L.A. and I met a guy named Jules Shear. We were sitting around in Doug Hayward's (Jackson Browne's bass player) living room with another member of the band, and together, we were just great. We said, "As long as we're waiting for our solo careers to start happening, why don't we form a band and do a few gigs?" We did one gig and a guy came up and said, "I want to manage you - don't do any more bars."

So, Richard Stekol and Jules Shear and I decided to get a rhythm section. Richard had some friends from Laguna. We spoke to Clive Davis, whom I had introduced to Glenn Frey. He said he was coming to town, and did I have any music going on at that time. This was our second day - I hadn't met the bass player or the drummer - so he said, "I'll come by." I told the guys and we worked up a couple of songs and he said, "Okay, I like it! You're signed - that's it." We had a record deal, and ended up getting Paul Rothchild to produce our first record at A&M Studios. That was pretty good because he produced the Doors, and all these folk records, and he was just a fabulous guy.

So we made our first record, and I think it's the best stuff Jules Shear ever did. Clive said, "I hope you guys can handle the success" - of course you like to hear that! We went out on the road and a single went to number 60, I think. Everything self-destructed after that - it was as much a part of our behavior as anything else. We got reviewed by *Rolling Stone* and didn't like it, so we burned it - and a reporter saw us backstage burning it and wrote it up (laughs). That band sort of fizzled due to internal pressure. We opened for (Darryl) Hall and (John) Oates. Then it turned out that Johnny Rivers heard the single ("Slow Dancing") and thought it was a big hit - and found out it wasn't, so then he cut it.

Jack, what other nuggets have you hidden from us that we should credit to you?

Well, there's a lot of songs that people might recognize - as well as all of Glenn Frey's hits except for "The Heat is On":

"You Belong to the City"
"Smugglers Blues"
"The One You Love"
"I Found Somebody"
"Sexy Girl"
"True Love"

I've also had material covered by other people:
"One More Chance" was performed by Trisha Yearwood
"White Shoes" was covered by Emmylou Harris
"Someone That I Used to Know" was done by George Jones
"You Can Go Home" was sung by Chris Hillman
"Rollin'" was performed by Glenn Campbell
"Somebody Tryin' to Tell You Something" was done by Tanya Tucker
"Your Tattoo" was performed by Sammy Kershaw
"To Feel That Way at All" was covered by Patty Loveless
Randy Meisner did "One More Song" and "White Shoes."

I've also opened for some great people, too: Ringo Starr and His All-Starr Band, Jackson Browne, Glenn Frey, Chicago, Dave Mason, Poco, Dolly Parton, Emmylou Harris, Karla Bonoff, Johnny Rivers, Joe Walsh, Kenny Loggins, Christopher Cross, Air Supply.

Last thought: is there any place special that you would like to visit in order to perform - perhaps some location that you have yet to see?

I'd like to go to Japan, but quite recently, I don't have the wanderlust.

Hallucination verification! John Wyker talks about Sailcat, the Early Allman Joys, and the Mighty Field of Vision

(In the spring of 2000, I received an email from friend and Gritz editor-publisher, Michael Buffalo Smith, about a concept called "The Mighty Field of Vision," fueled by John Wyker, from Decatur, Alabama. The project was designed to help down-on-their-luck musicians recover a sense of pride and potential royalties to help sustain their remaining years. I traveled to Decatur to meet John enroute to interviewing Whitlock. Life hasn't been the same for Buffalo nor I ever since—and we wouldn't trade that for anything.)

Hallucination verification, John D. "WildCat" Wyker's back on the loose! Actually, it's hard to keep him tied down - he's a writin', talkin', music-loving-and-playing power station of ideas. A musician by trade and a showboat promotion man by heart with close ties to Muscle Shoals, John's been riding the circuit for decades through several incarnations. Some of you may remember him on an early clip of American Bandstand (you remember that show from the '60's, don'tcha?), the singles, "Motorcycle Mama" and "Baby Ruth" (the latter recorded as a duet by Delbert McClinton and Bonnie Bramlett), and leadership of the Rubber Band and Sailcat.

The Rubber Band was a favorite of two other fledging artists who had just come to town with their band, the Allman Joys - and we're talking here about a very young Duane and Gregg Allman. John and Duane were closely entwined in many episodes of mischief and rascally ways, and one of John's Stratocasters wound up in Duane's possession (allegedly in Delaney Bramlett's hands!). To boot, John also was there for the jump-starts of two other familiar faces: a young Rhodes Scholar and ex-Ranger with a guitar named Kris Kristofferson, and a piano-playing wonder called Chuck Leavell. In those days, if you looked under most any roof that supported four walls south of the Mason-Dixon line and had a band performing inside, you'd find John Wyker and friends.

Not one to ignore the call of Fate, John's at the reins of two large-scale tasks: the curator and gatekeeper of the legacy of Eddie Hinton, an R&B soulmeister who cut "Shout Bamalama," "300 Pounds {of Hongry}," and other churning tunes through a meteoric-like brief lifetime of brilliance and flame-out. And if that's not enough weight to shoulder, John is the father-figure and mentor to The Mighty Field of Vision Anthem, a project with the heart and spirit of inspiration of efforts (like Charlie Daniels's Volunteer Jam) of musicians helping musicians, dedicated to raising funds and helping those brothers and sisters who have fallen on hard times. The MFV held their first session in Huntsville, Alabama, on March 14th, with players like Fame rhythm guitarist Jr. Lowe, Stephen Foster of the Doo-Dah Band, Little Richard's saxophonist, Guy Higginbotham, and the late Ray Brand of the Crawlers.

And, if you're part of the MFV mailing list, you've read John's "Cat Tales," where he lays down some funny and exotic yarns like he's got a bit of Davy Crockett and a sailor from the high seas in his soul - and a need as big as a barn door to share with man and womankind. Get it direct from the man: presenting the wild, the untamed, the amazing John D. Wyker!

John D., tell us a story about the roots of Southern music---and use a backhoe, 'cause these are some deep roots.

John Buck Wilkin, aka Ronny of Ronny and The Daytonas…in my opinion is the Brian Wilson of Southern Rock. In the late '50s and early '60s there was/is a genre of music called "Landlocked Surf Music"; Buck Wilkin was/is one of the founders of this goodtime Beach and Hot Rod style of music. He had hits like "GTO" and "Sandy" and "Bucket -T" and others that are certified anthems of rock 'n roll history…Buck and his mother, Marijohn Wilkin, also founded Buck Horn Music in Nashville in the '60s and the first writer to sign with their publishing company was a neophyte songwriter by the name of Kris Kristofferson.

Buck Horn Music published all of Kris's first songs…these songs are all classics now…I was fortunate to have spent a lot of time at Buck and Kris's apartment in the alley behind Music Row in the late '60s and was one of the first people to hear Kris play his new competitions…like "Me and Bobby McGee"…and all those great songs from that period.

I was crashed out on Kris' sleepin' bag one Sunday mornin' when he stumbled in half-drunk and kicked me in the side and demanded that I listen to his new song, "Sunday Mornin' Comin' Down"…he always played a 12 string guitar back then, and all 12 strings were always totally out of tune…he sounded awful…and I told him so… later that mornin' when I was as drunk as he was…he played that song again for me…and I got it that time…what a great batch of songs he turned out durin' that period!

Some great times were had with Billy Swan and Art "Neckbone" Shilling…and Buck…and…Kris and Tony Joe (White)…hangin' out at Bob Beckham's office every afternoon for guitar pulls…later, Buck and I moved a young Tuscaloosa high school graduate named Chuck Leavell to Nashville to join our band, the American Eagles…

he got his first session pay from these sessions but that's another story…LONG LIVE LANDLOCKED SURF MUSIC!"

Amen, John, thank you for that saga. Now, how's about laying it down about a guitar - you know the one I mean.

You know that Strat that Duane Allman gave Delaney Bramlett…I trust what Delaney says about that Strat…and there are probably a lot of stories about that Strat…but you can believe me when I tell you that that Strat used to be my guitar back in about 1966 or '67'… me and Duane and Eddie Hinton were sharin' a small garage apartment in Sheffield, Alabama…later, Duane asked Eddie to sing with what turned out to be The Allman Brothers Band.

Anyway, me and Hinton and Duane were sharin' this little one room garage apartment and Duane had some fantastic red hash…it looked like the red clay dirt that we have in Alabama…we used to joke that we did not need even need to hide it and that we could just cake it all over our boots and stuff and people would just think it was Alabama red dirt.

Well…me and Duane were sittin' around one night, smokin' Duane's hashish and he was playin' my Strat…I mean really playin' it makin' magic..he was gettin' sounds out my guitar that was blowin' my mind…It was easy for me to see that Duane had found his Muse and seen his musical matrix…and I was real high and spiritual… sometimes we'd get so stoned that we felt like high priests goin' into the mystic and we could see thangs for what they really were - .anyway, Duane was smokin' on that Strat and I was smokin' his hash… and I made an offer to trade him my Strat for the rest of his hash… probably about a 1/2 ounce…the funny thang was…we kept settin' there and jammin' and writin' little snatches to songs…and we both smoked up the rest of the hash together…and I think Hinton may have gotten a few tokes…when the hash was all gone, Duane still had that Strat of mine…I just learned from reading (the) interview with Delaney Bramlett in <u>Gritz</u> that Duane gave that Strat to Delaney and he still has it after all these years…God bless Delaney…I knew Duane was special…even back then…way before The Allman Brothers ever got together.

Didn't you say you knew them when they were the Allman Joys?

I used to hire The Allman Joys to open our shows when I had The Rubber Band - .we were big stars to Duane and Gregg…we had a hit single that was on Columbia Records called "Let Love Come Between Us"; it also hit with James and Bobby Purify and Delbert McClinton and Mavis Staples also did great cover versions--and The Rubber Band's version went to Number One in all the major cities of the Southeast or what Billboard called Area 6.

We did not need an opening act, but Duane and Gregg and the other Allman Joys had become good and fast friends…and they needed the money and the exposure--so I used to hire them to open for us: Duane would eat his guitar and play it behind his back and get down on the floor and do flips while he played and Gregg would be behind a little Vox organ on chrome legs..and Bill Connell pounding the drums…I thought they were pretty good…but the crowds gave them a hard time and gave a few boos from time to time.

You see, The Rubber Band used three saxes and a trumpet (I played trumpet & bass) in The Rubber Band and no other non-horn band could hold a candle to us back then…we were heavily influenced by a fantastic band from Muscle Shoals called The Mark V that featured Dan Penn, Norbert Putnam, David Briggs, Jerry Carrigan and Marlin Greene (they used to let me go on the road with them and get on stage and dance: I was called "The Action Man");…anyway, The Rubber Band featured Tippy Armstrong on guitar and our singer was Johnny Townsend…who later had the hit "Smoke From A Distant Fire" by The Sanford Townsend Band.

We all knew that Duane was 'way ahead of any of the other guitar players that were around the Shoals back then…except for two other amazing guitar-playin' cats...one was Pete Carr and the other was Tippy Armstrong...and...Pete Carr is the only one that survived the rock 'n roll wars--but on a lighter note, I remember Duane used to say that our Creator had a few thangs backwards...he used to say that "God should have put a fingernail on top of our heads so we could grow it out like the bill of a cap or a visor...and if it rained or somethang fell on our heads, we would have protection--like a helmet or hardhat," and he also said that "God should have put hair where our fingernails are." He had a lot of reasons for that, includin' how it could serve as a Q-tip and other thangs that involved pleasing women...but I won't go into that here...Duane was really a trip back "in the time."

Also, did you ever know about Bill Connell, the most excellent drummer for the Allman Joys? I recommended him to Doowang and Gregg and they hired him the night he graduated form Tuscaloosa High School and they all took off that night to go play at Trudy Heller's Club in Greenwich Village in New York City...I know Connell must have gotten a crash course in Rock n' Roll in the fast lane after he left his hometown to hit the road with Allman Joys! Years later, I hired Connell to go on the road with Sailcat in the summer of '72 when we did American Bandstand and Carnegie Hall (but that's a whole 'nuther chapter). Connell also toured with Bobby Whitlock a few years later.

We're getting' a crash course here, too--somebody remind me when to kick in the clutch - Oh, yeah, we've got a reply about one of Duane's guitars from (the late) Ray Brand, one of your buddies.

Brother Sting Ray Brand! He has one of the only original Coricidin slide bottles {from

Twiggs Lyndon) that Duane actually used. I've heard those legends about that famous Gibson Les Paul guitar of Duane's...and I think I read the same thang somewhere in one of Lanoir Allman's interviews…Duane used to call Gregg by his middle name when he really wanted to royally piss Gregg off…especially when Gregg was real depressed and wanted to go to "The Give -Up Rock"…(a legendary place said to be located near Opp, Alabama--where people go when they want to give up - legend has it that there is a big statue of Monty Rock III there and a person goes to that spot and takes off all their clothes and confesses that they want to GIVE UP and they make a covenant that they WILL NEVER EVER TRY AGAIN!"And then the person lays down on that cold hard stone…and they lay there until they finally just die and their beaten and broken spirit leaves their listless body!

Nevertheless, the first cat's name that owned Duane's famous Gibson Les Paul…was Richard Compton…who died in a car crash. Richard was from Decatur, AL, and he was a young musical genius that died too young…like so many that I've know. Richard has a brother named Tommy Compton and his nickname is "Crash"--he was once a sound engineer back in the early '70s at Capricorn in Macon--in fact, I think he was was hired to replace me when I quit my gig with Crapracorn in '69--sorry, I could not resist that--truth is, Phil and Blue and everyone in Macon treated me very well - actually, they treated me a whole lot better than I was treatin' myself at the time… way too much purple micro dot and stuff. I know ya'll understand what I'm talkin' about!

Back in my college days, as a freshman - seventeen or eighteen of us - What happened after you left Capricorn?

I really left Capricorn because Chuck Leavell and Buck Wilkin and I were under contract to record an album for Liberty Records… it started out to be by our band, The American Eagles…we did it at The old MSS on Jackson Highway…and we brought Norbert Putnam and Jerry Carrigan back home from Nashville to record at MS Sound and play bass & drums on the project…by the time we finished the record, Chuck and I looked at each other and said, "This should really be Buck's record and debut solo album"; it was only fitting...the record was released as <u>John Buck Wilkin, In Search of Food, Clothing, Shelter and Sex</u>...I love that title...and it was/is a great record!

Buck's mother, Marijohn Wilkin, was a big part of the Old Nashville Establishment and Buck was really tryin' to break some unspoken rules (and some written rules as well)...At the time, Buck was sharin' a cold water walk-up flat with Kristofferson and there was definitely revolution in the air when I used to go and visit them...a great period in Nashville around 1969...in fact, Buck and Kris wrote a great song that we recorded called "Apocalypse 1969"...we recorded that song at Broadway Studio which Marlin Greene had designed for Quinn Ivy...We had a whole room of Tuscaloosa musicians on that track, including Court Pickett, Frank Freidman, Art Shilling, Glen Butts, Lou Mullenix, and, of course, Chuck Leavell--about six or seven guitar players...a massive wall of guitars...back then, Tuscaloosa was producing some of the finest and most creative players that I had ever seen in one spot!

I think we kind of freaked a bunch of folks out on that session...there was so much energy in the room and we had one of those massive American flags like you see at big automobile dealerships--and we would spread it all over the entire floor of the studio (or anywhere) and it was so big that we could drape it over most eveythang in the studio and still it would stretch out in to the hall...I mean, we were "The American Eagles"...and that was way before there was ever groups called "America" or "The Eagles"...sometimes I think it's a terrible blessing to be ahead of your time...but how can a blessing be terrible?

Well, looks like I've done it again...but I can't help it when my train of thought collides with my stream of consciousness--down by the railroad riverbed!

Someone get the license plate of that train - either that, or fish me out of the stream! John, this is better than Saturday night at the

ROCK 'N' BLUES STEW II

movies! What else have you got tucked away for us - how about your friend, Eddie Hinton?

Yes, sweet Mamalama...Hinton knew and lived exactly what he was he was singin' about on that song and so many others...but my favorite thang about Hinton and his music was that on most of his songs he sounds so optimistic and upbeat...and positive in the face of what seemed to be a totally hopeless situation...that's what's so great about Southern soul music and R & B that had its musical roots in black church...as opposed to that old worn-out cry-in-yo'-beer-blues genre that gets so much attention these days...those kind of hopeless blues leaves me cold...

Eddie Hinton was the REAL DEAL--his songs were well-crafted, well executed and delivered with every once of soul on his body! I remember once, Hinton and me were livin' together in a house in Florence, right after I came off the road with Sailcat...1972 or early '73...and Eddie woke me up in the middle of the night to tell me about a dream that he had...he did that a lot...his dreams that happened while he was sleepin'...were very real to him and they all had special meanings to us. This one night he woke me up and he was very extremely excited...and he shook me until I woke up and he was just wild with joy...and he said, "Johnny, I just had this amazing dream and Otis Redding was in my dream and he taught me how to make his secret recipe for mayonnaise!" I knew exactly what he was talkin' about!

I'm fretting about why Otis was concerned about mayonnaise, considering everything else that he was famous for - but Otis did do things his own way - God bless him - and the mayonnaise, too! I'll never look at a tomato sandwich the same way now. So check out John and the MFV at http://www.mightyfieldofvision.com/

The Rambling Pony

(Somewhere, James Dalton is onstage either in Europe or America, blowing a harmonica, or playing guitar or mandolin—or something else that he's learned. Be safe and happy, my good man. You can tell 'em you played the Stone Pony.)

Welcome to Asbury Park, The Heart and Soul of the Jersey Boardwalk: sunshine, party food, vacation homes, beaches, and the legacy of the place called the Stone Pony. She's not pretty on the outside, but her music will get under your skin. She's tucked away down by the back end of the town, and they say it's where you can hear the bands play. At first glance, it wouldn't make you look twice, because the surrounding buildings are in disrepair or worse, waiting to be officially condemned.

The Rand-McNally folks probably forgot this street exists on a map. This was once a vital, sparkling city that bustled with people. However, economics and revenues change, and so do the population dynamics. Asbury Park has lost its trademark rides and arcade displays to other locations where real estate is more attractive, and the town has suffered badly. Maybe I should get out of here and just keep driving.

But the marquee says there's a show tonight, and the featured band is...wait. Maybe I need to go back for a second look. No—that's impossible—not down here in this forgotten part of the town, even if the beach is right across the street. What on earth would a talent like Gov't Mule be doing here? Or for that matter, The Band? All right,

ROCK 'N' BLUES STEW II

let's try a musical A-Z and see if you recognize any of the names that the Pony's hosted:

Edgar Winter	Black Crowes
Blue Oyster Cult	Brian Setzer
Gregg Allman	Dickey Betts
The Marshall Tucker Band	
Stevie Ray Vaughn	Cheap Trick
and Double Trouble	Levon Helm
Dave Edmunds	Hot Tuna
Wilson Pickett	James Cotton
John Entwhistle	Dr. John
Merl Saunders	Robin Trower
Jazz is Dead	Leon Russell
The Outlaws	Peter Frampton
Rick Wakeman	The Kinks
Huey Lewis & the News	

…and a local made-it-big friend named Bruce Springsteen pops in every now and then, too. It's good to support the players, he says, recalling his nights here when the E Street Band was sweating and struggling behind The Boss, trying to get a label to notice them. Remember your roots and pass the hat.

So, take a look inside: it's bigger than it seems, and as your eyes adjust, the comfort range of the place grows. It's got a stage that has plenty of space for instruments, a good-sized dance/crowd space, and there's a side door right there that gives excellent access to the street for loading and unloading—just step down and walk outside. There's even room for gear storage between sets. Additionally, several bars inside are reasonably priced and provide more than ample seating arrangements, and even the food is better-than-expected.

For insight, I spoke with James Dalton, Jr., one of the shore's multi-faceted musical consultant/musician/program coordinator/poet-writer-singer/rhythm guitarist-harmonica players--and a man involved in a spectrum of activities for the Pony. We had met when his band, a lively blues/jazz-rock alternative group called Secret Sound had opened for Dickey Betts, and direct from the horse's—I mean, Pony's mouth—I learned the reasons why there's still an oasis of music in a place like this, and how it has struggled for survival.

The Pony has hosted some serious talent. Yes, the town has gone to seed, especially down here by the ocean, but with its history, why doesn't this place get the attention it deserves? It still brings in top names.

I think the main problem itself is that the actual talent does not accommodate for the Stone Pony to exist on a professional business level. The reason for that is (a) it's in a state of complete disarray—it's in a transitional phase of revitalization. The town of Asbury Park would rather see itself succeed rather than to compromise and let one particular business get back on its feet. I don't agree with that, but I think it's the point they're trying to drive home.

And (b), it's an independent establishment. It's not affiliated with any corporation or conglomerate booking agencies—it is, however, the hub of independent agencies—it's a completely independent rock club. You talk about the House of Blues: it's a chain, a giant franchise, owned by Clear Channel. They also happen to own the largest amount of radio stations in the country, as well as having the strongest buying power. Someone can say to them, "I need 10 dates for a band—can you take care of me?" and they can do it.

I heard the manager of the Pony say that the objective of the club is to cultivate baby garage bands. Is that really true?

I think they say that metaphorically. The stereotypical image of the rock 'n roll club and the job in which it functions is to support the touring act—the live band. Pop bands just sit in the studio and then get radio airplay, and there may never be a need to develop an audience—everybody listens to it and buys the CD.

But when a live band comes along in its developing stage, say like U2 when they first started, or the Allman Brothers Band, or even Bruce Springsteen—he didn't start off as a pop star, he played little rock clubs like the Pony, all these small places, for years and years! And people went out to see a small show—they went out to stand 10 feet away from the singer and not be overpowered by the sound or the crush of the crowd. It was and still is an exciting experience.

A guy here who's doing it now is Matt Witte—people are coming out to the clubs to see him, and it's great! What the Stone Pony means about hosting baby garage bands is that they want to be the stopping grounds for the live bands that are up-and-coming that are in-between the small bars and the garage or the private parties, and the large venues—the coliseums and arenas. Without places like the Stone Pony, the Dave Matthews Band, so to speak, wouldn't be around. *That's* the band that I think displays the success of the club circuit as a breeding ground. U2, also. They were two of the most popular bands on tour last year, and they both had humble beginnings. And that's what the Stone Pony does: it brings those kinds of bands in and builds them up.

Is that kind of up-close-and-personal exposure the reason why the big name bands come there—to let the audience experience them?

Absolutely! It has that vibe—it's the place that everybody came through when they needed to be both visual and heard in a small environment, where the impact of the audience would be directly felt. The intimacy is everything. It gives everyone, including the band and the listeners, an exciting experience that can't be matched in the larger places. Look how close the stage is to the audience—they can reach right up and connect, for both the band and the customers. The thing that also makes it great is that the Stone Pony has been lucky enough to have been around for so long, and to have hosted people in the industry that have continued to grow in popularity.

Bruce Springsteen is a historical example of someone who started out here, or Southside Johnny Lyons (of the Asbury Jukes). He had a weekly gig here for years—there's actually a picture of a big light-up vanguard that says, "Home of the Asbury Jukes." There's one of those down in Nashville: you go to this one bar there and it says, "Home of BR 549." BR 549 is a classic country-rock band who's always been on the fringe. We're kind of like the small home that you always come back to, especially after you made it big in the world. You just don't forget your old neighborhood—or where you made your music.

How much influence does the Stone Pony contribute to the big cities nearby: Manhattan and Philadelphia?

It's definitely reflective of the fact that it's an hour-and-a-half south of New York City. Asbury Park was a popular beach resort for the rich and famous, as well as a vacation spot for U.S. presidents during the 1880s. President Garfield came to Elberon, just up the road. So, yes, this is a town that brings in people, especially being right on the shore, with the ocean right across the street.

The Pony was first called "Mrs. J's." It was opened just around the turn of the 20th century or so, and it's played host to music ever since. Top-notch, nationally-known musicians were attracted to the amusement park settings and the atmosphere of people enjoying themselves at the beach. It was kind of like a Coney Island of New Jersey: rides for kids, nice summer homes for rent, and the fresh salt air coming in off the ocean. The building we know as the Stone Pony has been renovated a lot, but it's still the place where everyone came to hear and see a show.

The hotel that used to be across the street—that's where Frank Sinatra and his buddies--the Rat Pack—played. The whole block—Second Avenue in Asbury Park was where you came to see a show and take your girlfriend down for a stroll on the Boardwalk. If you weren't in New York City, or Atlantic City, or Philadelphia, you had to be in Asbury Park! It was a midpoint of entertainment for the other big cities.

What happened with the "Save the Stone Pony" Movement?

That foundation still exists because technically, it hasn't been saved yet from being sold and torn down for urban development. The battle isn't over, but they got their needs to be heard. Go to the website, savethestonepony.com, and it will be there. I'm actually going to make it a stage shirt when I go on tour next year.

I note that it has great access from the stage to the street, and a lot more room than first impressions appear to give—is this part of the appeal?

Well, really, a lot of the draw for the bands, at least for the last couple of years, has been the fact that it's the only rock club that's been inducted into the Rock 'n Roll Hall of Fame in Cleveland. It has that reputation of being the place where the legends play.

You kind of pay your dues and also get a chance to pay homage to the business and the place at the same time. Bruce still comes here to play and he's as famous as anyone. But, because it's not run by a major corporation, it's one of the liabilities, and so a major band might decide to do three shows by booking through a big agency and pass up the chance to do one show here. It's an economic factor. It's like the Wal-Mart big franchise versus the small-town shop. The Stone Pony is the meat-and-potatoes of the music business. In a corporate world, no one is interested because we don't have the major backing. They like us; they like the idea of the place, but they don't put their money where their mouth is. It's like saying, "Only the money matters" when they should be saying, "It's the music that counts, too." That's the real reason why the Stone Pony is special. Look at the folks we bring in every week, and you'll be convinced.

I came back to see Warren Haynes and the Mule play. Up close. And no crowds and stadium-sized parking required. If you're in town and want to see a great 'name' band performance with a very reasonable price, and getting up close and personal to your music is what you love, then you'll have the best seat in the house at the Stone Pony. Make it a note for your travel plans and check it at http://www.stoneponyonline.com. Let the Pony kick up her heels for you: There's good rockin' and blues tonight—and the way that trends are going, whatever the neighborhood garage bands are rehearsing.

About the Author

Mitchell David Lopate was an adjunct English professor at Snead State Community College in Boaz, AL, and Brookdale Community College in Lincroft, NJ. He recently taught for two+-years as the Director of Teaching Affairs and English & Speaking instructor at Jiangxi University of Finance and Economics in Nanchang, China, and taught elementary school in Las Vegas (where he avoided casinos).

He is also an independent consultant for holistic and metaphysical concepts at http://tgstars.blogspot.com, an international psychological astrologer and advisor at, an academic support consultant for writing and educational concepts at http://tccwrite.blogspot.com; a music journalist and blogger (including videos) at http://rbs2.blogspot.com, and a separate existence as a Life mentor and Cosmic Tuning Fork.

He traveled with the U.S. Navy to the Aleutian Islands, Mississippi, Hong Kong, Japan, Indonesia, Malaysia, Thailand, the Philippines, Singapore, Korea, Japan, and Washington state, escaping each time by the narrowest of margins from overwhelming odds and risks. He avoided a tour (and hostage status) of the American Embassy in Tehran in 1978, and barely remained upright during a 6.5 earthquake in Alaska in 1977. His books include Psychological Astrology for the Psyche, a handbook guide for holistic counselors, parents, and healers, published in 2010, Smile! Your Life is on a Cosmic Camera!, a collection of short stories and comic non-fiction/autobiography, and The Creative Classroom Experience, a guide for educators and students, issued in 2018. The Sting – Revisited, a perspective on character and scenes from the 7 Academy-Award-winning film, was published in 2019.

MITCHELL D. LOPATE

He recently lived on a five-acre farm in Boaz, Alabama, where he and his (ex)-wife raised chickens, llamas, kept horses, a mule, and cats. He enjoys playing with a magical web of metaphysical colleagues, associates, and other Lightworkers on Earth and beyond. He is extremely fond of teasing, challenging, and ungluing the minds of students with ideas of how to set a paper on fire for an "A", medical documentation on topics like The Blue People of Kentucky, and assorted social injustices and upheavals. He returned to Humboldt county, California, where he was a DJ on Blue Ox Radio (KKPD 97.7) with his show "Rock & Blues Stew." He recently incarnated as Oscar Wilde, as well as a simultaneous existence and very personal association with the construction of the *Titanic*.

www.ingramcontent.com/pod-product-compliance
Lightning Source LLC
Chambersburg PA
CBHW030107100526
44591CB00009B/306